GUNFIRE AROUND THE GULF

BOOKS BY JACK D. COOMBE

Consider My Servant

The Temptation

Derailing the Tokyo Express

Thunder Along the Mississippi

GUNFIRE
AROUND
THE GULF

THE LAST MAJOR NAVAL
CAMPAIGNS OF THE CIVIL WAR

Jack D. Coombe

BANTAM BOOKS

New York Toronto London Sydney Auckland

GUNFIRE AROUND THE GULF

A Bantam Book / August 1999

Book design by Tanya Pérez-Rock.

Map by Jeffrey L. Ward.

Library of Congress Cataloging-in-Publication Data
Coombe, Jack D.
Gunfire around the Gulf : the last major naval campaigns
of the Civil War / Jack D. Coombe.
p.   cm.
Includes bibliographical references and index.
ISBN 0-553-10731-3
1. United States—History—Civil War, 1861-1865—Naval operations.
2. Gulf Coast (U.S.)—History, Naval—19th century.
3. Mexico, Gulf of—History, Naval—19th century.
I. Title.
E591.C75 1999
973.7'5—dc21   98-55774
                                                          CIP

Published simultaneously in the United States and Canada

Bantam Books are published by Bantam Books, a division of Random House, Inc. Its trademark, consisting of the words "Bantam Books" and the portrayal of a rooster, is Registered in U.S. Patent and Trademark Office and in other countries. Marca Registrada. Bantam Books, 1540 Broadway, New York, New York 10036.

PRINTED IN THE UNITED STATES OF AMERICA

BVG   10   9   8   7   6   5   4   3   2   1

To my agent, the late Gerry Wallerstein,
who patiently inspired me to renew my temporarily
neglected expertise in and fascination with
Civil War naval history

CONTENTS

PREFACE

It has long been my opinion that the naval history of the Civil War, especially those aspects of the Mississippi River campaigns and those in the Gulf of Mexico, has unfairly taken a backseat to the more-publicized land battles. A little reflection will convince one that when the Confederacy lost the major ports of New Orleans, Vicksburg, and Mobile Bay, it began a tragic march toward losing the war. Through these ports had flowed exports and imports vital to keeping the Confederacy and its war machine operating. Cotton was its premier product, coveted by the clothing mills of England, and in return for its export came a flow of medicine, ammunition, guns, powder, and clothing desperately needed by that hungry war machine. Because of the blockade, commercial traffic could be accomplished only by a fleet of blockade-runners that consisted of privately owned vessels, sponsored by the Confederacy. Although slowed to a crawl and its effectiveness diminished, this traffic did manage to continue throughout the war, even causing Union ships to break away from their stations to give chase. Eventually, as more Union ships were added to the blockading fleets, these activities were curtailed. But the Union did not accomplish the partial choking-off of blockade-runner activities without great cost.

New Orleans, Mobile Bay, and Galveston were eventually eliminated as ports used by the blockade-runners, but only after fierce naval battles that took a devastating toll in men and ships on both sides.

Those marvelous wooden deep-sea warships and ironclad vessels that plied the waters of the early nineteenth century are gone now, but they left an impressive legacy in land-sea warfare. Most important was the negation of the old dictum that wooden ships could not go against stone forts. Flag Officers Samuel F. Du Pont and Silas H. Stringham disproved this dictum at Fort Fisher and Fort Royal on the East Coast. Later, in the Gulf of Mexico, the indomitable Admiral David G. Farragut successfully attacked and subdued Forts Jackson, St. Philip, Morgan, and Gaines and forever changed naval history.

To this work I have brought to bear all the expertise at my command. As a veteran of Guadalcanal and Midway in World War II, I have tried to portray naval life and warfare realistically. Even though technological advances have produced modern state-of-the-art warships for the most awesome seapower fleets in the history of the world, the basic concepts of warfare and the psychological impact on the crews who man these fighting machines have not changed through the decades. That is why the important events in this work are told partly through the eyes of contemporary observers.

As in my last book I have taken some liberties with respect to naval terms although, unlike with riverine fleets, nomenclature has not changed much. For example: the term *hurricane deck* is no longer used but *quarterdeck* remains; today's *fantail* has replaced the *poop deck* of yesteryear and the old ordnance term *guns* has been replaced with *naval rifle*, because today's weapons are all rifled, as opposed to only a few on Civil War vessels. The terms *starboard* and *port* remain, although in the riverine navy, *larboard* was often used instead of *port*. *Freeboard,* the distance between the weather deck and the surface of the water, was used in Civil War days, as it is today.

Throughout this work I have attempted to adhere to chronological events as closely as possible. But some events do overlap others. In the Gulf actions the reader will notice some repetition of events such as Farragut's arrival and preparations at Ship Island. Because important events were happening at New Orleans concerning the Confederate shipbuilding efforts and because scattered naval actions at Galveston and at Pensacola overlapped the formation of the New Orleans strike force, it was necessary to move back and forth between events.

Many people contribute to the writing of a book of history. To name every single one would be impossible, because of space limitations. But those who made substantial contributions to this work deserve a grateful nod.

First and foremost the "research assistant" whom I have mentioned many times is none other than my wife and best friend of fifty years, Peg Coombe. Her dedicated assistance, understanding, and approval of this writer's monastic existence, coupled with her editing of my rough and final drafts, were invaluable. If ever a medal of honor should be struck in this field of endeavor, it should go to Peg.

I am obliged to Cindi Wolff, acting head of government publications and maps, and her efficient staff at Northwestern University in Evanston, Illinois. Cindi opened her vast and substantial files for my perusal, including the official records of Civil War armies and navies, which proved most valuable to my work.

Special thanks are due Bill Menary, curator at Howard Tilton Memorial Library at Tulane University in New Orleans, who was most helpful during our research trip to the Gulf states, as were Peggy Krohn and her staff at the Pensacola Historical Museum and Archives, who suggested valuable sources of information and maps. At the New Orleans Historic Collection, Mark Cove hosts a most efficient staff. Special thanks go to Carol Bartels, who was gracious to my research assistant and myself.

For making New Orleans newspaper archives available to us, as well as showing us a rare document on Fort Jackson during our visit to the Louisiana division of the New Orleans Public Library, Wayne Everard, archivist, receives kudos. His was a cheerful and always helpful demeanor.

Because Forts Gaines and Morgan, in Mobile Bay, were so important in the Gulf struggle, we did much of our research there. We are most grateful to Melinda Johnson, manager of Fort Gaines and the Dauphin Island Park and Beach Board, for her help in obtaining important letters and manuscripts as well as other material.

At Fort Morgan we were courteously helped by Blanton Blankenship, historic site manager, who performed the monumental task of supplying letters, diaries, and journals of soldiers who served there. In addition, he supplied technical information on the two forts themselves, along with data on the ships of both antagonists who fought at the battle of Mobile Bay. Much hitherto unpublished material was obtained for us by Mr. Blankenship and his staff, and we are grateful to him beyond measure.

I would be remiss in not recognizing the contributions to our comfort by Rose Raica and Jack Gaines, proprietors of the Harbor Lights

Inn on Dauphin Island, during our most delightful stay there. Billy Shelby, night manager at the Day's Inn at New Orleans and fellow fishing enthusiast, was enormously helpful to us and has earned our heartfelt gratitude.

A special measure of thanks goes to Kevin Foster, maritime historian of the National Park Service, for his many helpful suggestions during our long stay in the Gulf states area.

As usual, the Northbrook Public Library Reference Department in my hometown expended tireless efforts on our behalf in obtaining rare documents and books through the interlibrary loan system. Outstanding professionals there include Judy Nichols, Nancy Bishop, Elaine Stenzel, Claire Rothnagel, Thom Morris, Aimie Norton, Eric Robbins, Ruth Hafner, Karen Schachtshneider, Mary Schramm, and Joyce Nevins. Also, thanks to Marilyn Takiss, of Reader's Services, who went out of her way many times to renew my interlibrary loan books.

My agent, Gerry Wallerstein, was always available with advice and counseling during the hectic months of research and writing. Gerry embodied that rare combination of an invaluable agent and a close, personal friend. Our happy partnership was rare in the world of writing and publishing. Since her untimely passing, I have missed her more than words can say.

Katie Hall, my editor at Bantam Books who believed in my humble talents, was always thoughtful whenever problems arose during writing. Her optimism and cheery disposition are always inspiring. Editorial assistant Ryan Stellabotte was also always available for technical advice and information, as was Kristen Joerg in Publicity.

Dorothy E. Sappington of the United States Naval Institute Archives was as helpful as ever in supplying important photographs of Civil War ships and men.

Heartfelt thanks go to Aaron Brill, Dubi Fishel, and Francine Fishel for the loan of a venerable classic book on the Civil War, *The American Iliad.*

Jack D. Coombe,
Northbrook, Illinois

GUNFIRE AROUND THE GULF

INTRODUCTION

After Fort Sumter capitulated to Southern forces on April 14, 1861, war clouds gathered rapidly on the horizon. Armies were quickly recruited and thrown into the arena, but any chance of a surface naval battle between the two antagonists was nil, since neither side had a formidable navy. In fact, the U.S. Navy at that time was in pitiful shape, having been sadly neglected since the War of 1812. Out of a total of 90 vessels, only 42 were in active service, most of them scattered around the globe: in the Mediterranean, off the African coast, and in the Pacific off South America. Many units of the fleet were unserviceable.

As for the active fleet, the powerhouse consisted of huge steam/sail-propelled frigates of 29 guns, plus small but fast screw sloops of 14 guns each.

With respect to personnel, 259 officers resigned or were dismissed from the U.S. Navy soon after South Carolina seceded. During 1861 an aggregate of 993 acting appointments were made, not only filling the ranks but swelling them to greater proportions than before.

Of the ships in commission, most were wooden, of either sail or paddlewheel propulsion, and only a few were screw propelled. In many world navies, at the outbreak of the war, a few wooden battle-line warships continued to reign as far as tradition-bound navy men were concerned.

Then on April 19, 1861, newly elected President Lincoln announced a blockade of the Confederate states, extending from North Carolina, around Florida, to the coast of Texas; it was later extended north to Virginia when that state seceded. But implementing that blockade proved a challenge to the inadequate U.S. Navy, considering that it had to watch the Confederacy's 3,500 miles of coastline, with 189 harbors and myriad navigable rivers. The overall resource picture of both sides was interesting: The Union, with 23 states, had a total population of 22.7 million, while the Confederacy, with its 11 states, could boast only 9 million. The Union enjoyed numerous manufacturing facilities that the Confederacy, an agrarian society, could hardly hope to match. However ill prepared, the Union *did* have a flotilla of ships, while the Confederacy had none. In record time the Union soon had armed some vessels and was capable of blockading the East Coast ports of entry.

The Gulf states, however, presented a real problem for the U.S. Navy. That area, bordered by the Gulf of Mexico and stretching from Florida to Texas, proved early on to be a vital strategic region for both Confederate and Union forces, offering Confederates many inlets and bays for blockade-running. Acting swiftly, the Southerners established important coastal military bases at Pensacola and Mobile to the east and New Orleans and Galveston to the west. By controlling this land arc, they were able to bring in supplies and materiel by sea. The Union blockade, at its weakest in the Gulf, was unable to stem the tide of the indefatigable blockade-runners.

For its part, the Union recognized the military importance of the Gulf of Mexico but took limited action at Galveston and along the coast of Florida because of a lack of ships. Still, U.S. Navy Secretary Gideon Welles went industriously to work to assemble a fleet and restore the existing frigates and sloops-of-war to service.

The real Federal thrust came on June 7, 1861, when Captain William Mervine, aboard his flagship, the steam frigate *Mississippi*, was ordered to the Gulf area to command a force of nine warships. Union plans called for the eventual capture of the Gulf ports, including New Orleans, as combined Union land and naval thrusts down the Mississippi, under the command of General Ulysses S. Grant, conquered Confederate strongholds along the way including the bastion at Vicksburg.

That powerful Union thrust opened the great river to the Gulf and split the Confederacy in two, thereby denying it access to the rich resources of manpower, agriculture, and industrial products of Arkansas, Texas, and Louisiana.

The victories of General Grant, assisted by Admiral David Farragut's deep-water warships and the Mississippi gunboat fleet, forced the Confederate armies to abandon their Trans-Mississippi positions and move eastward, to eventual defeat at the hands of powerful Union armies.

After those long and bloody river battles on the Mississippi between 1860 and 1863 and the subsequent capture of New Orleans by Admiral Farragut, the Confederate and Union forces enjoyed a brief rest. The Confederate navy, hastily assembled by Navy Secretary Stephen R. Mallory, was decisively defeated. But the wily Rebels still had a card up their sleeves: a naval detachment, under the command of Admiral Franklin Buchanan, stationed in Mobile Bay, with the objective of preventing a seaborne assault on that vital Gulf port. (Ironically, General Grant had cast covetous eyes on Mobile after the surrender of Vicksburg, but bureaucratic bumbling discouraged him from pursuing this objective. The city of Mobile was not occupied until after the surrender.) The Southern-occupied base at Pensacola had been deserted early on and had been occupied by Union forces, giving them a strategic staging area. Meanwhile, the Confederate port of Galveston lost its importance as a result of the Union's Mississippi River campaign victory, which further cut off blockade-runner access for the Confederacy.

The spotlight now fell on Mobile Bay and its haven for the audacious blockade-runners, who defied Federal naval power, and on the awaiting Confederate flotilla.

In August 1864, Farragut forced his way past the two forts guarding the entrance to the bay and entered the bay itself. There he encountered the new and potentially indestructible ironclad ram *Tennessee* and four gunboats under the command of "Old Buck" Buchanan, Farragut's former academy friend. The flotilla, small in comparison to the awesome Union fleet, was nevertheless a formidable force with which to reckon.

Although outgunned and outnumbered, the Confederate sailors gave a good account of themselves and even sank a Union ship, but they were no match for Farragut's overwhelming power. In the end they lost two vessels, and the *Tennessee* surrendered. The last major naval battle of the Civil War, it was also one of the most savage since the battle of Memphis in June 1862. Having lost the vital seaport access and the routes of the blockade-runners, Mobile withered on the vine. With the fall of the Gulf ports—Mobile Bay, Pensacola, New Orleans, and Galveston—the Gulf campaign was over, a fatal blow to the Confederacy.

All of this came about, however, only after some fierce naval struggles between the formidable Union fleet and the disadvantaged but determined naval forces of the Confederacy. It is to these vital naval efforts that we give our close scrutiny in this work.

CHAPTER ONE

THE PRELIMINARY WAR

Soon after the war began on April 14, 1861, with the capitulation of Fort Sumter, tall, thin President Lincoln stood beside the short, massive General of the Army, Winfield Scott, scrutinizing a map of the United States. The septuagenarian general, hero of the War of 1812 and the Mexican War, was convinced that the Union was facing a potentially long and bloody conflict with the rebellious Southerners, and that a swift, decisive victory, with minimal bloodletting, was needed.[1] Scott, euphemistically called "Old Fuss and Feathers" by his men, may have placed a pudgy finger on the East Coast and suggested as the first phase of the plan a massive, snakelike blockade winding around Florida, along the rim of the Gulf of Mexico, to the Texas coast. Such a blockade would prevent the Rebels from receiving military and material aid from foreign sources.

Then he may have pointed to the midwestern section of the country, particularly the Mississippi River at its confluence with the Ohio. There, in this second phase of the plan, 660,000 well-trained troops, backed by a fleet of gunboats and transports, would push downriver, taking enemy fortifications along the way until they reached the

Gulf of Mexico. This move would split the South in two and cut it off from those states bordering the river, rich in agricultural, industrial, and manpower resources, thereby strangling it into submission.[2]

Although Lincoln approved the plan, it was never officially adopted. Yet during the war, curiously, it was followed almost to the letter. A carping press derisively labeled it the "Anaconda Plan," in reference to the South American reptile known for squeezing its prey to death before devouring it. But as the plan uncannily proved its validity in the long, bitter conflict, the carping went into nothingness.

To the South, the Mississippi River was of immense strategic importance. It was a major highway of commerce, upon which steamboats and river rafts endlessly plied, carrying raw and manufactured goods as well as manpower. The railroads had not yet spread their tentacles sufficiently far and wide to handle the monumental traffic, except for a few feeder lines leading up to and away from the Mississippi; therefore the river remained the main mode of transportation.

FROM its humble beginnings at Lake Itasca in Minnesota, as a stream less than a foot deep and eighteen feet wide, the Mississippi River snakes southward for a distance of roughly 3,710 miles, touching Wisconsin, Iowa, Illinois, Missouri, Kentucky, Arkansas, Tennessee, and Louisiana. (When one steps into that fairly narrow stream in Itasca, as this author has done on occasion, it is difficult to imagine its evolving into that wide, deep body of water that it becomes after it meets the Ohio.) The Father of Waters has more than 250 tributaries and literally splits the country in two.

To the Confederacy, control of the river meant control of a vital waterway. The South desperately needed the resources that the river brought, because of its shortage of machine shops, foundries, rolling mills, and powder factories, so necessary for production of arms and ammunition.

For the Union, gaining control of the river would mean cutting off the Confederacy from these vast resources. Isolating this region, coupled with a successful blockade, would prevent a prolonged conflict and hasten the end of the war. Unfortunately for the Union, however, at this juncture most of its military eyes were on the blockade of the East Coast. But Southern eyes were quick to fasten on that western anchor that would become known as the Trans-Mississippi Department of the Confederacy.

Not all states along the Trans-Mississippi fell within the Confederacy's influence: Kentucky and Missouri seesawed in their loyalties to either side. Thanks to quick handling by a few astute Union military leaders and an underlying sentiment of loyalty to the North, these states remained in the Union. But because Kentucky bordered on the Ohio and Mississippi Rivers, it became a defense perimeter for the Confederacy. After Lincoln's call for troops, Kentucky Governor Beriah Magoffin flew into a snit and declared his state neutral. Yet he failed to utter a peep when Confederates established fortifications on Kentucky soil.[3]

For the Union, Cairo, Illinois, located at the confluence of the Mississippi and Ohio Rivers, became the fountainhead of military power in the Western Theater. Late in 1861 the astute Lincoln tagged industrialist James Eads to build a fleet of seven ironclad gunboats to support any military campaign downriver to the Gulf. The vessels, based on a design by the elusive Samuel Pook, were constructed at shipyards in Carondelet, Missouri, and Mound City, Illinois. Each vessel was of 500-ton displacement, 175 feet long, 50-foot beam, and seven-foot hold. The casements were of 13-inch charcoal iron plating, which protected 10 to 13 guns of various calibers. Five boilers, each with a 36-inch diameter and a 28-foot length, would feed two powerful reclining engines that drove two 22-foot paddlewheels located in the stern.[4] Crew consisted of 200 officers and men.

The gunboats, named after midwestern cities, were especially designed for maneuvering in shallow waters; their nine-foot draft allowed them to navigate in the shoal waters prevalent in major river systems. Eads turned them out in a record one hundred days, using his own funds whenever the government was delinquent in payment.

This remarkable fleet of ironclads had an aggregate of 5,000 tons, an average speed of nine knots, and an approximate total of 107 guns. Also part of this riverine fleet were three "timberclads," former freight/

passenger steamers of 500 tons' displacement, with conventional side paddlewheels, sporting an armament of eight guns. They were so called because of five-inch oak bulwarks that protected the boiler and engine rooms.

This formidable fleet, plus a well-trained army, came under the command of General Ulysses S. Grant, a veteran of the Mexican War who had received two citations for gallantry and one for meritorious conduct. Grant had resigned from the army after the Mexican War and settled on a farm in Missouri with his wife. When the Civil War broke out, he volunteered his military expertise and was given command of the 21st Illinois. Not long afterward, he was appointed a brigadier general by Congress and given command of a district in the Western Theater, with headquarters in Cairo. Armed with the trained army and the remarkable fleet of gunboats, he began planning the downriver assault on Confederate strongholds outlined in the Anaconda Plan. The small river town of Cairo was transformed into a bristling army and naval base.

The Confederacy, for its part, was shackled by a lack of shipbuilding facilities, manpower, and other war materiel, yet it did manage to put together a fleet of 20 fighting craft of all descriptions. Labeled the River Defense Fleet, it would be used to counter the Union threat on the Mississippi. It was to be backed by two ironclads at New Orleans and two more at Memphis, Tennessee.

Under the direction of the indefatigable Stephen Mallory, the Confederate secretary of the navy, this fleet took to the waters. The stage was now set for some fierce naval action on the mightiest of rivers, between two factions locked in a life-or-death struggle.

Union action began on November 7, 1861, when General Grant loaded two timberclads and transports with 2,000 troops and bombarded the Confederate installation at Belmont, Missouri. Afterward Grant's troops went whooping in on a startled contingent of Confederate soldiers, who quickly fled through cornfields to safety. The victorious Union troops riotously looted and hurrahed until the Confederates, reinforced from an army across the river, came howling back and drove the Union contingent back to their transports, in which they fled upriver to Cairo. One Federal unit did not make the boats in time but managed to walk back to Union territory. Grant had apparently pulled off a giant raid, not a military maneuver, with tragic results: The Union toll was 120 killed, 383 wounded, and 104 either captured or missing.

Grant wrote in his memoirs that the Belmont operation was a success in that it prevented the Confederates from detaching troops from their base at Columbus, Missouri, and threatening a contingent of Union troops in that region.[5]

The Southerners, for their part, proudly proclaimed a victory: After all, the Yankees had retreated in disorder after a counterattack, they crowed. Yet the real point, not lost on Confederate generals, was that with Missouri solidly in the Union camp, Grant would be able to out-flank Belmont from downriver. They saw the thrust as a possible recon-noitering effort toward that objective.

Militarily, the operation was actually a draw. Each side was faced with the fact that the other was a determined and efficient foe.

For Grant, it was the first episode of a preliminary bombardment upon a shore installation by a fleet, followed by a troop landing.

Belmont was the curtain-raiser on an ambitious, well-planned, and coordinated Union campaign down the river. One by one Confeder-ate installations fell like duckpins before the Northern onslaught. The powerful flotilla of Federal gunboats and mortar boats was under the command of the efficient Flag Officer Andrew Hull Foote, a Connecticut-born officer, a deeply religious man with a passion for in-temperance. His old friend Gideon Welles had tapped him to command U.S. naval forces on the upper Mississippi.

Three months after Belmont, in February 1862, Grant's campaign started when Flag Officer Foote took his flotilla of ironclad gunboats, herding a fleet of transports, down the Tennessee River, which after a brutal stretch of rain had reached flood stage, to the Confederate instal-lation of Fort Henry. The lethal guns of the men-of-war bombarded Fort Henry, as they had done at Belmont earlier, attempting to pound it into submission. Meanwhile, Grant landed 15,000 troops downriver from the fort, then moved up to invest it. The river had flooded through the fort's sally port and rendered the river-level batteries inoperative. The Confederate commanders, realizing that resistance was hopeless,

took most of the troops and fled overland to the neighboring Cumberland River and the more powerful Fort Donelson. Once Henry surrendered, Donelson became Grant's next objective.

The fleet of gunboats churned upriver to the Ohio, then back down
the Cumberland to stand off Fort Donelson. Once again the gunboats
delivered a fierce bombardment, while Grant's troops moved up to invest the fort. But Donelson was no Fort Henry. Skilled Confederate
gunners pounded the Union fleet, damaged some of the vessels, and
drove the entire flotilla upstream in retreat. Undaunted, Foote brought
his charges back and this time pounded the fort severely at close range,
causing much damage. Grant marched his army up, and the fort surrendered.[6] The Federals' way was now open into the heart of Kentucky and
Tennessee.

MEMPHIS was the beginning of the end for the Confederate resistance on the Mississippi. The Union fleet roared downriver and on June
6 squared off against the River Defense Fleet off Memphis. The Confederate fleet, under the command of James Edward Montgomery, consisted of eight gunboats that had been acquired as steamers and quickly
converted at New Orleans. Although outgunned by the Federals, the
Confederate vessels were equipped with rams, and their great versatility
in maneuvering gave them an advantage.

The Memphis populace gathered on the levee to watch their fleet an-
nihilate the enemy. The battle was quickly joined and became a melee,
with vessels weaving in and out, guns blazing, trying for a knockout opportunity, while heavy gunsmoke hovered over the river, sometimes
blocking out the view. Then through the fray came a new element in the
Union navy—a fleet of nine timberclad rams built and commanded by
Colonel Charles Ellet.[7] The river reverberated from shore to shore from
the heavy gunfire, and when it was all over, the shattered Confederate
defense fleet was no more: Only one gunboat escaped destruction.

With Memphis occupied, all seemed to be going well for the Union
forces. Vicksburg, however, was another matter. Located on a bluff
bristling with guns, that city was a major obstacle in the effort to open

the Mississippi. But Grant, Farragut, and Flag Officer William Davis, who had replaced the ailing Foote, were up to the task.

Grant made several attempts to outflank Vicksburg, but each effort was stymied by a resourceful Confederate army. The dauntless general then called upon Admiral Farragut, who was downstream, to sail up and join Davis's fleet above the city, even if it meant running past the batteries of heavy guns on the bluff. The admiral, having secured New Orleans, steamed up and successfully ran past Vicksburg, suffering only minor damage to his force. Soon afterward the combined Union fleets again ran past the batteries, sustaining the loss of one vessel and minimal damage. Grant landed below Vicksburg and began a siege of the city, which finally surrendered on July 4, 1863. It was the greatest military victory to date, with the surrender of 30,000 troops and a huge store of arms and ammunition.[8]

Earlier in May the strong Confederate fort at Port Hudson had presented a serious obstacle to the Federals. Its strong batteries were located at a hairpin turn in the Mississippi, on a series of high bluffs 25 miles north of Vicksburg. In fact, they were almost as formidable as those at Vicksburg. On March 14, Farragut, on his way to join Flag Officer Davis's fleet for a planned assault on Vicksburg, had had to pass those batteries. He devised an uncanny plan to lash gunboats to the port sides of the leading ships: *Hartford*, the 2,700-ton screw sloop *Richmond*, and the 2,078-ton screw sloop *Monongahela*. Steaming alone would be the 3,200-ton side-wheel frigate *Mississippi*.

During the heated fray the *Hartford* and her consort, the *Albatross*, managed to slip by the fort, but the *Richmond* and *Monongahela* were forced to drop downstream. The *Mississippi* almost cleared the fort, but then ran hard aground under the guns of two batteries. She took a fierce bombardment that tore at her vitals, and the captain ordered her fired and abandoned. Later her magazine blew, and the magnificent steamer was no more.

From May 27 to June 13, Union gunboats once more took on the powerful fort batteries, this time finally pounding them into silence. Port Hudson, however, remained manned until the surrender of Vicksburg, then capitulated to Federal forces on July 9.

The mighty Mississippi now flowed "unvexed to the sea," as President Lincoln proclaimed.

The opening of the Mississippi to the Gulf of Mexico fulfilled phase two of Scott's Anaconda Plan. It split the Confederacy in two, cut off its access to rich western resources, and severed its hold on the Trans-Mississippi. The loss of the Trans-Mississippi was a serious blow to the Confederacy: Its armies were forced eastward, to depend more and more on blockade-running for supplies.

And a lot more fighting still had to be done.

CHAPTER TWO

IN PURSUANCE
OF THE LAWS

On April 19, 1861, just five days after the surrender of Fort Sumter—and two days after Jefferson Davis's proclamation inviting shipowners to apply for letters of marque, which gave them the authority to seize ships and cargoes—President Lincoln took pen in hand and wrote a proclamation of a blockade of all Southern ports. In effect, it established a cordon of ships extending from South Carolina to Galveston, Texas. On April 27, after Virginia and North Carolina seceded, he extended the blockade northward to Virginia. Through the ports of Charleston, Savannah, Fernandina, Pensacola, Mobile, New Orleans, and Galveston, the Rebels would attempt to export and import supplies necessary for their population and their armies. But U.S. warships would close the ports, as required of a nation instituting a blockade.[1]

According to the blockade proclamation, any "hostile" vessel that attempted to enter or leave one of these ports would be challenged on the first attempt. Heaven help it if it made a second attempt; it would be captured and taken into port, and its master and crew would be subjected to court action and treated as prisoners of war.

Lincoln's action must have been inordinately painful for him, because by its very nature a blockade is an action of one nation against the other, not of a civil war. Indeed, such a blockade would recognize the nascent Confederacy as a "nation." But on the other side of the coin, the blockade would allow the Union to seize neutral ships attempting to break the blockade and those carrying contraband—something a mere closing of Confederate ports would not allow.

It did not take long for the South and Britain to ridicule the proclamation, citing the impracticality of its enforcement. But the British, even with their economy dependent on cotton, took a hands-off stance, not even giving formal recognition to the Confederacy as an independent nation. On May 13, Queen Victoria declared her country neutral in the American conflict, greatly allaying fears in the Union and, ironically, causing elation in the Confederacy, which incorrectly read this action as recognizing them in a state of war rather than a rebellion.

The government of the Confederacy certainly considered the blockade proclamation a declaration of war. President Davis raged and decried it, informing the world that all the seceded states should "be let alone—that those who never held power over us shall not now attempt our subjugation by arms. This we will, we must, resist to the direst extremity."[2]

In order to enforce the blockade, Lincoln would need a sizable navy. The five powerful steam/sail frigates in his arsenal were among the finest in the world. Sadly, all of them were out of commission. He would have had more men-of-war at hand, but for a disastrous turn of events at the Gosport Navy Yard in Norfolk, Virginia. Here units of the navy were berthed for repair or overhaul, including the later-famous *Merrimack*. On April 20, 1861, Confederates raided the Gosport Navy Yard, and the evacuating Union forces torched and abandoned it. The *Merrimack* was burned to the waterline, and eight warships were destroyed, but the Confederates salvaged a bonanza of powder, shells, guns and carriages, machinery, and fixed ammunition. The stain on the U.S. Navy resulting from the evacuation would take many years to erase. Ironically, the Federals could have brought up warships and troops, plus the vessels present, to defend the navy yard against the raid, but for some inexplicable reason it had not been so ordered.[3]

As a result of the successful Confederate raid, the only ships Lincoln had in home ports to enforce the blockade were the screw steamers *Brooklyn, St. Louis, Wyandotte, Mohawk, Pocahontas, Pawnee,* and *Crusader,* the frigates *Sabine, Cumberland,* and *Macedonian,* plus the *Powhatan,* a side-wheel steamer. To build a navy on this slim foundation, Lincoln needed an astute secretary of the navy. His very wise choice was Gideon Welles, a New Englander of the old school.

WELLES was born to the job. A former newspaper editor, state legislator, and member of the Navy Department under President James Buchanan, a crusty, energetic man with a full, flowing beard, he accepted the position with enthusiasm. With his remarkable knowledge of naval matters, he was a most important personage in Lincoln's cabinet, and he was quick to put Lincoln's blockade proclamation in place— although he privately opposed the plan because it recognized the Confederacy as a sovereign nation. Despite his private view, he immediately set to work converting the weak peacetime navy into a powerful modern force. He purchased ships, many from domestic shipowners, armed them, and then ordered a massive warship-building program.[4]

This program included the construction of what were known as "ninety-day wonders"—ships with small propellers, capable of great speed, and armed with rifled guns as light ordnance—to be built in just three months. These vessels would be perfect for scouting the Confederate coasts and enforcing the blockade.

Like his Union counterpart, Stephen Russell Mallory, the Confederacy's secretary of the navy, was quick to recognize the importance of a navy. Son of a shipbuilder, Mallory had held the post of inspector of customs at Key West, Florida, in 1833, while studying law in his spare time. After passing the bar, he was appointed collector of customs and in 1851 was elected to the U.S. Senate, where he served on the Committee on Naval Affairs for ten years. When war broke out, he resigned from the Senate and was appointed secretary of the Confederate navy, a navy that did not exist but that he was expected to build and direct.

Unlike Welles, Mallory was quick to recognize the importance of ironclad warships and the use of underwater torpedoes (mines). He did manage to arm and equip a few vessels for service, mostly revenue cutters captured at the onset of hostilities. Aware of a shortage of ironclad vessels, however, he decided to look to Europe—especially Britain—for his ships.[5]

On May 1, at the urging of Secretary Mallory, the Confederate Congress enacted legislation "to create a provisional navy of the Confederate States."[6] But it was easier to proclaim a navy than create one, because of the shortage of manpower and materiel. This was especially true with respect to iron plating. Mallory warned that "the want of iron is severely felt throughout the confederacy, and the means of increasing its production demand, in my judgment, the prompt consideration of Congress."[7]

The South was fortunate to have Mallory, who was an expert at the formulation of naval strategy (as Davis was not), the selection of commanders, and the control and execution of vital matters. At the outset, he had a sizable pool of more than 150 naval officers who had resigned from the U.S. Navy at secession. By April 1862 the Confederate navy boasted a roster of 9 admirals, 6 commodores, 20 captains, 20 commanders, 20 first lieutenants, 65 second lieutenants, and 60 shipmasters.[8] Many of these officers were given shore billets because of a lack of ships.

Mallory's main objective was to counter the Union blockade as best he could. He set about pressing into service blockade-runners that, for the most part, were privately owned. Other vessels, built in Britain, were designated "commerce runners."

Faced with both Mallory's industrial efforts to thwart the blockade and the daunting challenge of a 549-mile coastline, Welles pressed into service all available vessels that could float and carry a gun: packet boats, coastal luggers, tugs, even ferryboats with their rudders and screws at each end, for navigation on narrow rivers.[9]

This makeshift fleet of armed vessels, plus new warships to come off the building ways in various shipyards, were divided into groups, or squadrons. The North Atlantic Blockading Squadron covered the coast from Virginia to Fort Fisher in North Carolina; the South Atlantic Blockading Squadron covered from Fort Sumter, in South Carolina, to Key West; the East Gulf Blockading Squadron covered from Key West to New Orleans; and the West Gulf Blockading Squadron covered from New Orleans to Galveston and Brownsville, on the Texas coast.

The Atlantic squadrons were responsible for preventing ships from entering the seaboard ports, from Bermuda and Nassau, that were staging areas for blockade-runners carrying goods from Europe. The Gulf squadrons prevented traffic to and from Havana. All in all, the tasks were difficult for this navy, strung out all over the map, sometimes helpless to prevent blockade-runners from coming in and out with impunity.[10] But they would succeed, as time wore on. In 1861, for example, only one out of nine blockade-runners was captured, but in 1862 the rate ran up to one out of seven. By 1865 more than 1,149 Confederate ships had been captured and 351 destroyed by the Union fleet. But during the last three years of the conflict, the Confederacy still managed to ship half a million bales of cotton and violated the blockade more than 8,000 times.[11] Such was the admirable tenacity of the Confederates against the Union's overwhelming naval strength. Yet the successes were not accomplished without great cost in men and ships, before it was over.

David Dixon Porter, commander of the North Atlantic Blockading Squadron, praised the effectiveness of the blockade: "So efficiently was the blockade maintained and so greatly was it strengthened from time to time that foreign statesmen who, at the beginning of the war, did not hesitate to pronounce the blockade of nearly three thousand miles of coast a mortal impossibility, twelve months after its establishment were forced to admit that the proofs of its efficiency were so comprehensive and conclusive that no objections to it could be made."[12]

The Union feared that foreign intervention, especially by England, would break the blockade, but these fears came to naught as the noose was tightened. Neither England nor France wanted a shooting war with the Union, so aside from some attempts to supply the Confederates with ships, they both wisely decided to stay out of the affair. But the growing strength of the U.S. Navy and the blockade itself were the major factors in discouraging Her Majesty's government from interfering. As John G. Nicolay, Lincoln's private secretary, wrote: "The unexampled increase of the United States Navy, the extraordinary efficiency of the blockade, the vigilant diplomatic service of the Lincoln Administration and, above all, its vigorous prosecution of the war, left foreign powers no efficient excuse, and overawed all passing temptations to intervene."[13] For its part, the Lincoln administration wanted no trouble with foreign powers.

In order to make the blockade effective, Lincoln and Welles needed

bases on the shores of the blockaded regions, located near big Confederate ports. These bases required deep anchorages and docking facilities.
The large, heavily fortified ports of Charleston and Savannah were considered but quickly dismissed. Instead the strategists selected Forts Hatteras and Clark, between the Atlantic Ocean and Pamlico Sound,
because the sites fulfilled the above conditions, were easily defendable
from land, and contained only two log-and-sandbank Confederate
works. The commander chosen for the expedition was Flag Officer
S. H. Stringham of the North Atlantic Blockading Squadron, a veteran
naval officer who had served in the War of 1812 and the Mexican War.
Major General Benjamin Butler, a politician-turned-general from Massachusetts, was selected to lead the landing forces.[14]

To keep Confederate heads down while Butler's troops landed and
invested the forts, Stringham selected seven warships with enormous
firepower: the flagship *Minnesota, Monticello, Pawnee, Harriet Lane,
Susquehanna, Wabash,* and the frigate *Cumberland.* It was to be the first
amphibious assault in the war, foreshadowing General Grant's massive
landing below Vicksburg in May 1863.

On August 26, 1861, the flotilla of Union warships and transports
left Hampton Roads, Virginia, and sailed for Cape Hatteras, arriving on
the twenty-eighth. The warships laid down a fierce bombardment on
the largest fort, Hatteras, while the troops stormed ashore.

All did not go well for the invaders: A surf came up and swamped
some of the landing boats, drenching the troops, wetting their powder,
and destroying provisions. But 300 badly shaken troops did manage
to land, while Stringham's ships kept up their bombardment, pouring
more than 28 shells a minute into the forts. Against the Union ships'
heavy armament, the ancient 32-pounders of the defenders could offer
no more than token resistance. Finally, overwhelmed, the Confederates
ran up a white flag. While Butler's troops moved in on the surrendered
Hatteras, the ships sortied to attack Fort Clark. Not surprisingly, Fort
Clark fell after only a short bombardment. It was a prime example of
the falsity of the teaching of many naval commanders, such as Britain's
Lord Nelson: that wooden ships should never tackle land forts. It was
also the first time that a new naval strategy was used: keeping ships in
motion while enfilading, making them more difficult to hit.

Seemingly impregnable Forts Walker and Beauregard, at the entrance to South Carolina's Port Royal Sound, were picked for the next Union assault, in November 1861. This time Flag Officer Samuel Francis Du Pont, another veteran naval officer and participant in the Mexican War and a former commandant of the Brooklyn Navy Yard, was chosen to lead the flotilla of warships and transports. Brigadier General Thomas W. Sherman was in command of 12,000 troops in 36 transports. With a total of 77 vessels, it was the largest amphibious force to date.

Du Pont's 14 warships included the new screw sloops *Pawnee, Iroquois,* and *Mohican,* all with 11-inch Dahlgren smoothbores, plus a flotilla of recently built "ninety-day" gunboats. The expedition experienced bad luck early on when a violent storm struck off the Carolina coast. The fleet was widely scattered, and one transport was destroyed, stranding 300 marines on hostile shores. Du Pont, regrouping his forces, discovered that the damage to the fleet was less than expected. The stranded marines were picked up by a warship, and all seemed to be on track again.

It was an omen of good luck, according to some. On November 5, the squadron of warships had steamed into Port Royal Sound and commenced a furious bombardment of the two forts, one at each end of the sound's entrance. This was a classic elliptical pattern; that is, sailing on a course that includes sharp reverse turns in elongated circles. The ships enfiladed both forts, using starboard and port guns. A small flotilla of Confederate gunboats dared to challenge the fleet, but under the heavy fire of Du Pont's big guns, they quickly retired. The Confederates in both forts withered under fire and soon abandoned their charges. General Sherman's troops were landed and swiftly took possession. It was a great victory for the Union, with an important base of operations as the prize. Flag Officer Du Pont later wrote to Welles, "It is not my temper to rejoice over fallen foes, but this must be a gloomy night in Charlestown."[15]

The Union had now closed the ports along the Atlantic seaboard between Wilmington and Charleston to Savannah. Still, blockade-runners managed to slip in and out under the noses of the blockading ships, in a running cat-and-mouse game, causing many a headache for the Union fleet. They would sail to the neutral ports of Bermuda, Nassau, and

Havana and unload their cargoes of cotton in exchange for civilian and military goods. For the most part these craft were privately owned (although some belonged to the Confederate government). They featured a low profile and were capable of great speeds—factors that helped them evade Federal ships throughout the war. Other ships, called cruisers, masqueraded as merchant vessels until they were out at sea, where they would unmask a battery, then attack and destroy a Union merchant vessel. (The Nazis would adopt this technique at the beginning of World War II.) The most famous of these cruisers was the C.S.S. *Florida*, a British-built 700-ton sloop rig with an iron hull and two funnels (smokestacks) and armed with eight rifles and a 12-pounder. In her fabulous career as a cruiser, the *Florida* handed numerous headaches to Admiral Farragut in his Gulf Blockading Squadrons off Mobile Bay.

THE raiders propelled the name of one Confederate commander into naval history: Raphael Semmes. This impressive naval officer had been a lawyer and midshipman in the U.S. Navy; he served honorably in the Mexican War and later retired to practice law in Alabama. When that state seceded, President Davis tapped him to oversee ordnance for the Confederate armed forces, a job that took him into the North to obtain supplies. Amazingly, he was able to tap many Northern industrial moguls to sell products vital to the Southern war effort. He obtained huge supplies of percussion caps, powder, and light artillery pieces. Semmes was also ordered to purchase any steamers that were available for conversion to vessels of war, but he found none. (It is a tribute to his integrity that he never revealed his Northern sources, as long as he lived.)[16]

After this venture, Semmes was given the rank of commander in the Confederate navy and assigned the 437-ton bark-rigged *Sumter*, which had been converted to a cruiser at New Orleans and armed with a one-inch rifle and four 32-pounders. With this magnificent vessel, he broke through the blockade and for six months went on a seaborne rampage, during which he captured 18 prizes. He would later blaze into the history books with the cruiser *Alabama*, bagging 69 Union ships and causing a great deal of consternation for the Union navy until his defeat in 1864 at the hands of the Union ship *Kearsarge* off Cherbourg, France.

We shall hear more of Captain Semmes later, in our treatment of the Gulf campaign.

About this time, other seamen entered the scene to play parts in the coming Gulf campaign. Franklin Buchanan, another New Englander, entered naval service in 1815 and fought in the Mexican War. As a 14-year-old midshipman, he had sailed the Mediterranean; he fought pirates in the Caribbean and became the cofounder and first superintendent of the U.S. Naval Academy. During Admiral Matthew Perry's expedition to Japan in March 1852, he commanded a ship. He later took command of the Washington Navy Yard. Convinced that his home state of Maryland would secede from the Union, he resigned his commission, but when Maryland remained with the Union, he relented and tried to recall his resignation. Welles refused to reconsider Buchanan and dismissed him from the service. Buchanan then offered his services to Jefferson Davis, who promptly appointed him a captain and put him in charge of the Bureau of Orders and Details. When the ironclad *Virginia* was commissioned, she was his to command, and he took part in the celebrated battle with the Union ironclad *Monitor* on March 9, 1862, a battle that left him wounded. Upon recovery, he was appointed admiral in the Confederate navy and later commissioned as commander of the Mobile Bay Squadron, with orders to guard that bay from entrance by Union ships.[17]

Another figure to emerge was Admiral David Dixon Porter, son of the distinguished naval officer Commodore David Porter and half-brother to David Glasgow Farragut. Porter had been at sea since his youth, sailing with his father to the West Indies in 1824 to suppress piracy. He was commissioned as a midshipman and officially joined the navy in 1829. Porter proved a splendid naval officer and served with honor in the Gulf during the war with Mexico. In 1862 he was appointed a commodore and given command of a fleet of mortar boats, with orders to join his half-brother in the Gulf of Mexico for the expected assault on New Orleans.[18]

No discussion of important personnel in the Gulf campaign would be complete without the U.S. Army officer Adam Jacoby Slemmer. Though not as famous as the other personalities, Slemmer nevertheless forged a place for himself in the history books when he refused to surrender Fort Pickens, at Pensacola, to the state militia. He thereby allowed the Union, for the rest of the war, to keep one important body of water and a naval station from being used by the Confederates. Born in Pennsylvania in 1828, Slemmer entered the Naval Academy in 1850 and was appointed first lieutenant in 1854. After leaving the academy, he served with distinction on the frontier and took part in the Seminole War between U.S. troops and Osceola's Seminole Indians from 1835 until 1842. Later Slemmer taught at West Point until 1861, when he was appointed major, 16th U.S. Infantry, and given the post of inspector general of Ohio under the command of General Don Carlos Buell, the commanding general of that state. Slemmer was transferred to Fort Barrancas in time for the beginning of the Civil War. His heroic story will be told in the next chapter.

Another individual of note on the Confederate side was George Nichols Hollins who, strangely enough, struck a blow for the South by dressing as a woman. After the secession he resigned his commission as a captain in the U.S. Navy in order to cast his lot with the Confederacy, which quickly commissioned him as a commander. Dressed as a woman, he managed to distract the crew of the Union steamer *St. Nicholas* in Chesapeake Bay while it was being boarded and captured by armed Southerners. To reward him, Mallory appointed him commander of defenses along the James River. He was later given command of the Confederate naval station in New Orleans and took command of all river forces on the upper Mississippi. He saw action at New Madrid, Fort Pillow, and Memphis, but when Farragut's fleet threatened New Orleans, he returned to take over its defenses. Mallory believed that Hollins erred by keeping his fleet below New Orleans instead of above, with the result that Hollins was given a desk job and chairs in various naval boards and courts.[19]

No discussion of principal players in the Gulf actions would be complete without a mention of Admiral David Glasgow Farragut. His command would be the crowning effort in the struggle for the Gulf of Mexico. Because he will prominently dominate the pages of this book, more will be said about the man and his work.

These were the primary participants and events in preparation for the struggle to come. With the closing of key ports, the Gulf blockading ships took their stations, setting the stage for the battle to control the Gulf of Mexico.

CHAPTER THREE

THE CONFEDERATE TAIL WAGS

In order to understand the geographical platform upon which the great Gulf naval struggles took place, we must examine that curved arm of the Atlantic Ocean known as the Gulf of Mexico.

Viewed from space, the Gulf resembles a landlocked fishbowl that covers nearly 700,000 square miles. It is bounded by the United States on the north, by eastern Mexico on the west, and by Cuba on the east. In fact, a line drawn from the tip of Florida to the tip of the Yucatán Peninsula would mark the southern edge of the Gulf, with Cuba located smack in the center of that edge. The Gulf measures 800 miles long from north to south, and 1,100 miles wide, with an average depth of 4,874 feet, but its greatest depth—12,424 feet—is at the Sigsbee Deep, off the Yucatán. The major rivers entering the Gulf are the Mississippi and the Rio Grande.

This unique body of emerald-green water is surrounded by a coast-line of 3,000 miles, with low, sandy marshes and myriad inlets and lagoons leading to bayous that teem with wildlife; it is a tropical wonderland that borders on paradise. Naturally, it has good harbors: Mobile, New Orleans, Galveston, and Pensacola. Many lesser harbors lie along the coastline, which during the Civil War offered opportunities for the Confederacy to deploy blockade-runners, while other inlets and bays provided good opportunities for salt-making.

This bewitching area would hardly seem like the ground for a life-and-death struggle, but given the importance of its ports of access for the Confederacy and the Union blockade to cut off those ports, struggle was inevitable. As long as the Southerners tried to use the ports, Union ships would be there to close them off. The first target of the blockade in the Gulf sector would be Florida, with its 2,077 miles of coastline.

In 1861 Florida was a sparsely settled state, for the most part. Most of the population lived in the northern area; Pensacola and Jacksonville were the most strategic pieces of Florida real estate at that time.[1]

Even before the state seceded from the Union, Florida had endured much internal strife in two wars with the Seminole Indians. Then in November 1860, U.S. naval forces at Key West came under pressure from members of the Florida state militia who wanted Federal naval bases for themselves. U.S.N. Commander Thomas Craven wrote to Isaac Toucey, President James Buchanan's secretary of the navy, that because of worsening conditions, he had been forced to move swiftly to prevent the militia from capturing Forts Taylor and Jefferson. He had boarded the U.S.S. *Mohawk* and, along with Lieutenant Sabius Slanty on the U.S.S. *Wyandotte*, defended the forts against "a band of lawless men." This defensive action assured that Key West would remain a base and coaling station for Union vessels.[2]

As 1861 dawned, the Florida militia struggle intensified. On January 6, militiamen surrounded the Federal base at Apalachicola on the Florida panhandle, east of Pensacola. The man in charge of the base, Ordnance Sergeant E. Powell, sent a message to Captain Magnadier, chief of the Ordnance Department in Washington, to the effect that his forces were too weak to defend the base and that it had been taken. But Powell refused to turn over the keys to the armory and the magazine, which caused a flurry of notes and exchanges. In the end he was forced to turn over the items to the militiamen. The next day on the east coast, state militiamen surrounded Fort St. Augustine, forcing the weak garrison there to surrender.[3]

·   ·   ·

AT the same time, profound events were unfolding at Fort Barrancas and the Pensacola Navy Yard.

On the eastern side of the entrance to Pensacola Bay lies a long snake-like bit of land called Santa Rosa Island. Fort Pickens lies at the head of the snake. Across the mile-wide-plus channel, on the mainland, was Fort Barrancas. These two U.S. forts guarded the entrance to Pensacola Bay, one of the most important bodies of water in the Gulf at that time. It anchored an entire navy, and on its west bank a U.S. navy yard provided an important coaling station for warships.

Florida state troops, under the command of Colonel William Henry Chase, quickly realized the importance of Fort Barrancas to the Confederacy, and on January 8 they moved up to the facility demanding its surrender. The fort's commander, Lieutenant Adam Jacoby Slemmer of the First Artillery, had just learned that on January 5 Alabama state militiamen had seized and occupied Fort Morgan at Mobile. Slemmer wired the adjutant general of the U.S. Army in Washington that a contingent of troops had approached Fort Barrancas and had asked for its surrender.[4] Slemmer consulted with the commander of the Pensacola Navy Yard, Commodore Armstrong, about the desperate situation, and they decided that since Fort Pickens commanded the harbor better, it was the obvious site to bolster and defend.

Fort Pickens had a long history. In 1719, under Spanish rule, a small fort had been built on the site. For a time Pensacola came under French rule, but it was returned to the Spanish in 1722. The British took possession in 1763, at the end of the French and Indian War, and during the War of 1812, the British fleet used the spacious bay as a fleet anchorage.

After the United States took possession of Pensacola in 1821, a navy yard was established there in 1825. Forts Pickens, Barrancas, and McRee were constructed during 1825, 1837, and 1844, respectively.[5] Colonel Chase had himself originally supervised the construction of Fort Pickens, using slave labor because of a shortage of skilled workmen.

When Florida militia threatened a takeover of Fort Barrancas, the situation became more desperate. Slemmer put into action his plan to abandon Forts Barrancas and McRee. Commodore Armstrong sent the 450-ton gunboat *Wyandotte* and the 500-ton storeship *Supply* to his aid. These units would ferry the Union troops across the bay to Fort Pickens; the gunboat, also carrying troops, would stand guard over the small convoy. Guns were spiked, ammunition and stores were placed on a flatboat, and troops were put aboard the fleet. This small flotilla made it to Fort Pickens without incident on January 10, the very day Florida seceded.

After Forts Barrancas and McRee were occupied by Southern troops, Slemmer and his men were isolated at Pickens. Only 54 guns were present in the fort and two in shore batteries, plus the five guns of the gunboat. The Union contingent was in a precarious position indeed.[6]

On January 12 four men, acting on behalf of the governors of Florida and Alabama, arrived at the fort and vigorously demanded its surrender to those states. Three other demands followed, one by a pleading Colonel Chase.[7] But Chase's pleas for a surrender without bloodshed fell on deaf ears; Slemmer was determined to stand his ground.

Admirably, the Union force held on, hoping for reinforcements from the U.S. Army and Navy. In a report to Lorenzo Thomas, assistant adjutant general, Slemmer later told of the pressures upon him during a siege by 2,000 hostile troops. "Had we been attacked during those dreadful days," he wrote, "dreadful would have been the havoc and we were menaced every day and night, from the 12th to the 26th, by the increasing number opposite us . . . not to allow ourselves one moment to think of surrendering unless absolutely overpowered by numbers."[8]

Reinforcements were in fact on their way. On January 25, Adjutant General Thomas at Fort Monroe, Virginia, ordered the First Artillery Company A, under the command of Captain Israel Vogdes, to embark on the 2,532-ton, 21-gun screw sloop *Brooklyn* to reinforce Fort Pickens. Vogdes's company was to be accompanied by attached men from other companies, along with 15,000 rounds of cartridges, four mountain howitzers, and 200 rounds of ammunition.

The Confederates received word of this audacious development, flew into a rage, and thundered dire consequences. Curiously, they took no action to counter this Union move by making an assault on the fort with superior numbers while they still had a chance of taking it. Colonel Chase's reluctance to take any offensive move is a mystery, considering that he knew Fort Pickens intimately. Perhaps he was subconsciously afraid to damage his own creation. No one knows for sure.[9]

On January 31, the *Brooklyn's* three tall masts appeared hull down on the horizon to the inhabitants of Key West, Florida. Soon the magnificent sloop-of-war entered its spacious harbor and commenced coaling. The ship immediately afterward sailed up Northwest Channel, paralleling the southern Gulf Coast, into the Gulf of Mexico, arriving at Fort Pickens on February 6. Vogdes inspected the fort and found it in such deplorable condition that he was ready to disembark his command. But he was prevented from doing so by orders from the Union high command, who had taken note of the Confederates' bellicose threats, and because of an interim agreement between Washington and Florida to the effect that no offensive action against Confederates would be taken as long as reinforcements were not brought up. But a confident Slemmer, bolstered by the forces offshore, continued to build up his defenses.

Finally orders came from General Scott for Vogdes to land his men immediately. But realistically the artillery forces on board the *Brooklyn* were not enough to counter a Confederate attack, because by this time General Braxton Bragg, with his own reinforcement troops and artillery, had taken command of all Confederate forces in Pensacola. Finally, after interdepartmental wrangling and debating, Scott, with the president's approval, ordered a massive reinforcement under the command of Brevet Colonel Harvey Brown.[10]

Once again the Confederates fussed and hollered, but the prospect of more big warships coming to the area, as well as the presence of the big sloop-of-war, sobered them considerably. Affairs in the Pensacola region—at least for the time being—quieted down with Union forces still in command.

MEANWHILE, another action was afoot in the Mississippi Sound off Gulfport, Mississippi. Ship Island, an eight-mile spit of land, opulent with sugar-white beaches and a toupee of thick scrub grass, sat like a sentinel guarding the eastern water approach to New Orleans and the Mississippi River delta, the southern approach. This early prize, because of its strategic position, was coveted by both sides. It was at the moment occupied by a small contingent of U.S. Army engineers and some civilian workers. On January 20, 1861, a small force of armed Mississippians came over, landed, made a lot of noise, and captured the island. They raised the flag of Mississippi and declared the occupants prisoners. But Union eyes were also on this prize, and forces from the big transport U.S.S. *Massachusetts* seized it in September 1861. The Confederates abandoned the island after the massive Union show of naval force. The Federals now had a base for future operations against New Orleans. In all early reports, the facility on Ship Island was referred to as "the works." Years later, it was named "Fort Massachusetts."

About the same time, Alabama armed forces captured Forts Morgan and Gaines at Mobile Bay, as well as Forts Jackson and St. Philip on the Mississippi River approaches to New Orleans. The Confederates had moved swiftly to consolidate positions. Clearly, the Gulf Blockading Squadrons would have their work cut out for them in the months to come.

Meanwhile, Florida—derisively called "The Tail of the Confederacy"—continued to be the center of naval activity in the Gulf. Key West, with its fine harbor, remained a Union naval station throughout the war. Much of the military impotence of the Rebels was due to their inability to marshal sufficient land and naval forces to challenge the Union superiority. Until the Pensacola Navy Yard was also back in Union hands, Key West was the major coaling facility for Federal warships operating in Gulf waters.

Key West was and still is the southernmost city of the United States. It had been sold to Americans in 1822 by its Spanish occupants, and by 1860 its population had grown to 2,832. In January 1861, fearing an attack by state militiamen, Union military units were ordered to take refuge in Fort Taylor until all threats of an assault had passed. During and after this tense period, Union fleet units continued to use the spacious, ¾- by 1½-mile harbor. The reluctance of the militiamen to move on the city and the fort may have been due to fear of the big guns on board the one or two warships that were usually in the harbor. Later, when the U.S. Department of Florida was established, Key West became the headquarters; after the Confederates were no longer a threat, it was transferred to Fort Pickens.

An interesting and singular event, one that has been overlooked by historians, transpired on May 16, 1861, when the citizens of Key West pledged their support to the Union forces at Fort Taylor by forming a volunteer company. They asserted: "[We will] hold ourselves subject to the order of the commander of the United States forces at Key West. Signed, A. Patterson, et al."[11] Union personnel were overjoyed at this development; considering that Florida had seceded months earlier, it took a lot of courage on the part of the citizens. It shows that not all citizens of a Southern state were in sympathy with the Southern cause. In the annals of Civil War history, the unknown "A. Patterson" and his friends should take their places alongside the many other much-admired anonymous patriots.

Using Key West as a base, Union naval units became more prevalent in the Gulf, bolstering the blockading flotillas. Some were assigned a most unusual task—to destroy Confederate salt-works along the Florida coast, from Tampa to the panhandle. Here the abundant inlets and bays provided excellent opportunities for making salt, which was crucial to the Southern war effort. As the blockade shut off much of the goods necessary for the war effort, salt, the principal source of which was Florida, gained the utmost importance to the Confederate armies because of its ability to preserve meat.

The Confederacy showed remarkable enterprise in salt-making, an endeavor that it considered vital.

The most important salt-works were located between Tampa and Choctawhatchee Bay, east of Pensacola, particularly around St. Andrews Bay, near Panama City.[12] To disrupt these operations, the Union navy used small, lightly armed steamers and gunboats with light drafts, since the effort involved chases up rivers and into small bays and bayous, from which larger vessels with deeper drafts were excluded.

When the salt-makers refused to budge, the gunboats were often forced to fire shells into the works, destroying them and killing or wounding any occupants who dared stay on. Landing parties swiftly followed the shellings, to capture personnel if possible and, of course, to destroy the remaining equipment. In some cases 2,500 men were engaged in the salt operations, laboriously obtaining as many as 360 bushels of salt per day.[13]

Many of the Union naval movements against Florida's salt industry were directed by Rear Admiral Lardner, using a fleet of gunboats and contingents of marines. The Southern effort to defend the salt-making operation remained rigorous through most of the conflict because of its extreme importance to the South, and they managed to tie up some of the Union naval power.

THE struggle over salt aside, in Pensacola things were heating up as Slemmer continued to strengthen Fort Pickens. The massive reinforcement in April supplied him with more troops and artillery. Then, on September 2, 1861, bolstered by additional warships offshore, he boldly sent a contingent of troops to board a drydock that the Confederates had stranded in their effort to move it to Pensacola. Brevet Colonel Brown, surmising it was to be used as a floating battery, ordered it blown out of the water, but the frightened Rebels scuttled it first. In order to prevent its being raised later, the Union troops torched it to the waterline.[14] The hulk was so badly burned that the Confederates made no effort to raise and rebuild it.

On September 14 gunfire erupted in the calm of the harbor when a boarding party from the screw frigate U.S.S. *Colorado* attempted to board the schooner *Judah*, which the Confederates were outfitting as a blockade-runner. The boarding party of Federal sailors and marines was met by a hail of musketry, but the determined fighting men boarded the ship, commandeered it, and set it on fire. It sank to the bottom a few hours later.

This audacious act so angered General Bragg that he ordered General Richard "Dick" Anderson and 1,000 troops to land on Santa Rosa Island and invest Fort Pickens. On October 9 the troops, on board the steamers *Ewing, Time,* and *Neaffie,* with a train of boats and barges, landed and moved in on the fort in three columns. Unfortunately for Anderson, his undisciplined troops preferred to loot and burn rather than attack the fort, and once the confrontation escalated, they were forced to retreat. As the Confederates were boarding their boats and barges, Union troops outflanked them, took positions behind sand dunes, and opened fire, inflicting huge casualties. The raid was a disaster for Bragg: Anderson reported his casualties as 18 dead, 39 wounded, and 30 missing or presumed prisoners of war. The Federals reported 14 dead, 29 wounded, and 24 presumed prisoners of war. Never again did the Confederates attempt an assault on Fort Pickens. Slemmer's bold initiative thus denied the Confederates the most important navy yard south of Norfolk. The event had the further distinction of being the first land battle in Florida.

On November 22, in a climactic gesture, the reinforced batteries at Fort Pickens launched a massive bombardment upon Forts McRee and Barrancas plus the Pensacola Navy Yard, inflicting irreparable damage. Pensacola, miles away, repeatedly shook from the two-day bombardment, and huge numbers of fish were killed by concussions from shells hitting the water. The Federals had flung 5,000 rounds of ammunition at the Confederate facilities.

Adding insult to injury, the Federals on January 1, 1862, unleashed another bombardment, and this time Fort McRee was completely negated as a military facility. When the big guns of Fort Pickens were turned on the navy yard, it too suffered considerable damage.

AT the end of 1861 more warships appeared in the Gulf, and the blockade of ports from Florida to Texas began in earnest; the growing Union naval power tightened the noose even further. By early 1862 plans for an assault upon New Orleans were being considered in the Washington war rooms, made possible by the great success of the Union naval forces thrusting down the Mississippi River.

But problems remained for the Federal blockade. The coast of Texas, especially at Galveston, was troublesome. Six months earlier Secretary Welles had ordered Captain James Alden, aboard the 1,165-ton, five-gun screw steamer *South Carolina,* to steam off the mouth of Galveston Bay. On July 2, 1861, he arrived on station and began his blockade steaming pattern. It held without incident until August 5, when a Rebel gun battery, on the lee side of the peninsula upon which Galveston is located, opened fire on the ship without provocation. Alden held return fire, hoping someone would come out to the ship and apologize for an error of judgment. When no one showed, he moved his ship closer to shore, anticipating another barrage. He did not have to wait long; the gunners sent another salvo flying at the *South Carolina*. Fortunately for the Union, all missed. As far as Alden was concerned, the fat was now in the fire; he ordered a response from the ship's battery. But because the enemy gunners were on the west side of the city, some of the Union shells fell short, killing one civilian and wounding others. Various "foreign consuls" in Galveston vigorously protested the incident.[15] The blockade off Galveston was far from successful, however, because blockade-runners went in and out with impunity.

In December 1861 the Union added more ships to the blockade off the port. The 66-ton schooner *Sam Houston*, a Rebel ship captured in July; the 66-ton bark *Midnight*; the 235-ton screw steamer *Victoria*; and the flagship, the 726-ton frigate *Santee*, commanded by Captain Henry Eagle, all joined the squadron.

The only naval action reported by Captain Eagle was the firing of shells upon his ship by a small battery onshore, all of which missed. Eagle did not return fire, but he did send a salvo at a group of cavalrymen three miles south of Galveston, sending them into confusion.[16] Obviously, it was not all boredom for the crews aboard blockading ships.

MANY nonmilitary readers may wonder what life was like aboard a warship—without the benefit of modern air-conditioning—on patrol duty in subtropical or tropical waters, such as those Union ships in the Gulf.

For the seaman, time blends into more time; it means nothing. You get up when you are called for watch duty, and breakfast could be at 3:00 A.M. If you are on lookout duty, the watches are agonizingly routine: Hour after hour, day after day, week after week, you scan the horizon. You desperately hope that something out of the ordinary will occur. The hot, oppressive sun beats down mercilessly, heating the ship's iron or wooden hull, making it uncomfortable below decks in spite of ventilator cowlings. At night it may cool off a bit because of surface breezes, but that relief could quickly be offset by a strong tropical storm cell, which could spring up most unexpectedly. Then everyone springs into action to "batten down" the gear and hatches on the ship, and you ride out the storm, hoping all the hatches are secure and ventilator cowlings are blocked to keep out water.

During off-hours, you spend time reading, writing letters, or jawing with your shipmates. When you are not on watch, you are required to perform the duties of whatever ship's division you are in—in the gunnery division, for example, you clean and maintain the ordnance, making repairs if needed. Other times you participate in simulated gunnery practice in order to maintain your gunnery skills, regardless of your position on a gun. Then one day something unusual occurs, such as a strange ship being where it should not be, possibly a blockade-runner or even a vessel in distress. The adrenaline flows as you fling yourself into action. Honed to perfection during endless hours of practice, you go to general quarters and perform these duties until the emergency is over. Then the dreary routine starts all over again, and you hope and pray for another emergency situation.

In a Civil War navy, the crews were responsible for their own laundry, which they would string along the ship's riggings or on signal lanyards. Leisure time was slightly different: to while away hours, they played games on deck or listened to talented crewmates with instruments, such as banjos, fiddles, or guitars. But all in all, routines on patrol duty are much the same in any navy, in any time, and in any ocean.

As Union forces wrought havoc on the Mississippi and the blockade slowly tightened on the Gulf Coast, the time came for a Union assault on the gateway to the Mississippi, New Orleans. On February 20, 1862, Flag Officer David Glasgow Farragut arrived at Ship Island with a powerful flotilla of warships, including his beloved flagship, the 2,900-ton screw sloop *Hartford*, in preparation for the assault. This famous warship, 225 feet long, with a 44-foot beam and an 18-foot draft, was armed with 24 guns, including 20 nine-inch smoothbores. Her sister sloops-of-war, *Brooklyn* and *Richmond*, plus the screw sloop *Pensacola* and the side-wheel frigate *Mississippi*, were also present. Other vessels included the screw gunboat *Cayuga*, two corvettes, seven gunboats, the screw sloop *Iroquois*, plus Porter's mortar schooners.

Many warships of the Gulf Blockading Squadron, under the command of Flag Officer William Mervine, were already off the island, awaiting Farragut. This gathering of Union naval forces caused no end of consternation to Confederate General Braxton Bragg at Mobile, who wrote, "Some twenty of the enemy's vessels are below, landing supplies and large bodies of troops on the island."[17] Unfortunately for Bragg, he had no naval vessels with which to challenge the gathering Union naval and land forces.

New Orleans was of vital strategic importance to both the North and the South. The seizure and occupation of the city would fulfill the second phase of the Anaconda Plan: to open the Mississippi down to the Gulf, thus severing the Confederacy in two.

The operation was planned to coincide with Grant's capture of Fort Pillow, Memphis, Vicksburg, and Grand Gulf, backed by Flag Officer David Porter's powerful fleet of gunboats, transports, and supply train.

In his cabin on board the *Hartford*, Farragut must have read and reread his orders from Secretary Welles, to the effect, "When you are completely ready, you will collect such vessels as can be spared from the blockade and proceed up the Mississippi River and reduce the defenses that guard the approaches to New Orleans, when you will appear off that city and take possession of it under the guns of your squadron." He was to wait for a mortar flotilla to arrive, under the command of Flag Officer Porter.[18] These stripped-down schooners, equipped with 13-inch mortars, would play an important role in the capture of New Orleans.

THE accelerating events in the Gulf threw the already-embattled Secretary Mallory into a quandary. Fort Pickens was still in Union hands, blockading ships lay off every major port in the Gulf, including Galveston, and Federal naval strength was growing with every passing week. The naval vessels and troops gathering at Ship Island convinced him that New Orleans was soon to be the object of a major Union thrust. He had to do something to create a naval force, to counter the threat of a navy that had complete mastery of the sea.

And he had to do it swiftly.

CHAPTER FOUR

MALLORY'S GULF DILEMMA

As Stephen Mallory watched the Union forces encroaching in the Gulf, he must have endured a few sleepless nights. He had no deep-water ships with which to sortie out and challenge the blockading squadron, nor could he even hope to acquire such forces. He may have surmised that his only strategy lay in massing enough naval power to protect the South's most vital ports: Galveston, New Orleans, and Mobile Bay.

It must have given him some comfort that in addition to the unfinished *Merrimack* at the Gosport Navy Yard, a fleet of British-built, first-class ships were up for sale by the British East India Company. These vessels of "great size and power" had originally been designed for conversion to troop ships or ships of war.[1]

The East India Company had been formed to open trade with India and the Far East during the 1600s and had endured for more than 200 years. But it was fading as a viable organ of commerce, and in 1858 it had relinquished control of India to the British government. It also relinquished the recently built ships, which the crown promptly put up for sale. These vessels, properly outfitted and armed at a cost of $10 million, could have given the Confederate navy considerable punch. Alas, because of their desperately inadequate resources, the Confederate government was forced to reject the plan and never bought the ships.

Undaunted, Mallory forged ahead with his mission to create some sort of naval presence in the Gulf. Earlier he had managed to commandeer four U.S. revenue cutters, a steam tender, two coastal survey vessels, and two steam vessels. All of these vessels had been seized by Southern states as they seceded, including the 1,200-ton *Fulton*, a schooner-rigged, side-wheel steamer that the Union navy had used for anti–slave trade purposes; it had been stranded in Pensacola.[2]

To service this basic fleet, Mallory had two major navy yards: the Gosport Navy Yard in Norfolk, Virginia, which was still undergoing rebuilding after being torched by evacuating Union forces in April 1861, and the Pensacola Navy Yard. In addition, he could count on a few small, vessel-producing shipyards in New Orleans and a medium-sized, privately owned shipyard in Memphis, which could be enlarged to produce larger craft. At the latter facility, two ironclads were ordered to be built.[3]

Of all Mallory's acute shortages, none was felt as desperately as that of foundry facilities. He had only four: the Tredegar Iron Works in Richmond, Virginia; two rolling mills in Tennessee; and a foundry that had been converted to manufacturing naval guns in Selma, Alabama. (There were small facilities in New Orleans, not of major importance.) Of these facilities, the Tredegar works contributed most to the Confederate war effort. Before the war, the privately owned operation had produced cannons, gun carriages, locomotives, boilers, cables, and naval hardware for the U.S. Navy. When Virginia seceded, the firm's owner and manager, Joseph R. Anderson, pledged his company to the Confederate cause. It contributed, among other items, heavy army and navy guns, as well as armor plating and heavy equipment for arsenals and powder mills.

As for ready-at-hand supplies for the fledgling navy, Mallory had considerable guns, powder, ammunition, and necessary equipment for vessels from the Gosport Navy Yard and a lesser amount from the

Pensacola Navy Yard. But it was not enough; one of the priority tasks assigned to blockade-runners was to buy powder and shot from foreign countries.

Mallory was also plagued by shortages of iron. Tredegar contributed a sizable amount, but Mallory's crash shipbuilding program needed much more than was available. On August 16, 1862, he wrote: "The want of iron is severely felt throughout the Confederacy, and the means of increasing its production demand, in my judgment, the prompt consideration of Congress. The government has outstanding contracts amounting to millions of dollars, but the iron is not forthcoming to meet the increasing public demands."[4]

Later, with great effort, rolling mills and foundries were built at Macon, Georgia, and a powder mill at Columbia, South Carolina, plus an ordnance foundry in Charlotte, North Carolina.[5]

Perhaps the most interesting establishment created by Mallory—and one that had far-reaching consequences for the Union—was the Torpedo Bureau and Naval Submarine Battery Service, which would prove to be a vital factor in offsetting the lack of a powerful naval force. Through this bureau came the awesome weapons of "torpedoes" (known as mines today) and torpedo boats and the world's first operating submarine. The torpedoes were exceptionally effective and managed to sink or disable 32 Union vessels during the war. They were generally made from beer kegs, demijohns, or cannisters of all sorts filled with gunpowder, and they could easily be detonated either by contact devices or by cables to batteries on shore. (The U.S.S. *Cairo* was sunk by a torpedo with the latter device on the Yazoo River on December 12, 1862, and the U.S.S. *Tecumseh* by one with a contact device in Mobile Bay on August 5, 1864.)[6] Electrical torpedoes were not used on a large scale, because of a shortage of copper wire in the Confederacy.

Naturally, the Union became deeply concerned about these lethal weapons and was researching countermeasures, such as a crude minesweeping device invented by Charles Ellet. Ellet's device, had it been fully adopted by the navy, would have been the first practicable minesweeping device in naval history. It consisted of a strong wooden frame containing a series of iron hooks attached to an equally strong wooden frame bolted on the bow of a ship. The device was designed to snag the ignition wires attached to the mines, thereby disabling them. Ellet was set to test it, but an unexplained order from higher up canceled the test run.[7]

For their part, the Confederates, right up to the surrender, conducted research on improving the torpedo, testing a more effective electric device. We will discuss these weapons in more detail in the chapters on the battle of Mobile Bay.

The Torpedo Bureau was responsible for the prototype of another weapon that would have a major effect on navies for generations to come: the first operating submarine, the C.S.S. *H.L. Hunley*. This craft was produced from an old ship's boiler and was 35 feet long and five feet high, with a four-foot beam. The ballast tanks and horizontal fins on each side enabled her to travel underwater. The propeller of the cigar-shaped vessel was powered by a long crank, in the hands of a crew of eight men, producing a speed of four knots. One crew member, an officer, guided the vessel by means of a porthole, while controlling the bow ballast tanks. A petty officer controlled the stern ballast tanks. Air was let in only once.

The *Hunley*'s lethal punch was a 20-foot spar projecting from the bow, to which was attached a 90-pound copper torpedo. The submarine would approach a target, ram the torpedo below the waterline, and hopefully sink it.

The *Hunley* was tested twice, both times ending in disaster for the vessel and her crew. On February 17, 1864, the *Hunley* successfully attacked and sank the 1,800-ton U.S.S. *Housatonic*, a 23-gun wooden corvette. Unfortunately for the Confederacy, the *Hunley* was also destroyed in the explosion, along with her crew and the inventor, H. L. Hunley. But a new era of warfare had been born.

The third Confederate naval innovation was the torpedo boat. This wooden craft, 30 to 40 feet long with a six- to eight-foot beam, was designed for speed. It too was equipped with a long spar, to which was attached a torpedo. Like its submarine sister, the torpedo boat would approach a target and ram the torpedo into its side. A few torpedo boats were in experimentation on the East Coast, but the Confederate navy never adopted them. About 78 years later the torpedo boat would reappear as a viable weapon in World War II.

With respect to personnel, the Confederate navy suffered from the same problems as the Union: For the most part crews consisted of a motley blend of civilians and army and navy men. To compound the problem, the crews were under the command of the army, instead of the navy, which caused much dissent among both officers and men.

Hopes were growing that England, with her need for cotton, would intervene with her superior navy to back Confederate efforts to break the blockade. Consequently Mallory expanded his ambitious blockade-running program. It was easy at first, because of the Union's lack of blockading ships. But as time went on and more ships became available to the Federal navy, it grew more difficult.

By the fall of 1861, the situation in the Gulf had arrested most of Mallory's attention, especially at New Orleans and its shipyards. His fledgling navy clearly needed ironclad gunboats with which to meet the Union threat. But to his chagrin, the existing shipyard facilities at the Crescent City were inadequate, so he arranged to have yards established at Jefferson City, north of New Orleans. There two ironclads, *Louisiana* and *Mississippi*, would be built, plus 42 other vessels that could be armed with guns and commissioned in the navy. But the bugaboo he faced was a crippling shortage of workers and materiel with which to build these craft. Jefferson Davis had already written that "there was a lack of skilled labor, of ship yards, and of material for constructing iron-clads, which could not be readily obtained or prepared in a beset and blockaded country."[8] Davis also complained about the shortage of iron plating, or railroad iron, with which to equip the vessels.

Enter the brothers Tift, Asa and Nelson. This team of industrialists offered their services to the Confederacy and proudly announced that they would build the ironclads for Mallory. They created quite a stir of excitement when they ingeniously managed to procure lumber and building materials from existing firms, plus the smaller ironworks scattered throughout New Orleans. Keeping to their promised schedule, they managed to lay the keels of the two ironclads in October 1861— no mean feat, considering they had to use every trick in the negotiation book.

Unfortunately, Major General Mansfield Lovell, the Confederate military commander at New Orleans, blocked their efforts, through inefficiency and lack of leadership. But the Tifts forged on, and some materiel began to appear on the scene. They offset the shortage of manpower somewhat by borrowing slaves from nearby plantations. The *Mississippi* began to take shape, but once again that shortage of engines, boilers, and iron plating took its toll, and progress slowed to a crawl. This was a sad situation for the Confederacy, because the *Mississippi* would have given the Union fleet some real opposition. At a displacement of 1,400 tons, she would have been 260 feet long, with a 58-foot beam and a 12-foot draft. Her armor plates were to have been three inches thick, and her armament was to consist of 20 guns, two of which would have been seven-inch rifles. Her sister, the *Louisiana*, would have been a bit larger at 264 feet, with a 62-inch beam and armed with more guns. Together these men-of-war would have posed a serious threat to Farragut's wooden ships. In addition to the ironclads, Mallory was equipping a sizable fleet of vessels with ramming prows and arming each with a gun or two, depending upon size.

Meanwhile, in New Orleans a private group, not associated with the military but sympathetic to the Confederacy, procured a tug and converted her to an ironclad at the Algiers shipyard. This strange, turtlelike craft of 387 tons, 143 feet long with a 33-foot draft, was armed with a 64-pounder and a 32-pounder. Her convex sides gave her the appearance of a huge egg. The unlovely ironclad, with a two-foot, six-inch freeboard projecting above the water, was later commandeered by the Confederate government and named *Manassas* and was used to challenge Farragut's fleet.

At a Memphis shipyard two more ironclads were under construction, the *Tennessee* and the *Arkansas*. After Union forces on the Mississippi, in the spring of 1862, threatened the construction projects, the *Arkansas* would be finished on the Yazoo River. She would later enter naval history by taking on an entire Union fleet at Vicksburg—and surviving. Her sister was burned on the stocks when the Federal fleet approached for an assault on Memphis.[9]

Three more ironclads were rumored to be under construction up the Escambia River, north of Pensacola, and up the Mobile River, north of Mobile. The latter proved to be true, and the finished ironclad *Tennessee* would challenge Farragut at the battle of Mobile Bay in August 1864.

Still more Confederate ironclads were under construction in the rivers of North Carolina and Virginia, but none of them had any effect on the Gulf campaign. All in all, the shipbuilding efforts of the Confederacy were admirable.

LACKING a deep-water navy and faced with a blockade, the Confederates adopted a most effective counterstrike: blockade-running.

During the early days nine out of ten vessels managed to run the Union blockade without interference. Between September 30, 1862, and September 30, 1863, a total of 113,000 small arms were brought through the blockade. During the same period 5,000 pairs of shoes, 300,000 blankets, 8 million pounds of meat, and half a million pounds of coffee were brought into southern ports from England. Many blockade-run items helped in the military campaigns: At Shiloh, for example, Confederate General Albert Sidney Johnston's troops fought with Enfield rifles that had been made in Britain and brought in by the blockade-runner *Fingal*. The rest of her cargo included 1 million ball cartridges, 2,000 percussion caps, 3,000 cavalry sabers, 400 barrels of powder, and 100 rifled cannons, along with other fighting equipment.[10] Not only did blockade-running help the Confederacy, it was profitable, too. For a typical run a captain could realize around $5,000 profit, and his chief engineer around $2,000.

The Union blockade was especially ineffective in the Gulf, because the bulk of the Federal fleet was stationed off the Atlantic coast. Blockade-runners who operated out of the Gulf of Mexico used Havana as the chief port of entry and exit, although some trade also moved through the Bahamas. At these entry points to and from Europe, the smaller runners would unload cargoes onto lighters, which in turn would load large seagoing ships for transit to Europe. The reverse was true with traffic coming from Europe.

The smaller blockade vessels had to travel remarkably long distances. A trip from Mobile to Havana covered 637 miles; New Orleans to Havana, 886 miles; and it was a rather long 960 miles from Brownsville, Texas, to Havana.[11] Cotton, of course, was one of the main cargoes exchanged for European goods. It is estimated that more than 1 million bales of cotton were shipped through between 1861 and 1865. Millions of dollars were realized by the indefatigable blockade-runners, especially in the early years of the war.

As blockade-running became more perilous, the goods that were brought in became atrociously expensive. For the Southern housewife in 1860, for example, 10 pounds of sugar cost $1.25, but in 1863 the same 10 pounds cost $10.00. Clearly, the blockade was rough on the population of seceded states.[12] For the more affluent, however, a great many luxuries, such as French brandy, jewelry, and perfume, were brought in.

The vessels picked for blockade-running were of necessity fast and sleek, usually side-wheelers with a displacement of around 400 tons, although some vessels were sail-rigged. Most of them had a low freeboard, slim masts, and funnels that were either telescoped or lowered. They burned anthracite coal because of its low smoke production, and hulls were usually painted a dull gray to allow them to blend in with surrounding waters.

If discovered, the runners could often outdistance the blockading ships.[13] Naval historians E. B. Potter and Chester A. Nimitz speculate that Confederate blockade-running did not substantially harm the Union cause; in fact, it actually siphoned off able-bodied seamen, and by "stimulating the gold flow out of the country and thus debasing the currency, the blockade-runners weakened the South."[14]

PRIVATEERING became another important aspect of Confederate naval strategy. By definition, a privateer was an armed private vessel holding a government commission to attack and either capture or destroy enemy ships of commerce.

The Confederate privateering strategy was intended to destroy the blockade. Privateers would force the Union to draw more and more of its ships away from the blockade in order to give chase, thereby diminishing its effectiveness. In one incident, more than eight Union men-of-war were assigned to track down one Confederate privateer that had captured 10 U.S. merchant ships. During their heyday, the privateers managed to capture around 60 merchantmen on the high seas with few or no losses to themselves.

Ultimately, however, the strategy was unsuccessful because too few good ships and men were available to the Confederacy early on, and later because bringing prizes through the blockade became extremely difficult. As time went on, it became harder to replace the men and ships. By the middle of 1862, privateering had all but faded from the scene.

Many historians agree that the most effective seagoing blockade-busting weapon in the Confederate arsenal was the cruiser or commerce raider. These vessels, generally built in England or Scotland, were fast, heavily armed, and designed to prey upon Union shipping much as the privateers did, except that the cruisers were government owned and sanctioned. In the Gulf the most famous cruisers were the *Florida* and the *Alabama*. The latter, skippered by Raphael Semmes, became one of the most famous ships in naval history. The *Florida*, commanded by John Maffitt, gave the blockading forces in the Gulf quite a few headaches, especially off Mobile Bay.

The *Alabama* and the *Florida* had been constructed in the Laird ship-yards in Liverpool, England. Built with the best oak available, they were copper-bottomed and equipped with the finest materials, "in all respects first-class ships."[15] The *Alabama*, for example, displaced 1,050 tons, was 200 feet long and had a 31-foot beam, a draft of 14 feet, and a crew of 148. Her four boilers and two horizontal, direct-acting, condensing engines propelled her at an impressive 14 knots. Little wonder she blazed a reputation as the scourge of the high seas, evading entire squadrons of Union ships seeking to destroy her. Both vessels used the Bahamas as a base of operations.[16]

Another Confederate cruiser that earlier challenged the Union navy in the Gulf was the *Sumter*, a 437-ton bark-rigged vessel 184 feet long, with one screw. Converted from the coastal packet *Havana* at a New Orleans shipyard, this ship was commissioned by the Confederate government. The *Sumter*, with her dynamic skipper Raphael Semmes, steamed on to forge an enviable record of achievement, becoming a nemesis of the Union navy for many months in the Gulf. Here is a most fascinating story of courage and excellent seamanship.

In Montgomery, Alabama, only days after the surrender of Fort Sumter on April 18, 1861, Semmes received an order from Secretary

Mallory to take command of the steamer *Havana* at New Orleans, along with a complement of officers.[17] Semmes wasted no time; he packed and arrived in the Crescent City on April 22, in the company of an officer, Lieutenant Robert Chapman, who had joined him at Mobile. He inspected the ship and found her well suited to his purposes. She was 230 feet long, with a 30-foot beam, and her one screw was powered by a single vertical direct-acting engine.

Semmes fashioned his command well. He overhauled the *Havana* for what he called "war purposes." Then he generously installed a berth deck for the crew, plus comfortable quarters for the officers. He also expanded the coal and ammunition bunkers. In view of the expanded facilities, Semmes remained concerned about her speed and her coal capacity. Still, he armed her with one eight-inch pivot gun and four 32-pounders and shipped onboard a crew of 114. After rechristening her the *Sumter*, he pronounced her ready for action, proclaiming that he would "do the enemy's commerce the greatest injury in the shortest time."[18]

After two weeks of rigorous testing of men, machinery, and weapons, Semmes was ready for his planned run past the blockade.[19] On the night of June 18, the C.S.S. *Sumter* cast off and slipped downstream to anchor near Fort Jackson. Semmes needed time to study the situation with the blockading ships off the passes: the 21-gun, 2,532-ton U.S.S. *Brooklyn*, the fastest ship in the Union navy with 21 knots; and the 16-gun, 13,765-ton side-wheeler *Powhatan*, the ship Semmes most feared. Also hovering nearby were the 4,582-ton frigate *Niagara* and the 4,832-ton screw frigate *Minnesota*. For a time Semmes remained under the protection of Fort Jackson, which had been seized by the Louisiana state militia on January 10, 1861, while he considered his options. He continued to receive intelligence about the movements of the Union ships, firmly at anchor off the bars.

Then on the eve of June 21, he received word that the *Powhatan* had hightailed off to investigate some strange sails. He quickly slipped downstream to the Head of the Passes of the Mississippi River delta.

THE Head is part of an intricate work of nature. The Mississippi River delta is the result of generations of silt being swept downriver by the currents and piling up to form a land base. The outlets, or passes, from the delta usually branch out from one wider body, the Head, which lies at the foot of the river where it empties into the Gulf, 70 miles south of New Orleans. In the Mississippi delta there were, and still are, three main passes: the South Pass, the Southwest Pass, and the eastern pass called the Pass à l'Outre. Each pass had a lighthouse at its entrance, and the Head itself had one, located between the South and Southwest Passes. The Union ships were anchored off the bars of each pass. Semmes decided to anchor in the Head and wait for some lucky chance to dash out into the Gulf. Because navigating through a pass and across the bar is a dangerous business without a pilot, Semmes visited the lighthouse of the Head and requested one. He was ignored. Flying into a rage, he threatened to arrest all the pilots if they failed to comply with his wishes.[20] Sure enough, he got his pilot.

Reasoning that the lighthouses were as useful to the enemy as they were to him, Semmes climbed into a boat and was rowed out to remove the oil from both the South Pass and the Pass à l'Outre lighthouses. He was determined that the Union captains would have no help from light-houses to guide them in and out of the passes.

It was fortunate for Semmes that he did not make a run after he received word of the *Powhatan*'s absence, because in the meantime she had returned to her station. A chase with her at that time would have been disastrous for him and his crew. So he dropped anchor and set his crews to constant drilling, hoping for just the right break.

Finally it came. He received a report that the *Brooklyn* had sortied off to investigate a strange sail and had left her station at the Pass à l'Outre unguarded. Semmes cleared the *Sumter* for action, obtained a pilot, cast off, and started his fast run down the pass. It was a close call; as he approached the outlet, he was astonished to see the *Brooklyn* returning to her station, but she was not yet close enough to block him.

The race began, with four miles between them. For a time the *Brooklyn* gained on the *Sumter*—when the latter's boilers began to froth. But the problem was cleared up, and the *Sumter* surged ahead. Semmes's rigorous training of his crew, while waiting in the Head of the Pass, made all the difference to him and his ship now. The *Brooklyn*, with her less experienced crew, dropped behind, and through a masterful feat of seamanship by Semmes and his crew, the *Sumter* escaped. Later Semmes often pondered why the Union ship had failed to use her guns during the chase; she had been close enough at times. No explanation was ever given.[21]

The *Sumter* reached Cuba on July 3 and immediately captured a Union merchant ship, the *Golden Rocket*. After removing her crew and cargo, he burned her, setting off bitter repercussions for him.

The intrepid cruiser and her intrepid captain went on to capture more merchant vessels: five brigs, six barks, and three schooners. It was a scenario that Semmes repeated many times thereafter, until the *Sumter* was sold to the British at Gibraltar in December 1863. At that point he received command of the C.S.S. *Alabama* and proceeded to start a whole new chapter of battling the blockade.[22] We will catch up with Semmes and the *Alabama* when we discuss the actions at Galveston.

President Davis later crowed about the incident in which "this one little cruiser created a general alarm and, though a regularly commissioned vessel of the Confederacy, was habitually denounced as a pirate, and the many threats to destroy her served only to verify the adage that the threatened live long."[23]

The Union responded to this embarrassing situation by detaching a fleet of ships to search the Caribbean for the *Sumter*, but the search was fruitless. The wily Semmes and his ship were never captured by U.S. warships.

Stephen Mallory was no fool. Quick to realize that cruisers could be powerful tools to strike at the blockade, he searched for more such vessels. Britain, with her ability to build magnificent ships, was a logical source. Accordingly, he sent Commander James Dunwody Bulloch of the Confederate navy, along with some agents, to London, with orders to contract for the building of cruisers. There Bulloch swept aside obstacles, such as the British Foreign Enlistment Act which forbade English shipyards from building foreign warships.

Bulloch managed to have a cruiser built in British shipyards—a 700-ton sloop rig with an iron hull and two stacks, named the *Oreto*—under a ruse that she was being built for the Italian government.[24] Despite the strenuous assertions of the U.S. minister to Great Britain, Charles Francis Adams, that the vessel was destined for the Confederate navy, it was launched and manned by a British crew. The *Oreto's* armament was shipped separately in the hold of a British cargo ship, the *Bahama*. At Nassau the *Oreto* dropped anchor and awaited the arrival of the British merchantman. When the *Bahama* arrived, her crew started to unload the armament onto a lighter vessel for transfer to the *Oreto*, but the diplomats of the U.S. consulate there demanded she be inspected by a neutral party. The captain of a British ship was picked to inspect her, and he promptly announced she was outfitted as a warship in every way. The ship was libeled in a British court and a trial was held. Much to the chagrin of the U.S. consul members, the ship was released, and Captain John Maffitt of the Confederate navy was chosen as her skipper. U.S. consul diplomats strongly suspected the British of a blatant bias in the trial, but they could do nothing but protest vigorously.

Maffitt took the *Oreto* north to the security of Green Cay, where he had the *Bahama's* cargo loaded onboard and installed. He renamed her the C.S.S. *Florida* and commissioned her in the Confederate navy.

After the commissioning, Maffitt sailed for Cuba, where he hoped to fill out his crew and obtain those gunnery supplies that were missing from the *Bahama's* cargo. This vessel was destined to become another nemesis for the Union navy blockading Mobile Bay.

All in all, Confederate cruisers managed to wreak much havoc on the U.S. Merchant Marine, as many ownerships were transferred to foreign registry or laid up in ports for fear of capture. The U.S. government was helpless to stop the release of British-built vessels to the Confederacy and seemed unable to stop the cruisers, especially in the Gulf, whose captains outwitted or outdistanced Federal warships that were either searching for them or blockading the ports from which they operated.

But that situation was soon to change.

ALTHOUGH the operations of Confederate cruisers in all regions of the country, including the Gulf, caused a remarkable amount of damage to the U.S. Merchant Marine, the "damage aggregated less than 1% of the value of Union seagoing commerce during the war."[25] The process of transferring registries of ships to foreign nations worked to the advantage of the Union in that it gave a new lease on life to the highly prosperous merchant marine, while the South faced economic ruin from the blockade.[26]

Meanwhile events were unfolding in the Mississippi River Theater that would have a profound effect on the struggle for control of the Gulf of Mexico.

CHAPTER FIVE

PRELUDE TO NEW ORLEANS

A series of yellow-white flashes briefly lit up the western sky as a thunderstorm approached. The sultry air was heavily saturated, and soon large drops of rain pelted the armor plating of the ironclad gunboat. But she plodded on. It was April 4, 1862.

Only a short time before, the U.S.S. *Carondelet* had cast off and entered the main channel of the Mississippi River in an attempt to run past Island No. 10, a formidable Confederate bastion guarding the river approaches to New Madrid and farther north to Cairo. The Federal gunboat had a coal barge lashed to her port side, hopefully to absorb enemy shot and shell from the island's gunners. Now she was caught in a tempest that whipped the water around her into a froth. Were she not battened down, she would have been swamped by the wind-lashed river.

Suddenly, the sky was torn apart by unearthly displays of lightning that threatened to expose the *Carondelet* to enemy gunners on the island. To the Union flotilla commander, Captain Andrew Hull Foote, the darkness and the rain had been a blessing because it meant the enemy would be hunkered down, protected from the furious, slashing elements. But lightning was another matter—one alert sentry catching sight of the flotilla could jeopardize his entire operation.

Captain Henry Walke, a deeply religious man, must have prayed fervently that nature's fireworks would not betray his *Carondelet*'s position. So far so good. Suddenly the gunboat's stack flared up, shooting huge sparks skyward. Apparently after the exhaust had been shunted into the wheelhouse, in order to muffle the characteristic popping sound from the stacks ("chimneys," in rivermen's parlance) of river craft, soot had dried there. The heat from the boilers had then ignited the dried soot.

Rockets streamed into the air from the island; the gunboat had been spotted. Enemy shells thudded into the coal barge, while others splashed into the water around the *Carondelet*. Captain Walke immediately called for hard-a-port helm, in order to skirt the shore of the island as closely as possible. This was an expeditious move, because the Confederate gunners would be unable to depress their guns low enough to do any damage. At one point the barge scraped bottom, but the gunboat and its burden plowed on until she returned to the main channel, unharmed by gunshot—a triumphal parade of one.

The *Carondelet* had accomplished what many thought impossible: passing unscathed by a heavily fortified island.

Below the island, after a brief duel, the gunboat knocked out an artillery barge, then swung northward to New Madrid, which by now had been occupied by Federal troops. Weeks afterward, a seaman aboard a Rebel steamer nearby, which had kept out of the affair, wrote to his wife about the amazing odyssey of the *Carondelet*: "The gunboat had pulled a Yankee trick of using a barge full of coal or hay on her port side to absorb shot." He predicted that the fate of the island was settled and that the run would be duplicated by other gunboats.[1] He was right in his assumption, because the *Pittsburgh* repeated the *Carondelet*'s feat two nights later. Together the two Federal gunboats ranged down the river, knocking out Confederate batteries almost to Fort Pillow. Behind them Captain John Pope's troops swarmed across the river and invested Island No. 10 from the south.

After the surrender of the island, Union forces reaped a staggering amount of muskets, artillery pieces, horses, powder, and tents, not to speak of three brigadier generals.[2] The *Carondelet* had opened the flood-gates so that Grant's armies and Flag Officer Foote's flotillas could move south down the river. But still Fort Pillow, Memphis, and Vicksburg had to be taken by combined land and naval assaults. This proved to be a tough nut to crack, since enemy gunboats were lurking nearby. At New Orleans the Confederates had gathered a flotilla of ships against a likely Union thrust, either downriver or upriver from the Gulf.

In the difficult and bitter campaigns down the Mississippi, Grant and Foote would often request help from Farragut's big ships in the Gulf.

The biggest and toughest nut of all was New Orleans and its two powerful forts above the Head of the Passes.

New Orleans: an anomaly. It presented to the world one face, that of a rowdy city full of fun and frolic, music and good food, especially during Mardi Gras, during which all stops were pulled for a celebration that sometimes bordered on the absurd and irreverent.

But New Orleans had another face that it kept from the public—its lawlessness, mayhem, and sinister decadence. No matter which face one encountered, the city was (and still is) one to be reckoned with.

New Orleans was founded by the French governor of Louisiana, Jean-Baptiste Le Moyne, sieur de Bienville, in February 1718 and was named after the regent, Philippe, the duke of Orléans. At that time Louisiana was held by a company organized by one John Law in 1731. In 1722, although not yet incorporated as a city, New Orleans was named the capital of the colony of 500 citizens and 100 houses. In 1731, Law's company returned it to the French crown.

It was finally incorporated as an American city in February 1805. New Orleans thus has the distinction of having been under French, Spanish (1762–1800), and United States flags during its fabulous history.

Located in a crescent made by the Mississippi as it flows from the northeast and then southward again, the city earned its nickname of "the Crescent City." Its strategic position always made New Orleans a mecca for craft plying up- and downriver. Colorful steamboats landed at docks to unload cargoes from the Northern states. These cargoes were then transferred to the holds of ships that voyaged to the Gulf and thence to the oceans of the world.

Because it controlled traffic up and down the river and out to the rest of the world, New Orleans was clearly a vital city for the Confederacy. In 1862 it contained 170,000 souls and was the fifth largest city in the country. Moreover, it had more manufacturing facilities, shipyards, and trained workmen than any other place in the Confederacy.[3]

From the Confederate point of view, the river coursing freely north and south was the avenue for goods flowing from rich agricultural and industrial sources in Arkansas, Texas, Mississippi, and Louisiana, which were also huge pools of manpower for Confederate armies. Conversely, from the Union point of view, this avenue had to be cut off for as long as the so-called Trans-Mississippi Department remained in Confederate hands.

Lincoln and Welles were well aware of the strategic importance of New Orleans. As early as 1861, military minds in Washington were brainstorming ways to capture it. As the fleet grew stronger every day, the Union could concentrate enormous firepower anywhere at its choosing; New Orleans and its vaunted forts were of the utmost priority. It was Assistant Secretary of the Navy Gustavus Fox who first broached the idea of subduing the forts guarding the river approaches to the city, capturing New Orleans, and then steaming upriver to join the Western Gunboat Flotilla, poised to fight its way down. He argued that New Orleans was more valuable than Mobile, because the latter would play no part in the opening of the Mississippi. New Orleans, he insisted, should be the number-one priority for the Union.[4]

Fox knew whereof he spoke. He had commanded merchant marine ships up and down the Mississippi, had visited New Orleans countless times, and was thoroughly acquainted with Forts Jackson and St. Philip. He was sure that a fleet of ships, even if many were wooden, could subdue the works through heavily concentrated gunfire.[5]

But Fox's detractors maintained that it was foolhardy for the navy to attempt this plan. After all, had not Admiral Nelson said that "only fools would attack stone forts with wooden ships"? (Nelson did not live to see ironclad vessels.) The plan was doomed to failure, he was told, and precious U.S. warships should not be sacrificed in such a foolhardy manner. It is curious that the ironclad-ship concept had not yet penetrated some minds in Washington.

To counter this argument, Fox pointed to the successes of Flag Officer Du Pont's fleet at Hatteras Inlet and Port Royal, when wooden ships had bombarded the forts into submission. He went to President Lincoln and got tacit approval for the plan. The president, however, insisted that more intelligence needed to be gathered on the strength of the forts before any action was taken.

Fox's plan was backed fully by David Dixon Porter. For a preliminary bombardment of the forts, he maintained, the Union had to assemble a large naval force of an aggregate of 200 guns, with drafts no more than 18 inches, plus 30 schooners fitted out as mortar boats with 13-inch mortars. Like Fox, Porter too was familiar with the Mississippi, having made 30 reconnaissance trips up and down and through the passes. He suggested that an army of 2,000 troops be present for the occupation of New Orleans.[6]

In November 1861, a top-level meeting was held in Washington that included Lincoln, Fox, Welles, Porter, and General George McClellan, to lay plans for the New Orleans operation and to consider a commander. McClellan was invited because he had recently taken over as commander-in-chief of the army from the ailing General Winfield Scott. At first he was skeptical of the plan, proposing that it would take not 20,000 but 50,000 troops with siege weapons. He hastened to add that he could not spare the troops.

The general, who was once sarcastically dubbed "the young Napoleon," did finally agree to the operation when he was convinced that it would primarily be naval and would involve only 10,000 troops.

The task of appointing the commander was next on the agenda. Welles consulted his roster of naval commanders and discovered that top men such as Du Pont, Stringham, and Charles Wilkes were already engaged with important commands. But one name on the list stood out: David Glasgow Farragut. Sixty years old and nearsighted, he had been passed over for squadron command a few times; he did not appear to qualify as a commander for such an important operation. But certain qualities about the man arrested Welles's attention: Farragut was dependable, courageous, and energetic. (Whether the fact that Farragut was Porter's foster brother had any influence in the matter is unknown; surely it is a subject for conjecture.) He was a Southerner who had not only refused to throw in his lot with the secessionists but had censured them scathingly, warning them of impending doom, then packed and moved north with his Virginia-born wife. With that information in his portfolio, Welles presented Farragut's credentials to the committee; the decision was made to appoint him overall commander of the naval operations with the West Gulf Blockading Squadron. He was tapped to lead the difficult assault on Forts Jackson and St. Philip and to capture the city of New Orleans.[7]

Tennessean David Glasgow Farragut was practically born to the sea. He became the adopted son of famed Captain David Porter, who put him in the navy in 1810. Later Farragut shipped onboard the U.S.S. *Essex*, a 36-gun frigate. At only 12 years of age, he was given command of a prize, the American whaler *Barclay*, in the Pacific. He later rejoined his foster father on the *Essex* before her fatal duel with the British frigate H.M.S. *Phoebe* off the coast of Chile in March 1814. The two were taken prisoner for a brief period, then paroled with the remnants of the *Essex* crew.

Therefore, at the age of 13, Farragut had already participated in one of the most important naval engagements of his time and was welcomed as a hero in New York.[8] The lessons he learned from that battle would serve him well in the contests to come. So did an incident aboard the merchantman *America* during which, as the only naval officer present, he took charge and calmed a dangerous situation that almost caused a panic among the crew and officers. He had learned that "good training and leadership are good ingredients in producing good fighting men."[9] He spent the years before the secession learning languages and studying for command of a warship, while serving in the Mexican War.

When the Civil War exploded on the scene, he refused to join the Confederate cause, warning his military wooers that they would "catch the devil before this was over." Then, with his wife in tow, he moved to Washington and offered his services to the Union cause.

After a series of disappointments that discouraged Farragut, his star

rose during that historic conference in Washington. He was given command of the West Gulf Blockading Squadron in December 1861.

His choice of a flagship, the magnificent screw sloop U.S.S. *Hartford*,
was typical of Farragut's acumen: She was one of the finest vessels in the
U.S. Navy. Built at the Boston Navy Yard for $500,000 and launched
on November 22, 1858, she was commissioned on May 27 after her
fitting-out period and her shakedown cruise. She was chosen to carry
Flag Officer Cornelius K. Stribling, new commander of the East India
Squadron, and later carried the U.S. minister to China around the Far
East on diplomatic missions. The *Hartford* was the perfect symbol of
American sea power.

With her graceful, sweeping lines, she displaced 2,900 tons and was
225 feet long, with a beam of 44 feet and an 18-foot draft. Her top
speed was 18 knots, which made her one of the fastest vessels afloat at
that time. Her 24 guns packed a lethal punch—one that would be
sorely needed in the coming campaigns.

The stern-faced Farragut and his powerful fleet arrived at Ship Island,
just off the coast of Mississippi and directly across the wide delta from
Forts Jackson and St. Philip, on February 20, 1862.[10] With his usual
aplomb he set about planning for the coming assault on New Orleans.
In his hands he held a directive from Secretary Welles to the effect that
he (Farragut) should "proceed to the Gulf of Mexico with all possible
dispatch."

From a bird's-eye view, it must have been a breathtaking sight: the
proud *Hartford* and her consorts off wind-scrubbed Ship Island with
its crude fort on the west end and the supply depots and scattered
clusters of tents for troops. Offshore, small boats of all descriptions cir-
cled around the warships like water beetles around lily pads. A train of
lighters, barges, and coal ships dotted the anchorage, ready to meet the
needs of the flotilla. On the island there would have been a beehive of
activity—groups of soldiers stacking mountains of supplies and materiel, others drilling in the broiling sun. Horses and wagons would be
crisscrossing the island on makeshift roads that would be covered over
by drifting sand in a fickle shift of the wind.

Within the fort troops would be standing to their guns, lest the

enemy attempt to interfere in any way; rumors fle.
the large, powerful rams that the Confederates were
Orleans. No one dared take a chance.

More ships arrived, and Farragut's fleet swelled to an awes
of firepower: the *Hartford's* sister screw sloops *Brooklyn, Richmon.
Pensacola*; the 3,000-ton side-wheeler *Mississippi*; the 40-gun *Colora.*
at 4,772 tons; plus the gunboats *Oneida, Varuna, Katahdin,* and *Wissahickon.* Expected any day was Porter's fleet of 22 stripped-down schooners,
upon which were mounted 13-inch mortars.

Meanwhile Farragut was absorbed in his duty of making Ship Island "supercharged with his energy." Lieutenant George Dewey, present on one of the warships, described the commander as "decisive,
indomitable."[11]

As March approached, Farragut must have cast anxious glances west-
ward toward New Orleans and wondered about events there, especially
about the giant, powerful ironclads that, rumors whispered, were ready
to be launched.

Certainly in New Orleans events were infused with anxious energy.
The atmosphere could have become chaotic had not the level-headed
Major General Mansfield Lovell, in charge of the defense of New Orleans, managed to keep things under control. But he argued endlessly
with Brigadier General Johnson Kelly Duncan about the ability of ships
to pass the forts successfully.[12]

Lovell had floated an obstruction consisting of 40-foot cypress logs
chained together, leaving a space to permit the passage of friendly vessels, across the river between the forts. The obstruction was to prove un-
feasible, because the accumulated weight of driftwood parted the chains,
and so a series of wooden ship hulks soon replaced them.[13]

In spite of all the interdepartmental squabbling, however, the Confederate River Defense Fleet was taking shape. It consisted of a motley
group of vessels, mostly from New Orleans shipyards. These shipyards
were mostly located in the suburb of Algiers, less than a mile across the
river from New Orleans, and consisted of eight dry docks, with all the
facilities needed for the construction and maintenance of gunboats.
Among these were Hughes Ship Building, Hyde & Mackay, and

..rram & Company. (Today there still are shipyards at the sites, turning out tugboats and other small craft.) Discouragingly, the materiel had to be moved back and forth across the river, which at this point was a half-mile wide and 100 feet deep.

The Confederate fleet now consisted of the *McRae*, a former bark-rigged Mexican navy ship with eight guns; the side-wheeler *Jackson*, at 297 tons, equipped with two guns; the *Governor Moore*, a schooner-rigged, 1,215-ton cottonclad ram; the 945-ton side-wheeler *General Quitman*, with two guns; and the newly acquired *Manassas* plus six armed riverboats.[14]

Most Confederate hopes lay with the big rams *Mississippi* and *Louisiana*, which were still under construction. Asa and Nelson Tift were wasting no time in building their huge man-of-war, *Mississippi*. They had arrived in New Orleans on June 28, 1861, and with a government contract in hand had set about contacting the various Algiers shipyards. They met with disappointment after disappointment. Hughes Ship Building offered the use of its yard but could not meet the specifications. Hyde & Mackay gave an estimate but refused to be bound by time. Harram & Company did the same.

Not to be discouraged, however, the Tifts procured a plot of riverfront land at Jefferson City, on the eastern corporate line of New Orleans. There they established their own shipyard. But as happened too often for the Confederacy, their endeavors suffered from constant shortages of iron, lumber, drive shafts, plate iron, and trained personnel. Adding to the Tifts' troubles, another ironclad, the *Louisiana*, was being built by E. C. Murray, an accomplished shipbuilder, who had acquired property next to the Tifts'.[15]

Murray set about building the *Louisiana*, a vessel of his own design, at 264 feet long and 62 feet in the beam. She was to be casemated with four-inch charcoal iron plating and powered by two screws and two paddlewheels in tandem, located in a center well. She was to be armed with 16 guns, including two seven-inch rifles. Had she ever been commissioned, she would have posed a real threat to Farragut's fleet. In fact, many historians are of the opinion that Murray's *Louisiana* would have presented a greater threat to Farragut's fleet than the Tifts' *Mississippi*, because of her proposed armor and armament.[16] But Murray and the Tifts were in competition with each other over supplies. Not even Murray's intimate and successful acquaintance with suppliers, however, could get him the supplies he needed.

At still another facility, two floating batteries, *New Orleans* and *Memphis*, were being constructed by General David E. Twiggs. These batteries would have no motive power of their own but would be towed into position for action. Fortunately for the Confederacy, this project died aborning. It was later proved that floating batteries cannot stand against the heavy firepower of a ship in motion. Positioning one next to a riverbank would have been a mistake, because all guns would not be brought to bear on a target. Anchoring it in a stream to allow all guns access would be very difficult to maintain.

By October 9, 1861, however, progress on the *Mississippi* was accelerating at a remarkable rate. The Tifts had brought in an agent from the Tredegar Iron Works and put him in charge of completing the ironclad. The keel was laid, lumber from the brothers' own sawmill was coming in satisfactorily, and some machinery was available. Day and night the shipyard buzzed with activity. But experts in naval machinery were still wanting, and the Tifts petitioned Secretary Mallory for experts from the Norfolk Navy Yard or from the Bellona Foundry in Richmond.

Mallory wired the Tifts that the Federals had scored a great victory at Island No. 10 on April 4. "Work day and night with all the force you can command to get the *Mississippi* ready. Spare neither men nor money."[17] The brothers needed no further urging.

The last communication from the Tifts concerning the construction efforts indicated that the *Mississippi* would be launched shortly and fitted out for action. The event would be long overdue, but taking all into close consideration, it was also a miracle the vessel was launched at all.[18]

Secretary Mallory must have slept a little better, knowing that the monster ironclad was almost ready to meet Farragut and his fleet. He must also have had some reservations about an interservice rivalry over commands of the various elements of his New Orleans fleet. Generals, navy men, politicians, and civilian contractors were all getting into the act. No one strong person was in charge to bring it all together, to have absolute authority. Each thought he was the one to unite the efforts, but none was backed by the right authorities.

The one man absent from the scene who might have made a difference in the mess was Commodore George Nichols Hollins, who at this time was languishing in a bureaucratic desk job upriver, because he had had the audacity to counter an order from Mallory earlier.[19] Some historians believe that Hollins was prevented from being there at a time when he might have made a difference because of the short-sightedness of Richmond officials concerning Farragut's ability to pass the forts downstream. In addition, Mallory was convinced that the danger to New Orleans lay upriver. Even though Hollins later returned to New Orleans after the battle, the River Defense Fleet never did get a unified command.

As Louisiana Governor Thomas Overton Moore later pointed out, another cause of the delay in launching *Mississippi* was "the failure of the Tifts to comprehend that the city was in danger."[20] The danger was abundantly clear to most; even the *New Orleans Picayune* had warned the citizens about the coming attack. It had quoted an ad in the *Washington Star* to that effect:

"It is now publicly announced that Commander Farragut is to command the great expedition that is to operate on the western part of the Gulf. . . . The fleet will consist of the *Richmond, Pensacola*, and other large steam frigates, a great number of gunboats. . . . The opinion is expressed in naval circles that few fortified places can hold out against such an expedition."[21] Few in the Confederate high command appear to have heeded the warning.

WHEN something urgent and vital is about to happen, events can be hastened to an amazing extent. All forces coalesce into one entity, and things get done in spite of obstacles. Old Mother Necessity is always a tough taskmaster.

As New Orleans and Richmond prepared for the attack on New Orleans, so did Washington. Secretary Welles, ever sensitive to detail, knew that the coming event would be a major thrust in the war against the

Confederacy. Looking to Farragut for the much-needed victory, he saw that ships were sorely needed in the area. On April 2 he ordered Flag Officer Du Pont of the South Atlantic Blockading Squadron to release gunboats to the Gulf, stating that "the exigencies of the public service are so pressing in the Gulf that the department directs you to send in all iron-clads that are in fit condition to move . . . to New Orleans, reserving to yourself only two."22

At Ship Island, meanwhile, Farragut was still putting together his New Orleans strike force. Being out in the Gulf and therefore out of touch with events, he wished for intelligence as to how the war was going, especially in the upper Mississippi. He sent an armed party ashore at Biloxi to get as many newspapers as they could. The group raided the post office there and came away with a bundle of papers, which Farragut devoured eagerly. He was heartened to learn about the major Union victories at Memphis and at Fort Donelson.

He augmented his intelligence of the delta and its passes by having U.S. Coastal Survey personnel mark out channels for his ships to use and for scouting for a possible base for supplies.

But the efforts of the survey personnel were complicated by the constant changing of channels and by the mud piling up at the mouths of the passes, creating mud bars that would obstruct the efforts of deep-water ships to pass.23

The intrepid admiral faced another problem as well: lack of coal for his vessels. The supplies at Ship Island had dwindled dangerously, and none were to be had at Key West; he had no source from which to draw the precious fuel. Then General Benjamin Butler came to the rescue. As was his wont, he arrived majestically at the island, leading a flotilla of troop ships that he had chartered. Instead of stones, which most ships of that day carried for ballast, Butler had used 2,000 tons of coal. Upon learning of the shortage, he generously offered the coal to a delighted Farragut who immediately had it transferred to his ships. Welles, in the meantime, had informed Farragut that a supply of over 6,000 tons of coal was on its way.

Everything was beginning to fall into place for the coming operation against New Orleans. Farragut now had his ships, plenty of provisions, and enough coal to get the operation started. His men were trained to their stations, and the hopes of a watching nation rode with him and his powerful fleet of first-line warships, gunboats, and lethal mortar boats. Once more, a flotilla of Union warships was headed for the Mississippi delta to do battle with the Confederates, but this time the officers and men on these ships were filled with resolve.

Resolve had been conspicuously lacking in the series of events that occurred at the Head of the Passes in October 1861. The fiasco had embarrassed the Union navy and had put a blot on its name. There is little doubt that Farragut had that fiasco in mind as he looked to the delta as a starting point for his assault on New Orleans. The same mistakes must not be repeated.

CHAPTER SIX

UNION HEADACHE IN THE PASSES

A great Union naval fiasco started in September 1861, when Captain William McKean had replaced the star-crossed Flag Officer William Mervine as commander of the West Gulf Blockading Squadron. McKean was given the directive to lock up "the outlets of the great central valley of the continent [Trans-Mississippi] so that their products shall not reach the ocean and that the craving wants of her population for the products of other lands shall not be supplied while their hands are raised against the government."

The 62-year-old William Wister McKean was a good choice. A career naval officer, he had become a midshipman in 1814 and risen rapidly through the ranks to commander, captain, and commodore by 1862. Later he was given command of the frigate *Niagara* and enjoyed the distinguished assignment of carrying the Japanese embassy staff to Japan in 1860. McKean, a respected commander, enjoyed a good reputation in the Navy Department; hence his assignment to take command of the West Gulf Blockading Squadron.[1]

McKean's responsibility was to patrol the four passes that stretch for 30 miles from east to west, where the Mississippi empties into the Gulf.

Each pass extends 15 miles from the Head of the Passes to the Gulf, and the deep-water Head itself measures two miles wide and two miles long upriver. The problem for the Union blockaders was that Pass à l'Outre bifurcates about halfway down, which afforded blockade-runners an extra pass through which to slip; consequently it was another area that the hard-pressed Union blockade flotillas had to cover. Theoretically, watching the passes would require more ships than the ones to which McKean assigned the task on September 19.

These assigned ships were: the 2,700-ton flagship *Richmond*, a sister to Farragut's *Hartford*, with 14 nine-inch smoothbores, on board which was Captain John Pope, the senior officer present; the side-wheel gunboat *Water Witch*, 378 tons, with one 32-pounder smoothbore, Lieutenant Francis Winslow commanding; the sloop *Preble*, 556 tons, with two eight-inch smoothbores and seven 32-pounder smoothbores, Lieutenant Henry French commanding; and the sloop *Vincennes*, 703 tons, with four eight-inch smoothbores and 14 32-pounders, under Commander Robert Handy.

In the first action, which we will label phase one, Captain Winslow on September 19 took the 225-foot-long *Water Witch* over the bar easily and up Pass à l'Outre toward the Head of the Passes. On board was a member of the U.S. Army Engineers whose mission was to scout the shores for possible artillery emplacements and a temporary site for coaling and provisioning.

As Pope approached the Head, a lookout spotted the smoke of a steamer churning upstream on the Southwest Pass, with a vessel in tow. It was Commodore Hollins's side-wheeler *Ivy*, a former privateer that was now a Confederate naval vessel. The 447-ton side-wheeler was 191 feet long and armed with an eight-inch smoothbore, a 32-pounder rifle, and two brass 24-pounders left over from her privateering days.

Upon sighting Pope's force coming up, the *Ivy*'s skipper, Lieutenant Joseph Fry, ordered full steam ahead, and the race was on. *Ivy* reached the Head first, and as she whisked rapidly upriver, Fry fired a shot at the Federals from a 24-pounder, but it fell short. The *Richmond* responded with a shot from a 12-pound howitzer; it too fell short. Then Pope gave chase to the *Ivy*, but the latter's speed was too much for him, so he merely watched *Ivy*'s stern disappear upriver. He had a scouting mission to perform, so he returned to the Head and anchored near the shore to complete it.[2]

In the meantime, Fry had halted upriver, reversed course, and headed back to the pass. There he anchored out of range of Union guns to keep an eye on the *Water Witch* and her activities. When Winslow had completed his scouting assignment, he headed back down Pass à l'Outre to join the rest of the flotilla in the Gulf. Shortly thereafter Fry upanchored and rushed to New Orleans to report his findings to Hollins, who was aware of the Union intrusion into the Head but lacked reports on ship composition and flotilla size. He then knew what to do.

The Confederate navy commander George Nichols Hollins had served with distinction under Captain Stephen Decatur during the War of 1812. Aware now that the Federals might probe the Head for possible base sites for an operation against New Orleans, he had wasted no time in assembling a flotilla of men-of-war to counter the Union intrusion. His vessels were, besides *Ivy*, the *Calhoun*, a former U.S. Navy ship captured in January 1861 of 508 tons and mounting one 32-pounder rifle and two 32-pounder smoothbores; the side-wheeler *Jackson* of 297 tons, mounting two 32-pounder smoothbores; the *McRae*, 680 tons, mounting one nine-inch smoothbore, six 32-pounders, and one six-pounder rifle; the side-wheeler *Tuscarora*, mounting one 32-pounder rifle; and the schooner *Robert Mclelland*, a former Union vessel, mounting one gun.[3]

This flotilla was formidable, but as the astute Hollins was aware, it was no match for the heavy ships and guns of the Union fleet. So he placed his tactical eggs in the *Manassas* basket. This unlovely ironclad was still proving sluggish, especially upstream, in spite of her twin screws. Her single 64-pounder was still unmovable and untrainable, but she had been fitted with a heavy iron ram on her prow. Before it was all over, Hollins was convinced, his ram would send one or more Union ships to the bottom of the river.

In addition, Hollins had assembled a fleet of fire rafts—that is, old wooden ship hulls loaded with combustibles of all compositions. These rafts were to be towed downstream by two tugs and anchored near Fort Jackson. Hollins's plan was simple: The *Manassas* would ram a suitable target, then send up a rocket to alert the fire raft crews to light their charges, tow them downstream, and hopefully envelop enemy ships with fire. After the fire rafts, the rest of the flotilla would advance with *McRae* in the van, to destroy the remaining enemy ships.

When word of the *Richmond*'s entrance into the Head of the Passes reached him, Hollins surmised that more Yankee ships would soon assemble there. He gathered his captains and crews and gave them a pep talk. Then the Mosquito Fleet, as it was affectionately called by the citizens of New Orleans, moved downriver to anchor under the guns of Fort Jackson to await developments.

Thus concluded phase one.

DEVELOPMENTS were not long in coming. On September 23 Pope decided it was time to make a move. He hoisted his flag on the *Richmond* and headed for the Southwest Pass, followed by the *Water Witch*, the *Vincennes*, the screw steamer *South Carolina*, and the rest of the flotilla. But in 10 feet of water the *Richmond* held fast to the bar. Frustrated, Pope ordered the *Water Witch* and the *Vincennes* to pull her free. They succeeded, and the big flagship floated into deeper water. She then headed upstream to anchor off Pilottown (rivermen's spelling of what the navy called "Pilot Town") and await the others.

Most of the other vessels made it over the bar, but the *Vincennes* held fast. The *Water Witch*'s crew cast lines over and attempted to pull her free, but to no avail. On September 30, the *Vincennes* finally slipped over the bar under her own power—only to get stuck fast again on an old submerged wreck. It took 10 days to pull her free and tow her to the anchorage site. Then Pope fired off a directive to Commander French at Ship Island to bring up the *Preble*. All things considered, it was not an auspicious beginning for this Union flotilla's sortie.

Then Pope, for some reason, failed to do what was accepted policy in enemy waters: Send pickets upriver to keep an eye out for advancing enemy ships. In addition, he failed to outline a plan of defense for his commanders, in the event of an enemy attack. This blatant neglect played right into the hands of Commodore Hollins, who took full advantage of it.

So concluded phase two of the comedy of errors known as Pope's Run. Phase three was about to begin.

OFF Fort Jackson, Hollins's little fleet swung at anchor, anticipating Pope's moves.[4] Upon learning of the Federal passage across the bar, he ordered Lieutenant Fry to take his *Ivy* downstream to observe enemy fleet movements in the Head and to harass them whenever possible. Fry reached the Head, dropped anchor, and kept a distance from Pope's big guns. Warily, he had his crews beat to general quarters.

Hoping to stir things up a bit and show the Yankees he meant business, Fry sent over a greeting in the form of two 24-pounder rifle shots. The log of the *Water Witch* records on October 8: "4:20 P.M. the *Ivy* opened fire with a heavy rifle gun, and it was returned by the rest of the fleet, the [enemy's] shots falling very near and over us and the *Richmond*."[5] Lieutenant Winslow got up steam and gave chase to the *Ivy*, but he was hopelessly outdistanced by the speedy Confederate ship.

The log of the *Vincennes* also recorded the attack by the *Ivy*, saying, "The shots passed over us" and that Pope had signaled all ships to cease firing.[6] Pope was coming unraveled. After the *Ivy* incident, he dashed off a letter to McKean in which he decried the attack and lamented that "we are liable to be driven from here at any moment, and situated as we are, our position is untenable." Then he made the amazing statement that he might be captured at any moment by a "steamer mounting one gun."[7] He also requested that more rifled guns be sent in from Pensacola.

This incident has puzzled naval historians endlessly. Why would the commander of a fleet mounting more than 40 guns have been rattled by a vessel with only a few guns? Pope's mental and emotional state has been debated over the years.

But Hollins was not contemplating his antagonist's mental state; he decided to refuel the Mosquito Fleet, move downriver with *Manassas* in the van, and challenge the audacious Union movements there.

Meanwhile, Pope had decided that the *Ivy*'s attack had been an isolated one, so he turned his full attention to refueling his ships. He ordered the coaling ship *Joseph H. Toone* alongside the *Richmond*, and in the early hours of October 12, a refueling operation got under way. Another historians' puzzle: Why were the crew members engaged in this difficult and strenuous labor so early in the morning, thereby robbing them of valuable sleep? Other units of the fleet were also coaling.

The *Preble* arrived and anchored near the flagship. In order to protect all approaches—deep channel and shoal waters—from enemy craft attempting to slip by, the rest of the fleet situated in an inverted V pattern.

Commander French, of the *Preble*, decided to retire after having been on deck all night supervising coaling procedures. He climbed into his berth fully clothed, expecting to grab a few winks. The night was dark with a clouded sky and a wind blowing from the north. Downstream from him were the *Vincennes* and the *Water Witch*, both taking on coal. Coal-oil lanterns were the only source of light.

Upstream, the little Confederate attack force, led by the sluggish *Manassas*, with her long stack belching smoke, was moving along. Her skipper, Lieutenant Alexander Warley, peered through the narrow piloting slit in the forward hatch and saw the enemy ships ahead with lights twinkling here and there. Looking around, he failed to spot the expected picket boats; that was fine—no signs of alertness among the Federal fleet.

Warley then rang for full steam ahead, and with the full force of a four-knot stream with him, he headed for the largest ship, the *Richmond*.

On the *Preble*, French had just gotten to sleep when an excited midshipman burst into his cabin. "Captain!" he shouted. "Here is a steamer right alongside of us!" French dashed to the deck, and as he passed a porthole, he peered out and saw what he later called "an indescribable object not 20 yards distant from our quarter, moving with great velocity toward *Richmond*."[8]

French sprang into action; he ordered a red lantern hoisted at the gaff—a signal for danger that had been agreed upon much earlier. But it was too late. With a loud splintering crash, the *Manassas* plowed into the port side of the *Richmond*. The impact cut away the *Joseph H. Toone*, which spun off downstream. The blow stove in three planks below the waterline, making a hole about three inches in diameter. The crash had been heard onboard the other ships, which were by now fully alerted.[9]

Warley backed his ram and prepared to take another swipe at *Rich-*

mond's stern, but the flagship had slipped her chains and was moving out. Meanwhile her gun crews blasted away at the ram, the shots rebounding with loud *clangs* off the 1½-inch plating, creating showers of sparks. Warley fired a rocket to alert the fire raft crews, then moved ahead of the *Richmond* to seek another target. There were plenty more among the confused Union flotilla; Warley was committed to an attack.

Upriver, the fire raft crews applied torches to the combustibles onboard their charges. The tugs then swung into position, and the strange-looking, blazing armada moved downstream.

In the Head of the Passes, bedlam reigned among the Union ships. Guns blazed at imaginary enemies; gun flashes bounced off clouds of dense smoke; and ships slipped their cables or chains and moved off toward the Southwest Pass, as ordered by the rattled Pope.

The approaching fire rafts caused even more dismay among the Federal fleet. Gunners aboard the *Vincennes* opened fire from the port battery, hoping to sink them before they reached the area. Fortunately for the Federals, the rafts drifted over to the west shore, where they burned out.

Pope's fleet, now in complete disarray, moved downriver, with the *Richmond* broadside-to, unable to keep her head upriver. Commander French on the *Preble* was startled to see the flagship rolling off downriver. He later wrote: "I could not and would not believe it possible until I ran aft and saw her [*Richmond*] astern and headed downriver."[10] He spotted the fire rafts coming, slipped his cables, and followed the swirling flagship. As he passed the *Richmond*, he received an order by word of mouth to "proceed down the pass." Farther down, French discovered the *Vincennes* fast aground, her stern upriver. Then he got stuck on a mud flat but pulled himself free "with one or three smart rolls."[11]

Meanwhile, the *Manassas* had been crippled by her encounter with the *Richmond*. Her stack had been knocked askew by shots from Union ships, her ram had been dislodged by the impact, and one engine and boiler had been knocked off their mountings. Smoke from the shattered stack had filled the interior, almost causing an abandon-ship order. Warley steered her over to the bank, where she became stuck fast. She would no longer be of any use in the fray.

The *Richmond* had become stuck downriver from the *Vincennes*, and as the Mosquito Fleet approached, Pope planned to counterattack with her stern guns. The Confederates opened fire on *Water Witch* and *Vincennes*, to which *Vincennes* replied with her nine-inch shell gun. *Preble* by this time had passed safely over the bar, along with the prize schooner *Frolic*. But with the other ships behind, it was now Union guns against Confederate guns. Pope had placed a nine-inch smoothbore on the *Richmond*'s fore topgallant, which kept up a steady fire during the engagement, but the shots were ineffective. On *Vincennes* Handy ordered his gunners to take down all cabin bulkheads and bring up two eight-inch guns. They were pointed out the stern ports, where he claimed he "kept up a sharp fire upon the rebel steamers with the stern guns."[12]

Pope was frustrated that two of his ships were in a direct line of fire from his deck guns. He finally decided that enough was enough and signaled all vessels to clear the bar and slip into the Gulf.

At this juncture Handy too seemed to become unglued. Even though his *Vincennes* and the *Richmond* had enough combined firepower to ward off the Rebel attackers, he fired off a dispatch to Pope on October 11:

> Sir, we are aground. We have only two guns that will bear in the direction of the enemy. Shall I remain on board after the moon goes down, with my crippled ship and worn-out men? . . . while we have moonlight, would it not be better to leave the ship? Shall I burn her when I leave her?

Whereupon an angered Pope replied on October 12:

> You say your ship is aground. It will be your duty to defend your ship up to the last moment, and not to fire her, except it be to prevent her from falling into the hands of the enemy. I do not think the enemy will be down tonight, but in case they do, fight them to the last. You have enough boats to save all your men. I do not approve of your leaving your ship until all efforts to save her from falling into their hands is [sic] made.[13]

Pope included this exchange in his report to Flag Officer McKean after the battle, thereby assuring the end of Handy's career as a naval officer.

Then came the most bizarre incident of this entire star-crossed sortie, one that would enter the annals of naval history.

After sending his answer to Handy's message, Pope ordered the signalmen to hoist a signal for his vessels outside the bar to get under way for Ship Island. The signal was blue, white, blue hoisted high on the mizzenmast. On the *Vincennes* a first lieutenant glanced at the signal book and told Captain Handy it was Signal Number 1, which meant "abandon ship." Handy wasted no time. With enemy shells splashing all around him, he ordered two cutters, a launch, and the port and stern quarter boats hoisted out for his men and himself. Before he left, he had a slow match fuse set to the magazine, then gave the order to abandon ship. (In the later report to the flag, an interesting phrase was interjected, saying the abandon-ship order was given "in obedience to signal from the *Richmond*." It was placed there by the officer who was to succeed Handy, Commander James Alden.)

Handy filled the boats with his crews, sent some to the *Water Witch*, and sent the rest, including himself, to the *Richmond*. With a display of patriotic showmanship, he wrapped himself with his ship's flag and appeared on the quarterdeck of the flagship, to a startled Pope and his crew. The flotilla commander wanted to know why he was there, and he was told it was in obedience to Pope's Signal Number 1.[14] Pope became enraged and no doubt was ready to throw the errant officer into the brig. All asked, "What about the *Vincennes?*" When told about the slow match, everyone waited expectantly for an explosion to scatter the fine warship all over the Mississippi River delta.

The explosion never came. Something had clearly gone wrong with the slow match fuse. A furious Pope ordered Handy and his crew back to the ship, where they discovered that the slow match had gone out or, as some believe, a recalcitrant, level-headed signalman cut off the burning end and tossed it into the river. Once aboard *Vincennes*, in an attempt to lighten the load of the grounded vessel, Handy ordered the 14 32-pounder guns and all 32-pounder shot to be tossed overboard. To no avail; the ship remained aground until the *South Carolina* pulled it off on October 13.

MEANWHILE Hollins had also decided enough was enough. Not wanting to confront the remaining big guns of Pope's ships, he gave orders to proceed upriver to New Orleans. After all, he had embarrassed and routed the Union fleet, and that was enough for him. He was looking forward to receiving plaudits from his fellow countrymen.

A still-infuriated Pope wrote McKean about the Handy affair, declaring that Handy was not fit to command a ship and that he was "the laughing stock of everyone." Handy was soon shipped out to face a court of inquiry, which he himself requested.[15] Many of the flotilla's personnel testified about the signal that Handy had misinterpreted. Testimony came from William Burrows, a signal quartermaster who said he heard a first lieutenant tell Captain Handy it was "Signal No. 1," which meant "abandon ship." Obviously, Handy was satisfied that he had received that particular signal. A quartermaster on the *Vincennes* also reported seeing the flag hoisted on the mizzenmast of the flagship.

Handy, in his request for a court of inquiry, maintained that he had seen the signal of abandonment on the *Vincennes* and that he had acted properly. When his boats were taking his crews to the two vessels, in full view of Pope, he said, he received no notice of his movements from the commanding officer. This allegation was never answered by Pope. Admiral Porter later commented that it was the most ridiculous affair that ever took place in the navy.

About the only beneficiaries of this comic opera were the Confederates. When Hollins triumphantly returned to New Orleans, he was hailed as a hero. Undoubtedly he could have been given the keys to the city. The *New Orleans Daily True Delta* remarked that Hollins's victory was "the most brilliant and remarkable naval exploit on record." But the paper erroneously reported that one enemy ship, the *Preble*, had been lost, another captured, and the balance driven ashore. This was partly true; the ship captured was the coal ship *Joseph H. Toone*, but the vessels reported "driven ashore" were grounded by their own actions. The article concluded with: "All honor to the heroic Hollins."

On October 15 the *True Delta* reported a narrative of the battle of the Passes and—surprisingly—gave some credit to the resistance efforts by the Federals, offering a grudging sympathy for their plight. But the *True Delta* also commented that the Yankees' firing, maneuvers, and general conduct showed they were "thunderstruck and frightened."[16] It was a slap in the face for the Federals, but it rang with a certain amount of truth.

Hollins was feted and serenaded by bands and military units marching past his hotel balcony. An onlooker described the event as intensely joyful.

The Union, however, had no joy. Pope was chagrined to no end over the events in the Head. To answer the *True Delta's* charge of "thunderstruck and frightened" Yankees, he fired off a dispatch to McKean: "It having been rumored there was a panic on board this ship at the time she was engaged with the enemy, I state it to be false; both officers and men exhibited the utmost coolness and determination to do their duty. My orders and those of the officers were carried out with as much coolness as if it had been an everyday affair."[17]

DESPITE the Union humiliation at the battle of the Passes, Hollins's victory was hollow. While he did damage the Union flotilla and sent them tails-tucked-under down to the Gulf, the success was only temporary. At Ship Island, Farragut had been biding his time, building the New Orleans strike force. Now he was ready to make his move on Forts Jackson and St. Philip.

In retrospect a few remarks are in order about the Head of the Passes fiasco. The irony of the battle is not what was done but what was not done. If Pope had sent pickets upriver to scout for Confederate naval activity, or if he had a prepared battle plan in case Hollins did challenge him, the outcome would have been different. What is surprising about the situation is the unbelievable timidity of both Pope and Handy. The spectacle of an old sea dog coming unglued over one enemy ship firing at him with one gun is contemptible, especially considering that his big guns far outnumbered those of the Confederates.

Handy's meek response to coming under enemy fire is another

enigma. Although his ship was grounded, many of his guns were still able to bear on the attackers. But for some inexplicable reason he failed to grasp the situation and cracked under pressure. He tried to abandon and destroy the *Vincennes* without putting up much of a fight, and his appearance on the quarterdeck of the *Richmond*, swathed in his ship's flag, was a loony act of empty patriotism. The incident over the slow match is so ludicrous as to be unworthy of comment. He was lucky that the level-headed signalman saved the warship and consequently spared him a probable court-martial.

Nor is Hollins beyond criticism. His attack plan was well executed at the beginning, but when the *Manassas* broke down after making one hit on the *Richmond*, it fell apart. Once again the same problem that dogged the Confederate navy throughout the war arose: lack of good materiel and skilled workmen. The vessel was poorly designed and flimsily built. Having one gun, immovable and untrainable, poking through a single porthole is ridiculous. The vessel's only effectiveness lay in its iron ram on the prow, but even that weapon was ineffective after the first impact—again, poor planning and inferior materials worked against Hollins's ambitious plans. In theory the ram should have sunk at least one or two wooden Union ships before she herself was disabled or sunk by Pope's big guns. But hindsight is always ineffective, and what should have been is only what *could* have been.

Hollins also lost a chance to destroy the *Vincennes* and the *Richmond* as they lay hard aground and at his mercy. At one time he seemed to hesitate as if wondering what to do next.

The entire ignominious affair put a blot on the U.S. Navy that disgusted the citizens of the North. More sadly, it ended the hitherto-unblemished careers of two naval officers. Good naval officers were sorely needed in the growing Union navy. Happily for the Union, many lessons were learned at the Head, and corrections were made for future sorties into enemy waters.

The battle of the Passes, or Pope's Run, would soon be forgotten, once Admiral David Glasgow Farragut forged ahead with some of the most daring exploits in naval history and helped turn the tide of the Civil War.

CHAPTER SEVEN

NEW ORLEANS—
PHASE ONE:
THE FLEET GATHERS

In March 1862, Commodore David Porter, with 19 mortar schooners, eight steamers, two barks, and a brig, arrived at Ship Island. He must have been deeply impressed with the fleet that was already there. Farragut had assembled the largest and most powerful naval force ever seen in the Gulf of Mexico, some 17 men-of-war, along with train vessels. The arrival of Porter's flotilla boosted the toll to 47 ships of all sizes, tonnages, and configurations. Present were the sloops-of war *Hartford*, *Brooklyn*, and *Richmond*, the screw sloop *Pensacola*, the side-wheel *Mississippi*, and the gunboats *Katahdin*, *Kineo*, *Wissahickon*, *Sciota*, *Iroquois*, *Kennebec*, *Pinola*, *Itaska*, and *Cayuga*—some 192 guns in all. The fleet was still awaiting the arrival of General Benjamin Butler's 15,000 troops and accompanying vessels, which would swell the flotilla even more.

The fleet train consisted of the necessary attending vessels, such as colliers, store ships, and despatch vessels of all sizes. The mortar schooners—called "chowder pots" by cynics—were unable to move under their own power, being sailing vessels with their spars removed. They were of average 200-ton displacement, and with the exception of the *Horace Beals*, each carried a 13-inch "seacoast" mortar, a gigantic weapon of eight tons that could fire a 200-pound shell almost two and one-half miles. Considering the weight of the weapon and its recoil, the mortar schooners had to be strengthened with heavy timbers to the keel. Two men of the crew, called "bummers" by the fleet, loaded the weapon by means of heavy-duty shell hooks that were inserted into a set of "ears" on each side of the fuse opening of the shell. Twenty pounds of powder were tamped in, and it was then hoisted into the 13-inch bore. The mortar was fired by means of friction primers attached to a long lanyard. Usually, in order to protect their ears from damage by the heavy concussion, the crew stood on tiptoes and opened their mouths during firing.

The mortar was a most awesome weapon, and it struck fear into the hearts of the uninitiated. The presence of the mortar fleet caused much consternation among the Confederates at Forts Jackson and St. Philip.[1] Strangely, no evidence of mortars being used by the Confederate navy exists. They depended upon the traditional smoothbores and rifles.

The colliers, or coaling ships, were vital to keeping the fleet active. Coal was the lifeblood of the steam-driven fleets of that day (although those equipped with sails were able to move in its absence). Colliers were generally old sailing vessels that had been pressed into service for the purpose of providing coal. It was transferred to the bunker of a ship by means of large canvas bags, four by five feet, or sometimes in baskets. In 1862 an average coal-burning steamer used 18 to 20 "bushels" of coal, or 1,900 pounds, per hour. And as various ships patrolled the Pass à l'Outre and Southwest Pass on blockade duty, coal *was* being used up.

LIFE onboard a ship on blockade duty was a series of monotonous days and nights—except when a blockade-running ship was sighted and the chase began. But these incidents were few and far between. According to Commander John Russell Bartlett, captain of the *Brooklyn*: "Most of the time there was a dense fog so thick that we could not see the length of the ship [233 feet]. The fog collected in the rigging, and there was a constant dripping from aloft like rain, which kept the decks wet and made things generally uncomfortable."[2] But ships' routines of both navies continued, and the energy of it kept the crews from grumbling and griping about their lot in life, such as crews have always done in every navy in every epoch of history. Usually reveille was piped around 5:00 A.M., and deck crews went to work routinely holystoning the wooden decks.

The process of holystoning consisted of dragging large stones, usually sandstone, across a deck that had been heavily sanded and watered. Crewmen followed the stones with brushes and brooms; the deck at times would become literally scrubbed white.

Around 8:00 A.M. breakfast would be piped. Typical fare would be beans or peas, dried fruit, butter, cheese, biscuits, and coffee or tea. Fresh meat and fruit would be served when available. Officers' rations were slightly better, having been cooked and served in a separate galley. Although the diet seems austere, with mostly dried foods, crews would obtain fresh fare by catching fish whenever the ships were at anchor. When close to land, hunting parties would occasionally be sent ashore.

The crews stood watches on one of the typical regulation watch schedules, according to the 24-hour clock from midnight to midnight. Watches were maintained while the vessel was afloat or at anchorage—except in combat conditions, when they were shortened and staggered.

During leisure hours the crews busied themselves with playing cards, smoking, talking, and perhaps wood carving. The literate wrote and/or read letters for themselves or others. Some crew members played musical instruments, usually fiddles, guitars, banjos, or harmonicas. Singalongs were always popular. When allowed, some crews would have mascots, generally dogs, and they spent a lot of time playing with these animals.

Part of the "turn-to," or work time, was spent painting topside, the bane of all navy men, when dry docks for painting the hulls were unavailable. Most of the work was relegated to bulkheads and decks.

Saturdays were spent mending or washing clothing in what was called "make or mend" day. Sundays the captain inspected, followed by a religious service—usually conducted by the captain; on larger vessels there would be a chaplain. The rest of the day was devoted to recreational activities like games; if at anchor, rowing regattas were very popular.

Civil War uniforms were similar to those worn in today's navies. Enlisted men would wear traditional blue "sailor" uniforms with collars

(Confederates wore gray), neckerchiefs, and flat or "pancake" hats. Petty officers wore fouled anchor rank badges on the right or left sleeve. Seamen in the Union navy wore cotton whites in the summer and wool blues in colder weather.

Officers' uniforms in Civil War navies were also similar to today's: a peaked cap, a frock coat with shoulder bars, a blue cloth ground, and silver rank badges with an eagle and anchor in the center of three ¾-inch gold lace bands on the sleeves. In the Confederate navy, officers wore much the same design as their Union counterparts, except for color—steel gray with gold lace bars on sleeves, with the top bar being looped. In the summer months straw hats sometimes replaced the regulation peaked caps.

Full dress uniform would feature bicorne hats with feathered fringes, gold-braided shoulder straps, and ceremonial swords.

Enlisted men in the Confederate navy did not always wear a traditional uniform, because of the disparity in the makeup of the crews—a lot of them were army personnel. Confederate sailors, for the most part, eschewed the "spit-and-polish" navy image, preferring instead to wear more nonregulation clothing.

ON March 7, 1862, when the battle of Pea Ridge was being fought in Arkansas and General McClellan's Federal army began its slow move into Virginia, Farragut decided to send the *Hartford* and *Brooklyn* into the Head of the Passes for preliminary work at Pilottown. Pass à l'Outre was picked, because it was believed to be the deepest of the three passes. But the pass had become clogged with sediment, and dredging procedures were lacking. Inasmuch as *Brooklyn* and *Hartford* both drew about 16 feet, the ships ran into trouble. The *Brooklyn* became stuck first, for 17 hours. The *Hartford* passed over lines and then strained her engines to pull the big 2,000-ton frigate loose. Then the *Hartford* became stuck, and it was the *Brooklyn's* turn to do the tugging. Once both ships were free, they backed out into the Gulf and proceeded to the Southwest Pass, where the water was deeper—even above the bar, where it was determined that they would not have any trouble traveling over.

Both ships managed to slip over the bar and triumphantly reached

Pilottown, where they anchored. The marines and sailors were then ordered to occupy the deserted buildings and to prepare them for conversion into warehouses and hospitals.[3] As other ships set out to join them, Commander Bartlett curtly described their laborious struggle to get over the bar and into the river channel as a "considerable delay in getting the larger ships over the bar and filling up with ammunition and coal."[4] Eventually all the shallow-draft vessels arrived and proceeded up the pass. The fleet was beginning to assemble in the Head. On March 18 Porter took his 19 mortar schooners, towed by their accompanying steamers, up the pass to join the fleet.

Finally, the side-wheeler *Mississippi*, the sloop *Pensacola*, and the *Richmond* and *Colorado* arrived and prepared to enter the pass—but their deep drafts kept them from slipping over the bar. Farragut ordered them back to Ship Island, where they lightened themselves by putting ashore all nonessential items, such as heavy guns, coal, shot, shell, boats, and everything that was not nailed down. Then they returned to the pass. When the *Colorado*'s 23-foot draft would not allow her to slip over the bar, her guns were removed and rationed among the fleet.

Meanwhile, the *Mississippi* and the *Richmond* were laboriously dragged across the bar. Because she was a side-wheeler, the *Mississippi* had to be towed across keel-on instead of being tilted on the side, as would a ship without side-wheels.

The theory was that the vessel's side-wheels would churn themselves into the mud and create a vacuum, making her hopelessly stuck. It took four days to get her across, snaking her foot by foot, leaving a wide gouge in the mud.

The *Pensacola* was another story. Her stubborn commander, Captain Henry W. Morris, attempted to ram the sloop across, under full steam ahead, only to get hopelessly stuck. This move infuriated Commodore Porter, who immediately fired off letters to his friend, Assistant Secretary of the Navy Gustavus Fox, complaining about everyone and everything. After another unsuccessful attempt, Morris backed off, raised a full head of steam, and plowed over, using full speed ahead. Finally, by the end of March, all the vessels were assembled in the Head, ready for the expected assault on Forts Jackson and St. Philip, 30 miles upriver.

On April 8, 1862, the sight of this assembled fleet must have been awesome—or so it was to the officer of the day of the 1,000-ton, 16-gun sloop *Portsmouth*, at anchor near the *Colorado* (which was left downriver because of her deep draft). He reported, on "a splendid day," that the big steam frigate was a "splendid looking ship," and that "some of our men went on board of her to see some of their friends."[5]

With his fleet assembled, Farragut issued directives and, as was his wont, visited various ships of his command in person to deliver pep talks to the crews. It was one indication of Farragut's deep concern for his men.

The sight of this stern-faced, solid-statured commander no doubt gave heart to the sailors who were about to risk life and limb. One morning the deck officer of the *Brooklyn*, for example, was startled to see Farragut being rowed up to his gangway at 6:00 A.M. to ask how everything was going. At times the flag officer was reported to have "climbed over the side to see things for himself."[6]

One of Farragut's directives instructed captains to store all nonessential elements of their ships—including spars, rigging, and boats—in the Pilottown warehouses. Wherever possible, ships were painted a lead color, in order to prevent the Confederates from spotting them in the dark. The *Portsmouth*'s journal reports doing so from stem to stern and whimsically records that the hapless residents of Pilottown "skeedadled [sic] to New Orleans on the first appearance of the fleet, except for three families who were wise enough to remain."

The journal further records that Commodore Porter was "fitting up a 1st Class Hotel" in one of the abandoned ships for the establishment of a hospital.[7] Steam drums, hawsers, and rigging were taken from the holds and stored in the fore sickbay compartment, converting the entire hold into a hospital. Ramshackle wooden buildings mounted on stilts and connected by plank walkways were to hold the tremendous weight of the ships' materials. While the fleet lay at anchor in the Head, chain armor had been hung over the sides abreast the engine and boiler rooms. The iron links were 1½-inches in diameter, and the chain mail extended two feet below the waterline.[8] Sandbags were now piled alongside, and an ingenious device was rigged over the hold that allowed stretchers to be lowered down to the awaiting medical personnel.

This is proof of the old adage that innovations can sometimes come out of war situations. Another ingenious idea came from Commander Alden of the *Richmond*: whitewashing the deck and gun carriages fore and aft. This expediency made a difference in night combat: "When before all was darkness, now side tackles, falls, handspikes, ammunition and, indeed, everything of the kind about the decks, were plainly visible by contrast."[9]

Farragut ordered howitzers placed in the foretops and maintops, and large kedge anchors were hung on each quarter of the ship, in anticipation of any need to make a sudden turn. He then ordered each gunboat in the First Division to paint a 6-foot number on its smokestack, near the top. *Sciota* had number "1," and *Cayuga* sported number "9."[10] This method of identification would prove useful in the free-for-all, smoke-enshrouded darkened conditions of combat.

Everyone was aware that fire rafts were being prepared by the Confederates upriver. On April 17 Farragut issued a general order giving elaborate instructions on how to deal with this menace.

Basically, the advice he gave was to keep the rafts in the center of the channel, as much as possible, and to punch holes in the rear of the flatboat containing the incendiary materials. Water would flow through the holes and extinguish the fires. If that were not possible, the gunners were to fire shots into the flatboat. Grappling hooks would be used to tow the encumbrance over to the shore, where it would burn out.[11]

Every contingency was considered in the preparation; nothing was overlooked. Porter issued an order, called a "proposition," expounding at length on the role to be played by the mortar schooners in the coming battle. He offered suggestions about passing the forts with or without mortar boats, expressed concern over the chain barrier stretched across the river between the forts, and even suggested that the entire fleet, after subduing the forts, steam up the river with mortar boats in tow, directly to New Orleans.[12]

The Confederates were kept informed of these proceedings in the Head, but they had missed a golden opportunity to attack Farragut's force during its preparations, when it was most vulnerable. The one man able to form such an attacking force, Commander Hollins, was upriver grappling with the Federal ironclad fleet coming down from its successful securing of Island No. 10 and its equally successful skirmish with his Mosquito Fleet at Plum Point. Remarkably, even though his fleet was obviously no match for the Federals and could not stem the blue tide, Mallory wanted Hollins there.

Commander William C. Whittle, the only visible commander of naval forces at New Orleans, realized the gravity of the situation downriver and sent urgent messages for Hollins to come down and take charge. He too failed to subscribe to the Confederate government's general opinion that any attack on the city would come from the north.

Hollins took note of the pleas and came down to New Orleans as fast as he could. There he immediately made plans to counter the Union threat at the Head of the Passes. He asked Secretary Mallory for permission to "make a dash at the enemy," but he was refused, because of the myopic view prevailing in Richmond as to the northerly origin of any Federal attack.

In their eyes, too, Hollins had committed an unpardonable sin: He had left his assigned post upriver with the Mosquito Fleet to return to New Orleans. Hence the only navy commander capable of meeting and countering the Union threat was called to Richmond to do a menial administrative job. The military task fell on the shoulders of Major General Mansfield Lovell, a veteran of the Mexican War and son of a distinguished surgeon general. Before the war he had been a manufacturer of iron products and knew a great deal about organization, but this experience did not make him fit to head a naval force against one of the Union's most able and brilliant tacticians. All he reigned over, within commands at the New Orleans camp, was a lot of confusion. Still, he was going to do his utmost.

MEANWHILE, downriver, Porter had positioned his mortars on the west side of the river, below the Plaquemines Bend, 2,850 yards from Fort Jackson and 3,680 yards from Fort St. Philip. Tree branches had been fastened to mast tops, in order to camouflage them from Confederate observers at the forts. Confederate infantrymen were sent out to harass the mortar crews, but some well-placed shots from one or two of the mortar schooners' 36-pounders, loaded with grape, scattered them. The Confederates never used that tactic again.

On the morning of April 16, the officer of the day of the *Portsmouth* wrote in the ship's journal:

> A very nice day. We heaved up anchor this forenoon and with a spanking breeze sailed up the proud Mississippi to join the rest of the fleet. Early in the afternoon we came to anchor near the fleet which is about 4 miles this side of the Forts Jackson and St. Philip. There is a bend in the river with high wood on shore and which conceals our Mortar Fleet who are [sic] hugging the left bank.[13]

The unknown officer also expressed concern about the cable barrier across the river (other sources referred to it as a "chain") and suggested that it be cut before the fleet could move on the forts. Several officers in the fleet seemed worried about the prospect of safely getting by this man-made obstruction under the guns of the forts, feelings reflected in the journal.

IN Richmond, President Davis had previously sent a subordinate to New Orleans to confer with General Lovell about the available land forces and their ability to stave off a Union attack. Lovell reported that all land forces were ready for any attack, but his fear was "that the enemy would not make a land attack."[14] This series of events all too vividly illustrates the commander's paucity of information or concern about the Confederate navy taking part in an assault. The prevailing argument, as Davis admitted in hindsight, was "that the [Union] gunboats would descend the Mississippi and applications were made to have the ship *Louisiana* sent up the river as soon as she is completed."[15] At that time, however, the *Louisiana* was in no condition to ascend or descend anything.

All this was unknown to Farragut, who had now assembled his fleet and moved into position, and was looking ahead at his objectives.

CHAPTER EIGHT

NEW ORLEANS—PHASE TWO: THE DAY OF THE MORTARS

The barriers to Farragut's ascent up the river—Forts Jackson and St. Philip—were indeed formidable, born out of necessity—that of protecting the lower Mississippi delta from hostile action. The smaller of the two, Fort St. Philip, was (and still is) located on the east side of the river in Plaquemines Parish, 32 miles from the Gulf and 65 miles from New Orleans. In 1769, under the Spanish governor Baron de Carondelet, a crude breastworks called Fort San Felipe was built on the present site. A redoubt called Fort Bourbon was later constructed on the opposite side of the river, on the spot of the present Fort Jackson.[1]

Fort San Felipe justified its existence during the War of 1812 when a British fleet, attempting to storm upriver and reinforce General Pakenham's hard-pressed land forces to make an assault on New Orleans, unsuccessfully bombarded it. The aftermath of this struggle saw an energetic project to build a strong fort on the site of Fort Bourbon. The project, headed by General Andrew Jackson, was begun in 1823 and was completed in 1832 at a cost of $554,000. A small garrison occupied the fort until February 1842, at which time President John Tyler turned it into a military reservation.

The U.S. government had always recognized the need for a fortification at the head of the Mississippi. In 1860 a survey of Fort St. Philip was made by P.G.T. Beauregard, chief engineer of the U.S. Army (later General Beauregard, C.S.A.). He estimated that upgrading the fort with "concrete, setting gun platforms and sundries [sic] would cost $28,895.96.[2] The fort was not substantially strengthened, and both facilities fell into disrepair until Louisiana state troops seized them on January 8, 1861.

The strategic value of New Orleans was known to both sides of the conflict from the very start. The city was the largest and most vital seaport in the Confederacy. Confederate military minds in Louisiana were aware that some sort of barrier across the river was needed to defend New Orleans against a possible Union attack, because there were no established fortifications between the Gulf and the city. The *New Orleans Picayune* predicted that "by land, we [New Orleans] are impregnable and the coast and river's assailable points are susceptible to a degree of defense that floating wood or iron cannot make an impression."[3]

The Confederates set about rebuilding and strengthening the forts, especially Fort Jackson. Originally built in the traditional five-point-star configuration, the redbrick walls of the fort stood 25 feet above the waterline of the moat, or wet ditch, that surrounded it, and were 20 feet thick. The foundation of the fort was constructed of three layers of cypress logs topped by cypress two-by-fours. The gun foundations were reinforced with red and gray granite, and the casemates facing the river contained eight guns, howitzers, and 10-inch Rodmans, which glowered over the approaches. In the center of the fort was a citadel in which 500 men could take shelter during a bombardment; it was reinforced with logs and dirt. The armament of Fort Jackson consisted of six 42-pounders, twenty-six 27-pounders, two 32-pounder rifles, sixteen 32-pounders, three 8-inch columbiads, one 10-inch columbiad, two 8-inch mortars, one 10-inch mortar, two 42-pounder howitzers, and ten 24-pounder howitzers.

Fort St. Philip, also traditionally built, featured parapets 20 feet thick that rose 17 feet from the bottom of the surrounding ditch. Its armament consisted of six 42-pounders, nine 32-pounders, twenty-two 24-pounders, four 8-inch columbiads, one 8-inch mortar, one 10-inch mortar, and three field pieces.[4] Work continued on strengthening the forts right up to Farragut's attack, and the gun count changed a bit as time went on. Both facilities were thought impregnable by confident New Orleans citizens and military men.

On the riverbanks of both forts, waterfront batteries were established, featuring 32-pounders and 42-pounders. The effectiveness of these batteries depended on the level of the river, because at high tide or heavy flood stages, they would be inundated. As to manpower, a complement of around 1,000 men was divided between both forts, under the command of General Johnson Kelly Duncan, a veteran of the Seminole War who later became a civil engineer.[5]

It was decided to construct a barrier across the river, from fort to fort. The barrier that was constructed consisted of 42-foot cypress logs chained together, anchored by 15 heavy anchors in 100 feet of water and securely fastened to both banks. This encumbrance was short-lived, however, as the overwhelming weight of driftwood and flotsam broke it loose.[6] To replace it, the resourceful Lovell constructed a "raft" of eight schooner hulks anchored, bows upriver, with 60 fathoms (a fathom is six feet) of cable. The entire raft was held together by chains that passed over and between the hulks. Lovell had scoured Gulf and East Coast installations to obtain mooring chains and anchors. The schooners' masts and rigging were cut loose and allowed to trail in the river current, on the theory that the rigging would become entangled in the screws of passing vessels.[7] Undoubtedly it would present a much more formidable obstacle to Farragut's progress upriver than the first barrier had, and floating debris somehow did not break this barrier loose.

The barrier was of deep concern to Farragut. He had sent his chief of staff, Captain Henry Bell, with the gunboats *Kennebec* and *Wissahickon* upriver to reconnoiter the forts and the nearby river area. Bell reported that the obstructions were "formidable . . . the passage between the forts was thus entirely closed."[8] Farragut then decided to have a look for himself; he boarded the *Iroquois*, accompanied by Bell and his signal officer, and moved upriver, escorted by two gunboats. Gunners in Fort Jackson spotted the flotilla and opened fire on them; the shots missed. Farragut sat calmly watching the shells fall, commenting on the accuracy of the enemy's fire. Captain Bell reported that his commanding officer "was as calm and placid as an onlooker at a mimic battle."[9] Not satisfied, Farragut made another trip upriver on Porter's flagship *Harriet Lane*, again accompanied by two gunboats, to have another look-see. This time the gunboats answered the fort's gunfire in a lively exchange. No damage was done to Farragut's little flotilla, and the flag officer obtained much-needed information on gun ranges to and from the fort.

IN New Orleans, meanwhile, Confederate navy Commander John K. Mitchell had sent his aggregate fleet down to anchor above Fort Jackson. This River Defense Fleet, consisting of the *Louisiana*, the *Manassas*, the *Jackson*, the *McRae*, and two launches, joined the Louisiana state navy, commanded by Captain John Stephenson, with the cottonclads *Governor Moore* and *General Quitman*, the side-wheel steamers *Warrior*, *Stonewall Jackson*, *Defiance*, *Resolute*, *General Lovell*, and *R.J. Breckenridge*. The flotilla supported nearly 40 guns in all—impressive, but no match for the mighty Union fleet. The one vessel able to do serious harm to Farragut's fleet was the *Mississippi*, but she was crippled by faulty engines and a lack of full armament. In fact, she had to be towed downstream to a point above Fort St. Philip, where she was to serve as a floating artillery platform. Davis stoutly maintained that had the *Mississippi* been operable, she "would have driven the enemy's fleet out of the river and raised the blockade of Mobile."[10]

In addition to the River Defense Fleet, Lovell had prepared a large number of fire rafts. He had loaded these flatboats with dry timber coated with tar and moored them to the riverbank above each fort. The Confederates were about as prepared as they could be for an onslaught.

On April 15 Porter towed three of his mortar schooners to within 3,000 yards of Fort Jackson. To obtain "the range and durability of the vessels," he fired a few rounds. Contrary to the predictions of some, he smugly crowed, none of the bottoms of the schooners had dropped out after 10 rounds. Afterward he learned that General Lovell and his aides had been in the fort at the time to take a look at the Yankee fleet. After some of the shots dropped close by, they had immediately scurried for cover.[11] The exercise gave Porter the ranges necessary for the full bombardment to come. He then withdrew downstream to rejoin the other mortar schooners at anchor.

But soon afterward the fire rafts began to give the Union fleet some trouble. At 2:00 A.M. on the 16th, a fire raft drifted downriver, ablaze from stem to stern. It drifted between the *Hartford* and the *Richmond*, sending out waves of heat to crewmen on the decks. Below, the *Kineo* and the *Sciota* slipped their cables, in an attempt to get out of the way, but the two vessels became entangled, and the *Sciota* lost her mainmast in the confusion. The two vessels then slammed into the *Mississippi*, causing damage to the *Sciota*. To add to the confusion, the fire raft slammed into her and set her afire, but the conflagration was quickly extinguished by the alert crew. Even more embarrassing to the fleet, the side-wheel ex-ferryboat *Westfield* crunched into *Iroquois*. It was quite a morning for the Federals, and it showed that an accurately placed fire raft could cause great damage among wooden ships.[12]

On April 18 Farragut decided that all was sufficiently in order, so he issued the order for Porter to start the bombardment of Forts Jackson and St. Philip. The huge mortars began to belch their 200-pound shells, backed by 20 pounds of powder, high in the air at a rate of one every 10 minutes, and later 2,800 shells every 24 hours. Day and night the sky over the river was split by the bright, red-orange flashes of mortar fire; the incandescent shells arched like huge meteors and landed in Fort Jackson or exploded over it. As the fort answered the fire, the river reverberated with thunderlike claps.

Superficial observations could obtain no vital intelligence about the effects of the bombardment on the forts, but around 5:00 P.M. it became apparent that a huge fire was burning either in or near Fort Jackson. At first it was believed to be a nearby house, but later observation from a boat rowed upstream revealed that the citadel in the center of the fort was blazing. The fire continued until 11:00 P.M., according to the journal of the *Portsmouth*, whose writer conjectured that a "barracks was on fire."[13]

Hour after hour the exchange of gunfire continued, as the Confederate gunners tried to hit the mortar boats. A shot crashed into one, killing one man and injuring others but causing minimal damage to the craft. Occasionally a Confederate gunboat came timidly down the river to fire a shot, but the heavy gunfire of Union ships sent it scurrying back.

On April 20 Farragut reported that on the second day Union shells dismounted a columbiad and destroyed one of the furnaces for heating shot.[14] Then one of the Confederate shells smashed into the vitals of a mortar schooner, the *Maria J. Carleton*, sending her to the bottom. Another 10-inch shot hit the gunboat *Oneida*, wounding five or six men.

John Hart, a soldier on one of General Butler's transports, *E. William Forsley*, noted in his diary that one of the mortar boats had been rumored sunk. (His vessel had had to drop back downriver in order to anchor in a safe haven.) He optimistically commented that "if that was the only vessel sunk, we ought to be thankful." As the bombardment continued, he stood in awe and laconically wrote: "I expect ere this day a great many fellows bit the dust while we are looking on."[15]

The mortar fleet began to hurt as some vessels of the First Division were badly damaged. Porter himself inspected the vessels and ordered the damaged ones anchored across the river out of harm's way.[16]

On April 17 the unknown officer of the *Portsmouth* climbed the rigging of his ship to obtain a better view of the proceedings. He reported seeing mortar shells bursting over the forts "with good effect," and that "the forts every once and [sic] a while would return fire, but very irregular and with no effect whatsoever." (Obviously, he was unaware of the damage being done to some of the mortar schooners and the loss of one.) He wrote that the *Portsmouth* crew then "coated the outside of the ship with chain mail, making her almost impregnable and bombproof."[17] This was done in preparation for a run past the forts.

In New Orleans there was considerable concern over the ability of the forts to withstand the fierce bombardment. But the prevailing military thinking was that the two forts were invincible against an attack. On April 23, in an attempt to soothe the populace, the *New Orleans Picayune* ran a headline that read: "The Forts Hold Their Own and Are Likely to Do So."

The *Picayune* also ran a letter from Brigadier General Duncan, who was in charge of the forts. He reported that the bombardment, which had been going on all night and day, had caused few casualties. Then he added:

> God is certainly protecting us. We are all cheerful, and have an abiding faith in our ultimate success which I regret to learn, is not altogether the case in the city. A people in earnest, in a good cause should have more fortitude. . . . The health of the troops continues to be good and they are generally in good spirits than even in more quiet times.[18]

The enemy had fired between 22,000 and 25,000 shells, he reported, and "they must soon exhaust themselves. If not, we can stand it with God's blessing as long as they can."

The government in Richmond did not share Duncan's concern about the fact that a Union ironclad fleet was above and a wooden fleet below New Orleans. In response to Governor Moore's plea to President Davis to "engage the enemy now assaulting the forts," Davis reacted with an astonishing display of indifference. The forts should be able to deal with Farragut's wooden ships, he thought, and the *Louisiana* would take care of the threat from upriver.[19]

IN the Farragut fleet the question of the hulk-and-chain obstruction across the river came up again—it had to be removed before the fleet could move upstream. The task fell to Lieutenant Charles Caldwell, skipper of the gunboat *Itaska*, plus Lieutenant Pierce Crosby of the *Pinola*. The two gunboats were placed under the command of Captain Bell, and their captains were given orders to open the obstruction.

Under the cover of darkness on the night of April 20, the two gunboats moved upstream to the barrier. The plan—under the direction of Captain Julius Kroehl, an expert on torpedoes—was to place a petard, or explosive charge, of 180 pounds on one of the hulks. The explosion would blow the barrier loose, sending it against the riverbank.

The two gunboats approached the barrier under a fierce barrage laid down by Union mortar schooners to cover the operation. The gunboats separated as each went to her assigned station on the hulk-and-chain obstruction. Caldwell ordered his gunners to fire into one of the hulks to sink it, but *Itaska* got tangled in the anchor chains and went aground for a time. After two attempts she was pulled free by the *Oneida*. Meanwhile, because of faulty wiring, the charges Kroehl placed failed to go off. Finally, the crews' attempts to slip the hulks' anchor chains and cables met with little or no success. It began to appear that the entire expedition was a failure.

Caldwell was not one to get discouraged, however, and he decided on a bold move. He took the *Itaska* upriver and, hugging the shore to avoid detection, suddenly swung out into the channel. Calling for full speed ahead, he headed for the chain between the second and third hulks on the western end of the obstruction. Then, using the full power of his engines plus the swift four-knot current of the river, he bore down and, like a modern icebreaker, rode up on the chain. The sheer weight snapped the chain; the hulks spread apart, and the two gunboats rode triumphantly through and downriver to Farragut. The obstruction had been removed, they reported, opening a passage for the fleet. Farragut was understandably pleased. In regard to the safety of his chief of staff Bell, he later wrote that he had never "felt such anxiety in my life until his return."[20]

But the flag officer had not been wasting all his time in hand-wringing. He had been studying a report from the chief engineer for the Army of the Potomac, Brigadier General John G. Barnard, who had earlier worked with P. G. T. Beauregard on the two forts. The report maintained that the two forts could bring to bear on the channel some 177 guns. Barnard, in his report, suggested that Farragut station "two or four of your large ships alongside the forts" and blast away "with 24- and 32-pounders to make the enemy shore and main batteries untenable." Then the fleet could steam past the forts, with minimal damage and casualties. On the surface the idea looked feasible.

Barnard warned, however, that the forts might be stronger than anticipated and that in that case Farragut would do well to pass them, capture New Orleans, and then send land forces to assault the forts.[21]

Finally, after five days of incessant bombardment and 16,800 shells expended, Porter's crews became exhausted and their ammunition was running low. In spite of being, as historian John Fiske points out, "riddled like a worm-eaten log," Forts Jackson and St. Philip were obviously still far from being subdued.[22] Earlier Farragut had sent up the gunboat *Oneida*, escorted by the *Sciota* and the *Pinola*, to support the mortar boats. For three hours Commander Samuel Phillips Lee had dodged shells from the fort and lobbed his own salvos in return. During the melee the *Oneida* was hit three times, disabling one 32-pounder and a nine-inch pivot gun aft. Six crewmen were wounded. Commander Lee, in a matter-of-fact tone, reported that "the shots that came on board were 10-inch solid and did considerable damage to the vessel."[23]

During the early morning hours of April 20, Easter Sunday, a squalid-looking Confederate deserter hailed the mortar schooner *Norfolk Packet*. Told to come onboard, he announced himself as a Pennsylvania show performer who had been pressed into Confederate service while on tour and wound up in Fort Jackson as a laborer. During the confusion of a bombardment that threatened a magazine, he had slipped out of the fort, grabbed a boat, and fled.

The mortar schooner's skipper, Lieutenant Watson Smith, realized this incident was of consequence, so he whisked the deserter over to Porter's flagship *Harriet Lane* for interrogation. The man informed Porter that the incessant bombardment had done much damage to Fort Jackson—levees had been cut, the magazine had nearly exploded, the citadel had been destroyed, and the men were greatly demoralized. Porter, always ready to impress his commander with the effectiveness of his mortars, took the deserter aboard the *Hartford* to Farragut. But Farragut was not impressed with the story.

Finally, Farragut issued his plan of attack, complete with a hand-drawn map of the sailing order of the ships. He stated:

> The flag officer, after having heard all the opinions expressed by the different commanders, is of the opinion that whatever is to be done will have to be done quickly, or we will again be reduced to a blockading squadron without the means of carrying on the bombardment, as we have nearly expended all the shells and fuzes [sic]

and material for making cartridges. . . . The forts should be run, and when a force is once above the forts to protect the troops, they should be landed at Quarantine from the Gulf side by bringing them up through the bayou, and then our forces should move upriver.[24]

Farragut went on to explain the signals for the operation to begin and, once Fort St. Philip had been passed, the order of sailing. Farragut's thinking was revealed in the general order, where he says that after giving the signal for "close action" number 8, he would *"abide the results—conquer or be conquered*—drop anchor or keep under way, as in his opinion is the best" (italics mine). Such dramatic touches are found occasionally in Farragut's general orders.

As the time for Farragut's move drew near, the citizens of New Orleans became more alarmed, even if their military did not. The newspapers, in dour editorials, fueled speculations of doom. Union warships were present in the Head of the Passes, the *True Delta* reported, but on April 22 the paper hedged a bit and published a series of communications between Confederate Generals Lovell and Duncan at the forts, affirming their ability to withstand the bombardments. On April 21 the *New Orleans Crescent* proclaimed to the citizens that they had "nothing to fear from dozens of the mortar boats below the fort."[25] With warning signals all around, everyone appeared to be aware of the dangers from below except for the military.

BUT there was one more act to be played out before the flag officers put Farragut's plan into effect, and that had to do with a last-minute report on the collective strengths of the forts and the ability of the fleet to pass them.

Sometime earlier Farragut had allowed a French admiral and a British frigate captain to go upriver on business. The two commanders had passed Forts Jackson and St. Philip, and on the way back they conferred with Farragut, proclaiming that the forts would be impossible to pass.[26] Many of Farragut's fleet personnel were discouraged at this news, but the flag officer was not. He was more sure than ever about his ability to accomplish his plan.

Finally, Farragut's patience was exhausted, and his faith in the effectiveness of the mortars had worn thin. The deserter's story and the foreign navy men's assessment notwithstanding, he called his commanders to the flagship and laid out his final orders. Among the admonitions to his commanders, and one prime example of how Farragut considered every detail of the operation, was that the captains of the vessels bear in mind that "you will always have to ride head to the current, and can only avail yourself of the sheer of the helm to point a broadside gun more than three points forward of the beam." With similar detail, he further admonished them to trim their vessels "also a few inches by the head, so that if she touches the bottom she will not swing head down the river."[27] The latter action would occur if the stern of the vessel touched bottom and thus acted as a pivot, swinging the vessel around in the swift current so that the head faced downstream. This instruction was a stark indication of the difficulty of maneuvering vessels of large configurations and heavy displacements in the river's swift, four-to-five-knot current.

At the proper signal, pursuant to Farragut's orders, the fleet would up-anchor and move upriver in battle formation against Forts Jackson and St. Philip and then on to New Orleans.

"The fat," as Southerners were fond of saying, "is now in the fire."

CHAPTER NINE

NEW ORLEANS— PHASE THREE: CRUCIBLE OF STONE AND IRON

Thursday, April 24, 1862

The mighty Mississippi flowed silently through the early morning darkness; a decided chill hung in the misty air. The big ships, resembling phantoms, sawed at their anchor chains, and among the black hulls nary a light could be seen. Onboard the phantom ships, crews were busy preparing for the expected run up the river. A breakfast of hardtack and coffee had been gulped down earlier by the apprehensive crews, after they had stowed their hammocks and personal gear in the proper lockers. The men had gone to their battle stations, many no doubt shivering in the cool dampness of a river night. Gun crews were checking their implements, and deck crews were storing buckets of sand around the gun stations, lest the gunners' feet slip on blood. It was a necessary ritual that all gunners abhorred.

At the flag banks on deck, signalmen checked and double-checked their flags, bunting, and halyards, in preparation for the swift deployment of signals. In the engine room men were carefully checking gauges and valves, while in the boiler rooms sweating black gangs tenderly ministered to the hungry boilers. On deck seamen removed all possible obstacles, put up netting, checked chains, and performed the many duties of a deck gang.

In his cabin onboard the *Hartford*, Farragut no doubt was going over last-minute preparations with his chief of staff, Bell, and the ship's skipper, Commander Richard Wainwright. Similar conferences were being attended on all 18 of the ships in the sailing battle order. In the dark all eyes on all vessels were focused in the general direction of the flagship, awaiting that prearranged signal for "getting under way."

Then it came. At 2:00 a.m. by the ships' clocks, three red lights crept up the mizzenmast of the *Hartford*. It was the signal everyone had been looking for.[1] All hands sprang into action; rattling noises echoed around the river as heavy anchors were either windlassed up to their hawse pipes or secured along the hull. Screws churned the water; ships hove-to against the current until signaled to move forward. Unfortunately, an hour was lost because the *Cayuga* had difficulty raising her anchor, which had become fouled. Once it was finally raised and properly seated, the ships silently began to move along the preplanned battle line, against the inexorable four-knot current.

It must have been a tense time for all hands, even for the flag officer, who later wrote that "it was the most anxious night of my life."[2] An entry in the *Portsmouth*'s journal recorded Farragut in a different mode, stating that "this was a most memorable day."[3]

The ships formed the battle line as follows:

First Division, Captain Theodorus Bailey commanding
- *Cayuga* (flag), Lieutenant Commander N. B. Harrison
- *Pensacola,* Captain Henry W. Morris
- *Mississippi,* Captain Melancton Smith
- *Oneida,* Commander Samuel P. Lee
- *Varuna,* Commander Charles S. Boggs
- *Katahdin,* Lieutenant Commander George H. Preble
- *Kineo,* Lieutenant Commander George M. Ransom
- *Wissahickon,* Lieutenant Commander Albert L. Smith

Second Division, Flag Officer David G. Farragut commanding

- *Hartford* (flag), Commander Richard Wainwright
- *Brooklyn,* Captain Thomas P. Craven
- *Richmond,* Commander James Alden

Third Division, Captain Henry Bell commanding

- *Sciota,* Lieutenant Commander Edward Donaldson
- *Iroquois,* Commander John DeCamp
- *Kennebec,* Commander John H. Russell
- *Pinola,* Lieutenant Commander Pierce Crosby
- *Itaska,* Lieutenant Commander C. H. B. Caldwell
- *Winona,* Lieutenant Commander E. T. Nichols
- Commander David Dixon Porter's mortar schooners and gunboats
- *Portsmouth,* Commander Samuel Swartwout[4]

At first Farragut had planned for the *Hartford* to lead the First Division, so that her big guns could deal with any Confederate naval vessels that dared appear. But his senior commanders prevailed upon him to head the Second Division, stating that he should not bear the brunt of the first salvos from the forts. His death or serious incapacitation would throw the whole fleet into confusion. The flag officer nodded at their advice and took the lead position of the Second Division.

Farragut might be criticized for not having the fleet steam in two columns, as would normally have been the practice. But at the bend, some 700 to 800 yards below the forts, the river was narrow. The passage that had been cleared through the hulk-and-chain obstruction was also narrow. The fleet therefore had to steam single column, even if it meant that straggling might occur, putting those vessels in jeopardy.

To keep the enemy gunners hunkered down, Commodore Porter's gunboats had been ordered up to within 200 yards of the water battery of Fort Jackson to pour in grape, cannister, and shrapnel.[5] Mortar schooners were also moved up closer to lay down a parallel barrage to that of the gunboats, covering the advancing ships.

According to the battle plan, the First Division was to steam to the right (or starboard) to engage Fort St. Philip, while the Second Division was to steam to the left (or port) for an assault on Fort Jackson. No lights were allowed on deck, lest they betray the ships' presence. But it would not have made a difference, because at 3:30 A.M. the ships' silhouettes were spotted in the darkness by keen observers at the forts.

Slowly, their screws churning furiously against the powerful river current, the phantom ships moved upriver. At 3:30, the same time they were spotted in the fort, the *Cayuga* reached the hulk-and-chain obstruction and was passing through the opening. The darkness was ripped apart as the gunners in Fort St. Philip opened up a "tremendous fire" on the *Cayuga* and her column steaming close behind, according to officers aboard the advancing ships.

Then the Union mortar schooners got into the act, opening up with an awesome barrage of shells that kept the Rebel gunners down and prevented them from inflicting more damage on Farragut's fleet. White flashes shattered the darkness of the river, followed by heavy crashes of thunder, as big guns vomited forth their lethal projectiles. Smoke rolled across, obscuring what little visibility there was. Farragut's gun crews had to sight their targets in the forts guided by the flashes of the latter's guns. The river, its banks, and everything around the battle area vibrated from gunfire that resembled the heaviest, most bone-jarring thunderclaps imaginable.

By now, according to observers, every gun in the battle area was belching fire and smoke. Shells whistled overhead, sending off showers of incendiary sparks, only to hit their target on a wooden ship with a heavy crunch, or with an earth-jarring *thump* on land, or in the water with a loud *chunk*, sending up a huge geyser.

The officer of the day on the *Portsmouth*, in a frenzy of excitement, wrote: "There was one continuous blaze of fire . . . the shells as they flew around me in all directions looked like balls of fire . . . words cannot convey any idea of this terrific naval fight, the greatest fight ever recorded on record. It was truly an awful and sublime spectacle to behold." His ship, being a sailing vessel, was being towed into the area by the gunboat *J.P. Jackson*.[6] On the transport *E. William Forsley*, also being towed up, John Hart got carried away by his excitement and wrote: "Hurrah! Hurrah! Hurrah! Good news for us, and I have had the pleasure to witness one of the greatest naval fight [sic] if not the greatest in the world . . . the river is only 700 yards from fort to fort. There are 18 of our boats in all. One of our frigates, the *Pensacola*, came to stand and fire broadside after broadside."[7]

The *Cayuga*, because she was ahead of the column, received the first and heaviest fire from the forts. A lieutenant aboard the lead ship reported that "the air was filled with shells and explosions which almost blinded me as I stood on the forecastle, trying to see my way, for I had never been up the river before."

The officer, Lieutenant George Perkins, continued: "I soon saw that the guns of the forts were all aimed for the midstream, so I steered close under the walls of Fort St. Philip, and although our mast and rigging got badly shot through, our hull was but little damaged." Perkins looked aft, and his heart jumped into his mouth when he discovered his ship was entirely alone. He concluded the others "must have been sunk by the forts." That was why the fort gunners were concentrating on his ship.[8]

(The *Cayuga*'s plight was similar to that of the Imperial Japanese destroyer *Takanami*, in the battle of Tassafaronga, on November 30, 1942, during the struggle for the Solomon Islands. Having been far in the van of Admiral Tanaka's "Tokyo Express," she received hits from all American cruisers and destroyers in the opposing American flotilla. As a result, she was literally ripped apart by the concentrated gunfire.)

As the ships steamed by the forts, exchanging shots with gunners, the fight became furious and heavy. On the ships, in spite of the morning chill, the sweating gunners were naked to the waist with their jackets tied around their necks, loading and firing as rapidly as they could.

Anyone who has ever been on a warship during a naval battle would not find it difficult to reconstruct what must have occurred on the deck. With six to eight well-trained men to a gun, the action would have become a matter of routine after a time. The two men at the muzzle would swing into action: One man would drop a powder bag into the muzzle, and the second would ram it home with a long rammer, equipped with a strip of rawhide with which to mark the depth of the rammer thrust. Then the first man would drop a round shot or cannister of grape, depending upon which was called for, into the muzzle, and the second would ram it home along with some wadding. That would keep the shot in the bore when the gun was depressed. The chief gunner would pierce the powder bag through a hole in the top of the breech, using a vent pick, and then the primer would be inserted. The gun would be run out of the port by a system of ropes and pulleys by gunners' assistants. The gunner would then hook a lanyard to a flintlock-type hammer over the vent. On the command to fire, he would yank the lanyard, and the hammer would fall and strike the primer. The flash would illuminate the area around the gun; the report would be deafening. The gun would recoil savagely against its ropes and pulleys; billows of burnt-powder smoke would boil back through the gunport, setting eyes to watering and throats to coughing. Then the gun would be run in; a crewman, using a water-soaked sponge on a rammer, would swab out the bore in the event that a lingering spark would ignite the next powder bag prematurely, causing injury to those around the gun.

Meanwhile hits on the bulwarks, from enemy shots, would send splinters of wood as large as two-by-fours flying in all directions, causing much damage. A heavy thud would signal a hit on the hull near or below the waterline, sending damage-control crews scurrying.

The process would become mechanical, numbing, with crews going into a trancelike state, automatically loading, running out, firing, running in, swabbing out, and reloading. After the cease-fire, sanity would return and the zombielike crews would resume some kind of normalcy; but sore eyes, ringing ears, and a general state of numbness—called battle shock—would linger for some time.

The next ship in line, *Pensacola*, was having her own problems. After passing the obstruction hulks and engaging in devastating "almost yardarm conflict" with the forts, she had engine trouble and slowed. In an effort to keep the enemy gunners down, Morris ordered a full broadside into the fort that caused many casualties.

Ahead on the *Cayuga*, Captain Theodorus Bailey found himself alone and, not having time to contemplate his plight, poured grape and canister into the forts, causing damage to enemy gunners who dared raise their heads to peek at the action. Then his lookouts reported two steamers coming at him from upriver: units of the Confederate and Louisiana state flotillas. Lieutenant George Perkins, on board the *Cayuga*, for a moment thought his ship was "gone for sure."[9] Fortunately for the *Cayuga* and every Union ship that engaged them thereafter, these flotillas were disorganized and lacked leadership. The River Defense Fleet, under the Confederate navy, had already hightailed it upstream, at the appearance of Farragut's armada and the start of hostilities, leaving the state-sponsored fleet to do the fighting.

Fire from the *Cayuga*, and from the *Oneida* and *Varuna*, which had come up from behind to assist her, soon drove off these enemy craft. The *Cayuga's* log recorded that during the fight with her and her sisters, 11 enemy gunboats had surrendered and were run ashore and burned.[10] At one point the *Governor Moore* was almost muzzle to muzzle with the *Cayuga* but she took a terrific beating in spite of a 10-inch ram on her bow. Captain Beverly Kennon of the *Governor Moore* reported that 13 members of his gun crew were killed.

The *Cayuga* was the first Union vessel to encounter the *Manassas*. Coming downriver, the ram "butted" the Union warship, missed her stern, then dropped downriver for more targets. The *Cayuga* steamed on, firing at everything and anything in view.[11]

The *Varuna*, because of her swiftness, soon outran her sisters, but she unexpectedly found herself alone and surrounded by enemy vessels. In the furious exchange of gunfire, she managed to drive off her assailants, sinking four of them—one of which was crowded with troops. Then going upriver her commander, Charles Boggs, spotted the *Oneida* battling Confederate gunboats. He steamed to her rescue but was forced to slow down because of boiler trouble—and was suddenly beset once again by the *Governor Moore*, which appeared out of the mist, making straight for the *Varuna*. Aboard the *Governor Moore*, Captain Kennon hoisted two lights—white at the masthead, red at the forepeak—which would identify his Confederate ship as being Union. It was an old trick—trying to fool an enemy into thinking she was a sister ship.

Kennon's ruse worked; the *Varuna* ignored him. As the *Governor Moore* drew close, Commander Boggs suddenly recognized her and opened fire. Soon a lively exchange ensued, during which the Confederate ship took a beating. The *Varuna*, because of her sluggishness, was unable to prevent the *Governor Moore* from ramming her with her ten-inch iron ram. The blow came along the *Varuna's* port gangway, killing four and wounding nine crewmen. Then the ram hit twice again on the

Varuna's quarter and port side. Kennon's vessel was close enough to use her bow gun, but because she was head-on, Kennon ordered the gun depressed, firing through his own bow. The first shot glanced off the *Varuna*'s hawse pipe; the second went through and hit the forward gun, causing heavy casualties. The *Governor Moore* then rammed the Union gunboat midship—a fatal blow. Boggs steered his damaged vessel into shoal waters, where she settled to the bottom—but not until after she had been given another ram by the Confederate steamer *R.J. Breckenridge*.

Flushed with success, Kennon wanted to take on the entire Union fleet with his damaged vessel; but an officer at the helm swung the *Governor Moore* to starboard, declaring that he and the crew had had enough. In so doing, he exposed his flank to the oncoming Union ships. A volley of shots sieved her; she exploded and went to the bottom, taking most of the crew with her, ablaze with her colors burning at the peak.

Later Boggs, with admirable magnanimity, commended his second-class powder boy, Oscar Peck, to Farragut, claiming that the boy's "coolness and intrepidity attracted the attention of all hands." He asked that Peck be appointed to a naval school. He also commended his marine contingent on board for their gallantry.[12]

By this time most of Farragut's ships were past the forts, but not without damage. The *Brooklyn* followed the *Hartford* through the hulk-and-chain obstruction, but one of her anchors became snagged on a hulk. The tautness of the cable swung the big ship around until her bow faced the right, or starboard, side of the river. This gave the gunners at Fort St. Philip a broadside target, so they poured it on. After Captain Craven had the cable cut, the ship swung back to head-on, and as she passed the fort, she poured on three broadsides that completely drove the rebels from their guns, silencing their fire. The vessel came within 60 yards of Fort St. Philip.

As the *Brooklyn* steamed on, she came upon the Confederate ram steamer *Warrior* and the ironclad *Louisiana*, which was aground but trying to use her broadside and stern guns. The big steam sloop let loose with a devastating broadside that smashed the *Warrior*, setting her on fire. The broadside had no effect on the grounded ironclad, but the grape and cannister swept away some of the exposed crew who were topside, behind an iron "fence" or bulwark fastened on the deck. Conversely, the guns of the *Louisiana* had little effect on the *Brooklyn*.

Suddenly the tide swept the *Brooklyn* over to the Fort Jackson side of the river where, according to Captain Craven, she received a "raking and terribly scorching fire, without the possibility of bringing any of the guns to bear."[13] Then without warning the ironclad *Manassas* came out of the mist and rammed the *Brooklyn* fore and aft, in spite of a "port the helm hard" order from Craven. Warley later reported that he had struck *Brooklyn* "fairly abreast of the main mast, with a tremendous crash."[14]

At first Craven thought the blow was fatal to his ship, but he quickly learned that the damage had been minor. "The black, whale-like-looking beast dropped alongside," he reported, and fell astern. The ram hove-to, apparently to decide what to do next, and an officer and a crewman stepped out of a hatch forward of the stack, ostensibly to examine any damage. Suddenly the officer staggered and fell headlong into the river. Craven called to the lead man in the forward chains and asked if he had seen the officer fall. The lead man replied that not only had he seen the man, but he had flung his lead at him, which had knocked him overboard.

As the *Brooklyn* pushed on, Craven gazed at the battle arena and was moved to write:

> A more desperate, a more magnificent dash was never made, the rush of our little fleet over the barriers, through a fleet of rams, ironclad gunboats, batteries and fire ships, and under the concentrated fire of two powerful forts, where the passage between them is just 1,000 yards wide, is beyond all peradventure, the most brilliant thing in the way of a naval fight ever performed. As for myself, I must confess that I never expected to get through, but the Lord of Hosts was with us, and though no one can tell how it was done, by His Divine Providence, we passed through this ordeal.[15]

It is remarkable that a man could have been moved to such eloquence in the midst of such a furious firefight.

Meanwhile the *Hartford* was having her own troubles. She managed to pass the forts, with Farragut stationed up in the main mizzenmast. She took some hits in her hull during the passage, but she gave back what she got with furious broadsides in what Farragut, in a Shakespearean mood, described as "such a fire as they never dreamed of in their philosophy."[16] In retrospect he was more concerned that his own vessels would fire at each other in the confusion than he was about any punishment the forts could dish out.

Gunfire was one thing—but fire rafts were another. A lookout reported a large raft aft, being towed by an enemy tug directly toward the *Hartford*. The helmsman, in an effort to avoid the danger, ran the big ship onto the eastern shore.

The *Hartford* was now stuck fast, yet the fire raft swept on toward her. All efforts to free the ship were futile. Finally the Confederate tug *Mosher* pushed the blazing raft against the ship's port side. In a moment the *Hartford* was ablaze halfway up to the maintop and mizzen, fueled by the tarred shrouds and ratlines. The ship's fire department, headed by Lieutenant Thornton, swiftly took care of the situation. Amid the conflagration that threatened his ship, Farragut strode about, giving orders, completely oblivious to any personal danger. He paced the deck shouting, "Don't flinch from that fire, boys. There's a hotter fire than that for those who don't do their duty!" About this time Signal Officer Osbon bent over, covering his head with his coat, and commenced uncapping some shells on deck. Thinking him to be in prayer, Farragut admonished him, "This is no time for prayer." But Osbon replied, "If you wait a second, you'll see the quickest answer to your prayer you ever heard of." With that he uncapped a third 20-pound shell and rolled them all over the side and onto the raft, where they exploded, blowing the bottom out. The fire raft sank rapidly.

Farragut then pointed at the *Mosher* and said, "Give that rascally tug a shot." They did, and one shot went through the boiler of the hapless tug, sending her like a rock into the depths of the river. All the while the *Hartford* was still firing at the forts. Finally some excellent seamanship freed her, and she swung out into the river and proceeded on her course.[17] Only then did Farragut and his crew discover that they had passed the forts.

Porter's mortar schooners continued to pour a hail of fire into the forts, driving gunners from their stations. The cannonading became so fierce that the noise was heard all the way to Ship Island by Mrs. Porter, who thought it was coming from Mobile Bay to the east.

Richmond, whose crew was lying low on deck in order to escape being hit by shrapnel, passed by the forts without incident. But at one time she was so close that Commander Alden could have "thrown a stone at the fort." The enemy gunners were unable to depress their guns low enough to hit her, so most of their shots passed over harmlessly.

The final casualty list on the *Richmond* was two killed and four wounded. Commander Alden lauded the use of splinter netting, which had prevented further casualties. He also commended the technique of whitewashing the decks and gun carriages, increasing their visibility under darkened conditions. He urged Farragut to adopt these techniques in the entire fleet.

The Third Division, led by *Sciota,* also slipped by the forts with a minimum of damage. But as they advanced, the converted Confederate packet ship *McRae* steamed into the fray, firing at every Union ship in sight. Unfortunately for Lieutenant Thomas Huger, captain of the *McRae,* he made the mistake of taking on John DeCamp's *Iroquois.* De-Camp ordered his 11-inch Dahlgrens to blast the impertinent Confederate vessel with shells and shrapnel. The *McRae's* deck was swept by the shrapnel; a shot landed in her sail room, setting the vessel on fire and putting her out of action.

All of the Third Division got through, with the exception of the *Itaska.* Shots from the fort smashed a boiler, forcing her back downstream. The *Winona* was also hulled by shells, so she too dropped back.

Farragut's ships were above the forts by now, but one more obstacle faced him—the *Manassas,* which seemed to be everywhere at once and refused to go away. Farragut sent a message to Captain Smith on the *Mississippi* to "sink that damned thing."

The big steam frigate, flanked by the *Kineo,* therefore set a course directly for the *Manassas,* and her forward guns slammed shells into the whalelike craft. Aboard the *Manassas,* with her ram badly damaged, her gun dismounted and inoperable, and her engines about to give out, Captain Warley knew there was only one expedient—beach the vessel.

He headed for the shore as the *Mississippi* roared by, just missing him. He beached the *Manassas* on a bank, left her to fill with water and sink, and escaped into the woods with his crew. A crew from the *Mississippi* boarded her but quickly returned, announcing that the ram was too far gone to salvage.

Then the *Manassas*, as if she were not finished yet and wanted to get back into battle, slid off the bank and drifted into deeper water. There she was pounded by a couple of broadsides from *Mississippi*. She burst into flames and floated downstream past the forts, where she was mistaken for a Union vessel. Confederate gunners pounded her mercilessly, but she slipped by, battered and in a sinking condition.

The Confederate ram was still not finished. As she passed the mortar schooners, Porter thought she was an enemy boat and ordered his gunboats to blast her. Then the ill-fated ram finally gave up the ghost, blowing up with a roar that reverberated up and down the river.[18]

MEANWHILE what was the *Louisiana* doing all this time? Actually she was doing nothing. Because of her inability to deliver broadsides, she sat immovable along the riverbank above Fort St. Philip, a spectator of the battle. She delivered a desultory shot now and then, but she took more than she gave because every Union warship slammed her with shells as they passed. It was a case of a potential that never was fulfilled. That potential lay in her very design and purpose. She could have been one of the most powerful warships in the world, and she could have driven the Federal naval forces back into the Gulf and then gone on to break the Mobile Bay blockade. She had four engines driving two paddlewheels in tandem in centerline, plus two propellers and two rudders for maneuvering.[19]

But all this potential came to naught because of the shortages of iron, parts, and personnel that dogged her builders from the very start. The sad truth was that, despite her four-inch armor plating and her proposed armament of 16 guns, she was impotent. She had to be towed to a spot above Fort St. Philip to act as a floating artillery position, with mechanics still on board.

Captain Charles MacIntosh reported that the *Louisiana's* rudders were useless and that she leaked badly, even in her magazines. The oppressive Louisiana heat, added to that from her boilers, would frequently drive the gun crews from their positions.

In Fort Jackson, Confederate General Duncan was naturally elated to see the ironclad arrive, although he suggested that she be brought farther downriver to engage the annoying and lethal mortar schooners. Commander John K. Mitchell, who was in command of the Confederate navy and the vessels of the Louisiana state flotilla, demurred. (His jurisdiction did not include the River Defense Fleet, however, because navy men refused to be under the command of the army.) Once again the Confederate command structure in New Orleans was obstructed by stolid indifference from Richmond.

So the *Louisiana* was pounded mercilessly by Union ships. Captain MacIntosh, while he was topside, surrounded by the ridiculously thin iron sheeting, was fatally wounded.

WHEN the Confederate naval vessels had either been sunk or driven back upriver, Farragut gathered his fleet at Point Quarantine to take stock of the damage and to bury the dead. All but four of his vessels had made the run past the forts, and only one, the *Varuna*, had been sunk. His casualty list was surprisingly low—37 killed and 147 wounded. As for damage, the *Hartford* had been hit 18 times; the *Pensacola*, nine hits; the *Mississippi*, 11 hits; the *Richmond*, 13 hits; and the *Brooklyn*, 16 hits. This was a relatively low price to pay for such a splendid victory.

In Fort Jackson, General Duncan lamented the run past his forts, claiming that the Union success was due to the inability of the fire rafts to accomplish their task in the darkness. The enemy, he further claimed, "was suddenly inspired, for the first time, to run the gauntlet at all hazards, although it was not part of his original design."[20]

In Washington, when Secretary Welles first read of Farragut's victory in telegraphic dispatches from the *Richmond Examiner* and the *Petersburg Express*, he was astonished.[21]

Meanwhile at Point Quarantine, Farragut prepared his men for the next operation on his agenda: taking New Orleans. He did not know how many batteries the Confederates had constructed along the river, besides the one at Chalmette at the bend ten miles down from New Orleans. But he was not worried, because he knew his ships, with their overwhelming firepower, would sweep away all obstacles, just as they had done during the run past the two powerful forts.

CHAPTER TEN

NEW ORLEANS—

PHASE FOUR: A CITY

SURRENDERS

April 25, 1862

The passing of the forts and the eradication of the Confederate flotillas dealt a crushing blow to the Confederacy. Wrote Secretary Mallory: "The destruction of the navy at New Orleans was a sad, sad blow."[1] Major General Lovell, who had been at Fort Jackson during the passage, left before the last Union ship passed the obstruction, and realizing that nothing could stop the Federal advance, he wisely returned to the city, "narrowly escaping capture." There he instructed General Martin Luther Smith, who was in charge of land defenses, to strengthen the fortifications to the south of the city, particularly at Chalmette. This move was of utmost importance, because it was the last viable defense site the Federals would encounter before reaching the city. (The wildcat gun positions in place downriver proved to be only a nuisance to the Union fleet.)

But Smith found these instructions very difficult to carry out. The guns at Chalmette faced east, in anticipation of a land attack from the rear. Furthermore, the river was at a record high stage, which would place the attacking ships higher than the gun positions and allow the guns to be shelled from front to rear with impunity.[2] The situation in the city—already intolerable because of a lack of powder and small arms ammunition—was further aggravated by a lack of manpower for defense: Only 3,000 men armed with shotguns and hunting rifles were present.

President Davis also lamented the passing of the forts, but striking a high note, he lauded General Duncan, saying that the general had "protracted a skillful and gallant defense of the forts, above praise."[3]

For Farragut's command, it had been a brilliant victory. General Butler, anchored with his flotilla of troop transports, rode out the battle, receiving occasional reports from dispatch steamers plying up and down the river. At word of the successful run, he sent a flowery message to Farragut: "Allow me to congratulate you and your command upon the bold, daring, brilliant and successful passage of the forts of your fleet this morning.[4] A more gallant exploit it has never fallen to the lot of men to witness." Commodore Porter was also quick to congratulate his commander. "Dear Sir," he wrote, "Captain Boggs has arrived. I congratulate you on your victory. I witnessed your passage with great pleasure. My hopes and predictions were at last realized."[5] Those hopes were always present with Porter, who was constantly looking for an opportunity to share in the glory to come.

When the sun came up, Farragut's fleet lay at anchor at Point Quarantine, four miles above the forts. Crews on the *Brooklyn* were busy "washing our decks of the blood and the mangled remains of our killed and wounded, temporarily stopping leaks and repairing damage."[6] The flag officer was aware of all contingencies; he dispatched Captain Boggs of the sunken *Varuna* through the Quarantine Bayou around to Commodore Porter, with instructions for Porter to demand the surrender of the forts and to ascertain the whereabouts of the *Itaska*, *Winona*, and *Kennebec*. Porter was also instructed to send a dispatch to General Butler, who was in the Head of the Passes awaiting further orders. Butler was to proceed down Pass à l'Outre into the Gulf, then land troops on Breton Sound, to the east of the forts. They were to proceed through a large bayou to the rear of Fort St. Philip and thence into Quarantine Sound.

Butler borrowed the steamer *Miami* from Porter's flotilla, loaded the 26th Massachusetts Regiment, and followed the route set out for him—until the bayou became too shallow for the *Miami* to proceed. The troops were loaded onto boats that took them farther—until they too reached water too shallow. Butler then had his troops march through the swamp until they reached a point above Fort St. Philip. From that position they would establish a stronghold and later send a large contingent across the river above Fort Jackson, cutting off both forts from reinforcements upriver.[7]

Gunboats were ordered to cover the operation on the river, in case the *Louisiana* and the *McRae*, still tied up above Fort St. Philip, should venture out to challenge the operation.

FARRAGUT had already finalized his plans to take New Orleans and cleared all ships' decks for action. At dawn on April 25, the fleet up-anchored and headed upriver. As it proceeded toward New Orleans, evidence of the panic of the city's population appeared. Cotton-loaded ships afire, boats, fire rafts, and all sorts of encumbrances floated downstream past the awed officers and men of the fleet.

As Farragut proceeded upriver, he discovered that contrary to his orders, Captain Bailey on *Cayuga* in the van had moved far ahead and had reached the Chalmette works. At the old War of 1812 battle site, Bailey was receiving a scorching barrage from Smith's 20 guns. It was difficult for him to return fire, because the Confederate guns ranged downriver for a mile, while the ship could answer only with her bow guns. The *Hartford* moved up to the rescue and replied with a devastating broadside, followed by those from *Brooklyn* and *Pensacola*, in line behind the flagship. It was all over in 20 minutes. The overwhelming fire from the ships scattered the Chalmette defenders in all directions. Onboard the ships a rousing cheer went up.[8] The last obstruction before the city had been swept away.

Ahead, New Orleans was in shambles. The citizens were in a state of near panic, running in all directions, not knowing quite what to do and causing considerable damage.

Louisiana Governor Moore had ordered all cotton stores removed or destroyed. Some were spirited to the interior, but the rest, in some desperate hope of impeding or stopping the Union advance, were split open, soaked with whiskey, set afire, and pushed into the river, along with burning vessels of all descriptions. Meanwhile frightened crowds broke into warehouses and ship holds to carry away bacon, sugar, corn, rice, flour, and any other foodstuffs that they could find. Other bales of cotton, waiting on wharves for loading onto ships, were set on fire.

Commenting on this frenzy, historian Robert Asbury writes that alarm bells rang, with four strokes repeated four times, warning the people of New Orleans that "Farragut's ships had passed the forts and that the last defenses of the city had crumbled. Immediately, the town was thrown into confusion bordering on frenzy, for it was popularly believed that New Orleans, if it fell into the hands of the Yankees, was destined to suffer the fate of Carthage." Asbury says that 15,000 bales of cotton were destroyed on the streets and on the levee and that "molasses flowed through the gutters like water." The rioting continued, in spite of the efforts of Confederate troops to quell it.[9]

General Lovell saw the handwriting on the wall. With his pitiful forces, he knew, he would be unable to counter Farragut's demands for surrender. If he were to resist, the Union ships would pound the city into a pile of rubble.

Lovell met with Mayor John T. Monroe and urged him not to resist Farragut. As for himself and his forces, he would evacuate and turn the city over to the mayor and the city council and let them deal with the Yankees.

Meanwhile all available troops and militiamen, along with their supplies, were ordered to board any available railroad car and leave the city. Every steamer afloat was commandeered, loaded with what military supplies there were, and sent upriver, hopefully to safety. As the people watched Lovell's forces evacuating the city, they howled with indignation.

When the *Hartford* rounded Slaughterhouse Bend, Farragut was shocked by the scene of devastation ahead. He later wrote: "The levee of New Orleans was one scene of destruction: ships, steamers, cotton, coal, etc., were all in one common blaze, and our ingenuity much taxed to avoid the floating conflagration."[10]

Farragut's thoughts, like those of his crews, were doubtless on the much-vaunted *Mississippi*. Rumors had flown thick and fast that she was the most powerful man-of-war afloat. Farragut theorized that she was intended as "the terror of the seas and no doubt would have been to a great extent."[11] There was no doubt in anyone's mind in the fleet that she was something to be dealt with. Upon her and her sister warship *Louisiana* lay the hopes of the citizens of New Orleans.

But all Union speculations about the formidability of the big Confederate ironclad were wasted, because of a lack of intelligence about her. At the time of Farragut's ascent of the river, the "terror of the seas" was moored to a dock with two of her propellers and a rudder lying on the dock. Her hull plating was incomplete, and even her guns were not installed. Upon hearing that Farragut had passed the forts, Commodore Whittle ordered Commodore Arthur Sinclair to take charge of the incomplete warship. Sinclair managed to obtain two steamers with which to tow the *Mississippi* upstream, where they hoped to finish her. The vessels, as Sinclair later wrote, "tugged at her the whole of the night unsuccessfully, for, instead of making headway, we lost ground considerably."[12]

Unfortunately for Sinclair and the brothers Tift, the doom of their much-heralded ironclad was sealed; the vessel had to be destroyed in order to keep her from falling into enemy hands. The *Mississippi* was set on fire, and with flames billowing from every gunport, she ignominiously drifted downstream, past the city that rested its hopes upon her, past a startled advancing Union fleet, and then downstream to oblivion. Some frustrated citizens came out with ropes, ready to hang the Tifts, but reason prevailed and they were quickly talked out of it. It was the end of a dream.

On April 25, with a misty rain surrounding it, the fleet steamed up opposite the French Quarter and dropped anchor at 2:00 P.M. An assortment of crowds stood on the banks, docks, and wharves jeering, weeping, shouting, and shaking fists until the *Brooklyn's* band struck up a patriotic number, and jeers quickly turned to cheers in the fickle crowd.

Suddenly a group of mounted Confederates rode up and fired into the cheering crowd of men, women, and children. The gunners on the warships bit their lips in frustration, because their first impulse was to fire cannister at the horsemen, but the presence of women and children prevented them from doing so.

After an hour's conference onboard the *Hartford* with his commanders, Farragut chose Captain Theodorus Bailey and Lieutenant George Perkins to go ashore, march to the city hall, and demand the city's surrender. The two men were rowed to a wharf used by the Memphis Packet in peacetime. By now a heavy rain was coming down, and as the landing party reached the wharf, they were greeted by a jeering, threatening mob, some brandishing pistols and loudly demanding a hanging.

Coolly and calmly the two officers asked for directions to the city hall. No one answered; the mob grew even more threatening. On board the flagship, a gunner stood alongside a pivot gun, lanyard in hand, smiling at the crowd while patting the black breech of the huge gun. It was a tight spot for the two brave officers; the situation had reached an impasse, and despite the visible threat from the ship, anything could happen at any moment.

Finally, a German citizen who had been visiting the city and had sized up the potentially dangerous situation stepped forward and offered to guide the officers to the building. As they walked, the crowd, resembling a pack of snapping dogs, followed along and pressed in from all sides.

Bailey and Perkins strode forward, looking neither right nor left. The mob kept shouting, "Kill them!" "Hang them!" "Shoot them!" The situation was ominous. As one observer commented: "So through the gates of death those two men walked to the City Hall to demand the town's surrender. It was one of the most bravest [sic] deeds I ever saw done."13

When they reached the city hall, Bailey and Perkins were ushered into the presence of the mayor and the city council, who were meeting in emergency session. There the two men presented Farragut's demand for surrender, as the mob outside stamped and grumbled. The mayor in-

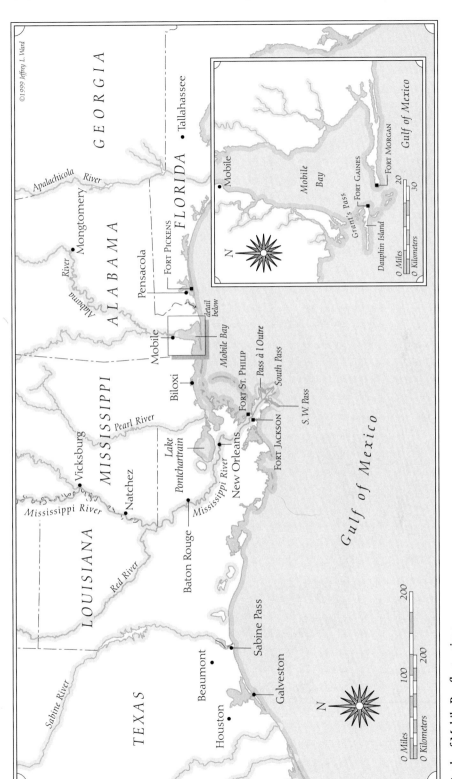

Battle of Mobile Bay fleet actions.

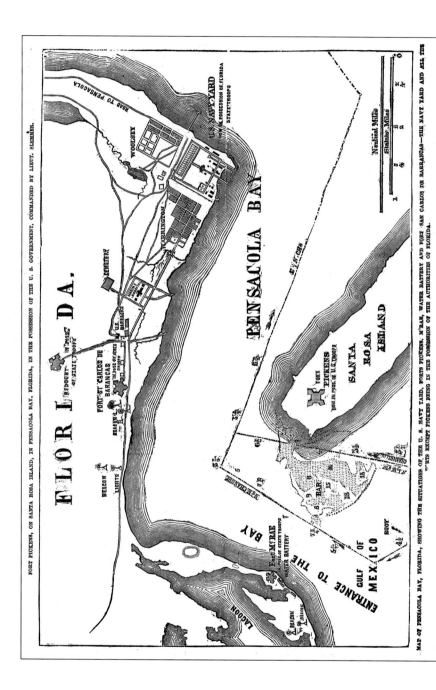

Map of Pensacola Bay area, showing all the Confederate forts. (U.S. NAVAL HISTORICAL CENTER PHOTOGRAPH.)

Parade ground of Fort Gaines on Dauphin Island, as it looks today. Anchor in center is from U.S.S. *Hartford*, Farragut's flagship. (AUTHOR'S PHOTO.)

View of Fort Morgan, showing the damaged citadel, taken shortly after its surrender. (U.S. NAVAL HISTORICAL CENTER PHOTOGRAPH.)

Raphael Semmes, CSN, captain of Confederate raiders *Sumter* and *Alabama*. (U.S. NAVAL HISTORICAL CENTER PHOTOGRAPH.)

U.S.S. *Hartford* engaging C.S.S. *Tennessee*, during Battle of Mobile Bay. (U.S. NAVAL INSTITUTE ARCHIVES.)

U.S.S. *Harriet Lane* being captured by Confederates from C.S.S. *Neptune*, in Galveston harbor. At left, the U.S.S. *Westfield* is being blown up to prevent capture. (U.S. NAVAL HISTORICAL CENTER.)

Admiral Franklin Buchanan, CSN, commander of Confederate flotilla at Mobile Bay.
(U.S. Naval Historical Center photograph.)

U.S.S. *Tecumseh* being destroyed by Confederate torpedo at Battle of Mobile Bay. (U.S. NAVAL HISTORICAL CENTER.)

Ramparts and outer walls of Fort Morgan. Much of the extensive battle damage has been repaired today. (AUTHOR'S PHOTO.)

A Fort Gaines cannon glowers at Fort Morgan on Mobile Point, across the bay. (AUTHOR'S PHOTO.)

sisted he could have nothing to do with the surrender of the city, because the city was under martial law proclaimed by General Lovell.
Shortly, the general strode into the chambers, followed by his aides.
Perkins described him as "pompous in his manner and silly and wiry in
his remarks."[14] The general proclaimed that he would never surrender,
but that he would withdraw his troops from the city and let the mayor
and the council take the hindmost.

When asked if he would take the Louisiana flag from atop the building, the mayor returned "an unqualified refusal."[15] He continued to
insist that he had no authority whatsoever for matters pertaining to
the military and that there was no power to prevent the Federal forces
from taking over the customs house and the U.S. Mint. They were government buildings anyway. Outside, the mob grew more menacing,
and there was talk of breaking down the doors and lynching the two
Yankees.

Then while some council members attempted to calm the crowd,
Bailey and Perkins were ushered into a closed carriage and whisked back
to the wharf and thence to the *Hartford* to report to Farragut about their
unsuccessful trip. Farragut proceeded to dispatch several steamers to
Point Quarantine to transport Butler and his troops up to the city.

It was a nervous night for all, during which all hands were issued cutlasses and pistols to thwart a possible boarding attempt, which never
materialized. When the morning of April 26 dawned, a rowboat came
up to the *Hartford*, carrying a message that the mayor and the council
would convene a special session to consider the surrender. Farragut
agreed to await the council's decision, but he sent along a message stating that as a naval officer, it was not within his province to assume the
duties of a commandant and that he had come to reduce the city to obedience to the laws of the U.S. government. He demanded that the U.S.
flag be flown all over the city and on all government buildings. All other
flags must be taken down.

As expected, Mayor Monroe refused to take down the state flags,
stating: "New Orleans is not now a military post; there is no military
commander within its limits. It is like an unoccupied fortress [of] which
an assailant at any moment may take possession." He then defended
his refusal to remove the city hall flag by stating that "no loyal citizen

would be willing to incur the odium of tearing down the symbol representing the state authority to which New Orleans owes her municipal existence."[16]

Such loyalty might have been admirable, but it should not have been flaunted in the face of overwhelming firepower. Farragut, also as expected, resented such stubbornness being flung in *his* face. But it did place him in a tight situation; he had many ships and many guns, but not enough to occupy the city. For that he needed troops. He decided to wait until General Butler and his troops arrived.

Patience, however, was not Farragut's strong suit. After a flurry of futile communications between himself and the city council, he decided to take matters into his own hands. On the morning of April 26, he sent Captain Henry Morris and some marines from the *Pensacola* to take possession of the U.S. Mint and to hoist the American flag atop the building; they would be covered by howitzers and marine sharpshooters atop the *Pensacola's* mainmast. The Morris party met no physical opposition but had to endure threatening howls from the mob that quickly collected. They returned safely to the ship. But the next day, during Sunday services in the fleet, a mob led by one William Mumford stormed the building, took down the flag, and tore it to shreds in the streets. The Union howitzers proved ineffective at discouraging this outrageous act.

On April 27 Farragut assembled a force of twenty marines, under the command of Lieutenant Albert Kautz and Midshipman John H. Read, and instructed them to proceed to the city hall to demand the hoisting of the American flag.[17]

Farragut promised the party that if anything happened to them, he would bombard the city with his big guns. As usual, the group was met at the wharf by another howling crowd, causing the marines to close ranks. Later, after conferring with an officer of the city guards, it was deemed prudent to send all but two marines back to the ship in order not to further inflame the mobs. Kautz and Read, along with two marines, then proceeded to city hall and presented Farragut's demand, but the mood of the crowd outside prevented any movement from anyone, particularly the council. Again the effort failed, and again the situation reached an impasse.

The deadlock gave Farragut a chance to take care of some unfinished business. Rumors had been floating about a formidable Confederate works at Carrollton, a town eight miles upriver. Farragut's concern was for Flag Officer Foote, who would have found the works threatening to his planned move downriver.[18] Therefore on April 28 Farragut took the *Hartford*, *Richmond*, *Brooklyn*, and *Oneida* and sailed up to Carrollton—only to find the works deserted, with the guns spiked and their carriages afire.

Returning to New Orleans, Farragut decided to solve the flag problem once and for all, with force if need be, even though he was still helpless without troops. He fired off a note to the mayor and council, demanding that the Louisiana state flag be hauled down and a U.S. flag be flown in its place. The expected refusal came.

By April 29, the endless squabbling exhausted what little patience Farragut had. This time he assembled an expedition of sailors—a battalion of marines with two boat howitzers—under the command of Captain Bell, accompanied by Midshipman John Read and Ensign E. C. Hazeltine. The force landed at the foot of Canal Street and marched to the customs house. There the marines were drawn up in line, their bayonets fixed, and the shrapnel-loaded howitzers were placed so that they faced up and down the street. While the silent crowd looked on, the officers entered the building and were guided to the roof by the postmaster, who was a Union sympathizer. There the U.S. flag was raised. Then, after leaving a guard in front of the customs house, the party moved on to the city hall, where the marines and howitzers were once again applied. Captain Bell offered the mayor the opportunity to lower the state flag, but he refused. Kautz went to the roof, accompanied by a boatswain's mate, and cut down the Louisiana flag, which they were instructed to take to Farragut on the *Hartford*. Once again they were followed by an angry mob.

The papers wailed with indignation. The *Picayune* reported the incident in particularly solemn tones: "Yesterday the flag of Louisiana disappeared from the staff on the Municipal Hall and the enemy flag flowed from the Mint and the Custom House." This was followed by a boastful, flowery, over-inflated eulogy that flatly stated: "The state flag was struck by no son of Louisiana or citizen of New Orleans. It was taken away as a trophy of an enemy, and the bare pole stands to remind us that, with the consent of our adversaries, we no longer have the State of Louisiana."[19]

The paper had earlier blasted Farragut for threatening to bombard the city after a 48-hour time period during which women and children could be evacuated. The editorial almost labeled Farragut as a monster, saying:

> There are seventy or eighty thousand non-combatants in this city and forty thousand women and children. It is impossible for Commodore Farragut, whose nativity is in some part of this region which he threatens to blast . . . not to know that it is an utter impossibility to remove one-half of the women and children in five times the space he offers . . . the other branch of his threat implied, with horrible significance, that his guns be so aimed as to break the levees, includes the menace that he will pour in the floods of the Mississippi, to drown those who may have taken to the woods and the swamp.[20]

Yet Farragut had written to the mayor and council that he had no intention of bombarding innocent women and children. The very insinuation, he said, would cut off any further communication with him.

This unfortunate misunderstanding over a threatened bombardment, as history shows, did not diminish Farragut's standing as a great commander and national hero in the North. But the citizens of New Orleans had other opinions. Julia LeGrand, who resided in the city, maintained that after Kautz cut down the flag, he should have been shot (although with all the Union firepower around the site, it is difficult to imagine anyone trying that). In an acidic comment she maintained that the Union had unwittingly complimented New Orleans: "To quell a small rebellion, they have made preparations enough to conquer the world."[21] With opinions such as these, it is no wonder that the citizens of New Orleans put up such resistance.

DOWNRIVER, events were moving swiftly. The two forts had not surrendered, the *Louisiana* and the *McRae* were still moored above Fort

St. Philip, and General Butler's troops were blocking any attempted land moves to reinforce the forts. The mortar schooners lay quiet as the crews rested, awaiting any further moves from the flag.

In Fort St. Philip, General Duncan met with his fellow Confederate officer Commander Mitchell and prevailed upon him to move the *Louisiana* downstream to a point between the forts. There she could enfilade any enemy ships coming upriver, thus adding to the guns in the forts. But the ponderous ironclad could not be moved, because of a lack of tugs. The forts themselves were in shambles but still operational, even though 7,500 mortar shells had been fired at them.

It was unclear, however, that the forts could take any more punishment. Porter must have sensed their weakness, because on the twenty-seventh he sent the *Owasco* under a flag of truce to Fort Jackson with a demand for surrender. The answer was returned by two gun salvos—and that was *that*. Then General Butler boarded the *Miami* with the intention of leading a landing party to a point behind Fort St. Philip and investing the works. This move proved unnecessary, however, when Confederate Colonel Higgins sent a boat to apologize for firing on the *Owasco*. Still, Higgins refused to surrender, and Porter flew into a rage and ordered a resumption of the mortar bombardments. Once again the skies over the lower Mississippi were ripped apart by the heavy barrage from the 13-inch mortars, and once again the ground of the forts shook as if from earthquakes caused by the heavy thudding of projectiles.[22]

By now it was clear to those in the forts that theirs was a hopeless cause. Cut off from New Orleans, with enemy ships above and below them, and hearing persistent rumors that Farragut's ships lay anchored off the city, they could obviously not hold off any longer. In an attempt to ease his men, General Duncan gave them a pep talk, praising them for their patriotism and courage under fire. He told them to "stand by their guns and that all would be well."[23]

But the soldiers knew it was over. On April 27, the tired and demoralized troops at Fort Jackson mutinied; they spiked the guns, while many slipped away into the swamps.

In Fort St. Philip, Duncan was in a bind: His men were immobilized, most of his boats were gone with the deserters, and he did not know the situation at Fort Jackson. He decided the situation was hopeless and sent a boat with a flag of truce downriver to Porter. Eager to seize upon any opportunity for glory, the commodore rushed up aboard his flagship *Harriet Lane*, accompanied by gunboats *Kennebec*, *Westfield*, and *Winona*, to accept the surrender.

As the participants sat down in the austere cabin of the *Harriet Lane* to sign the surrender papers, an officer rushed in to report that the flaming hulk of the *Louisiana* was floating down toward them, with smoke pouring out of her gunports and her guns discharging. The ill-fated ironclad finally blew up near the *Harriet Lane*, and the concussion almost set the flagship on her beam ends. Iron plating was thrown into the air in all directions, some landing in Fort St. Philip, killing an officer and wounding another. Strangely, none of Porter's vessels were damaged by the explosion. The Confederates had decided to destroy the *Louisiana* to avoid having her fall into enemy hands.

The forts, however, proved to be in surprisingly good condition, in spite of the devastating bombardments. Of the two, Jackson was the more heavily hit and damaged. John Hart, of the Union occupying forces, described the damage: "There was water in the fort 2 feet deep and it smells so bad it almost made me sick. There are about 75 guns in the fort and the same in Fort St. Philip." Hart went on to relate: "There are only 6 guns dismounted in Jackson . . . there were 13 men killed and about 1,000 taken prisoner."[24]

FINALLY, the news arrived at the forts that New Orleans had surrendered to Farragut. "We everlastingly gave three times three cheers for such glorious news in the afternoon," said an entry in the *Portsmouth* journal, relating that the captain had called all hands to muster to congratulate them on their meritorious conduct "under such a galling fire from the enemy."[25] Similar observances doubtless went on on all the Union warships in the area and among the troops occupying the forts.

Then on May 1, General Butler came up to New Orleans, landed his troops on Canal Street, and began the occupation of the city. An unfortunate occupation it was; Butler ruled with an iron hand, and his controversial deeds, rather than his more constructive ones, are the ones recorded in history. He was labeled—unjustly—the "Beast of New Orleans" by the resentful citizens, and rumors abounded that along with his brother (who masqueraded as a colonel), he used his influence to grow rich by taking bribes, selling contraband to the Confederates, and monopolizing trade in liquor, medicines, and food. He even received the sobriquet "Spoons," because rumor had it that he stole silverware from homes where he was a guest. In all fairness to Butler, this charge, widely circulated in the years following the war, was never substantiated.

One of the general's first acts was to track down William Mumford, the man who had torn down the U.S. flag from atop the mint. Butler ordered him hung outside the same building, in full view of everyone. But perhaps his most controversial edict involved some New Orleans ladies who had publicly made fun of Union officers and spat at them. One lady had even dumped a chamber pot on the head of Flag Officer Farragut. Thoroughly disgusted, Butler issued General Order No. 28, in which he ordered that thenceforth any female "indulging in such behavior be treated as a woman of the town plying her trade."[26]

The furor over Butler's order was heard all the way to England, where Lord Palmerston remarked vehemently that "no example can be found in the history of civilization til the publication of this order of a general guilty in cold blood of so infamous an act as to deliberately hand over the female habitants of a conquered city to the unbridled license of unrestrained soldiery." Palmerston particularly referred to an incident in which Butler sent to jail on Ship Island a "delicate lady of the highest refinement, the mother of nine children," because she was heard laughing as a Union officer's funeral cortege passed her house. She was imprisoned for two months, until outrage across the nation and in Europe induced the occupiers to release her. Local contempt for Butler remained long after his recall on December 16, culminating in putting his picture in the bottom of chamber pots.

The residual effects of Butler's rule were evident in a letter written by Emma Walton Glenny to her father, commander of the Washington Artillery. Despite General Order No. 28, she wrote, the Federals were not as strict with females, especially nurses, as was publicized. But for those who went along with Butler's rule, she had only contempt: "Many of our citizens will compromise their honor and dignity by swearing allegiance to a power they hate. . . . I must confess some of them have acted with great pusillanimity."[27]

In Richmond, Jefferson Davis was appalled at Butler's regime. He called it the "reign of terror, pillage and train of infamies too disgraceful to be remembered without a sense of shame by anyone who is proud of the name American."[28] He accused Butler of arresting civilians who were selling medicines to sick Confederate soldiers, and of putting citizens in balls and chains (a charge that was not substantiated). Davis issued an order that if Butler were ever captured, he was to be hung as a common outlaw and enemy of mankind.

Unfortunately Butler's nefarious deeds overshadowed his good ones. In an effort to control yellow fever, he managed to clean up the streets and canals of New Orleans, and he also initiated programs to feed the poor. But since his odious deeds outweighed his humanitarian actions, Lincoln removed him and sent him back to lead troops—a task for which he was equally unqualified. His replacement as military governor of New Orleans was Major General Nathaniel P. Banks.

THE rest of the country, North and South, did not immediately hear the truth about the surrender of Forts Jackson and St. Philip. The forts had surrendered to Porter while Farragut was in New Orleans, and the news that flew around was that they had surrendered solely to Porter's mortar fleet. Butler tried to grab credit, claiming he was the senior officer present when the forts surrendered. Indeed, as Butler and Porter obtained all the credit and adulation, Farragut's role in the victory was lost. It was weeks before the truth about the flag officer's startling accomplishments came out in Washington. He was then hailed as a national hero.

The news of the fall of New Orleans had a great impact both in Washington and in Richmond. "The fall of New Orleans was a great disaster, over which there was general lamentation, mingled with no little indignation," lamented President Davis.[29] President Lincoln and his cabinet finally came to the realization that their "near-sighted Flag Officer was a great fighting admiral, an authentic naval hero."[30]

The event had many ramifications. To the Confederates, the closing of the port of New Orleans naturally deprived them of their major trading port in the Gulf. Militarily, it exposed Natchez and Vicksburg to assault from below, and it choked off the flow of agricultural products from Texas and Louisiana to feed the armies of the Confederacy in the east. It also deprived them of a rich source of manpower for those armies, as well as those left in Trans-Mississippi.

From a diplomatic standpoint, the fall was important because it stopped the plans of Napoleon III in France to break the blockade and recognize the independence of the Confederacy, in exchange for its acceptance of his claim in Mexico.

Commenting on the military aspects of the fall of New Orleans, historian John Fiske maintains that the opening of the lower Mississippi would have been an even greater event if the army had cooperated with skill and promptness comparable to that of the navy. The capture of New Orleans, he observes, taken in conjunction with the capture of Corinth, "ought to have entailed the immediate fall of Vicksburg and the complete conquest of the Mississippi River."[31] But General Banks had only 25,000 troops on hand in New Orleans, and taking the Confederate bastions upriver—including Baton Rouge, Port Hudson, and Vicksburg—would require a great many of these troops. While Grant had a sizable army north of Vicksburg, a large contingent of troops would be required to ascend the river and join forces with him in what was shaping up to be a major military action in capturing Vicksburg and the strong fort at Port Hudson just below.

The 200-mile stretch of river from Vicksburg to New Orleans was the main axis through which flowed the rich resources of Arkansas, Texas, and Louisiana, resources that the hard-pressed Confederate armies sorely needed.

The Union had to conquer this section of the Mississippi and cut it off from the Confederacy. Its plan was to attack from two directions—from upriver and from downriver—using all available land and naval forces.

After the fall of New Orleans, Farragut took his deep-water ships upriver in June, past Baton Rouge, Natchez, and Port Hudson to the bluffs of Vicksburg. There he used his big guns to pound the city's defenses into submission, just as he had done with Forts Jackson and St. Philip. But his bombardment failed to dislodge the firmly entrenched Confederates, and he returned to New Orleans empty-handed but wiser concerning the strength of Vicksburg. He asked for more troops from General Henry Halleck, but the general fussed and dawdled, allowing the Confederates precious time to build their defenses along the Mississippi.

But all of this came later and is another story. For the present, events were occurring in the Gulf that would affect the course of the war there.

CHAPTER ELEVEN

PREBLE'S INJUSTICE— THE *FLORIDA* AFFAIR

After the fall of New Orleans, the Gulf fell silent for a time. With Farragut's fleet up the river, helping Grant in his investment and siege of Vicksburg, the Union could spare only a few ships for blockading duty off the ports of Mobile and Galveston. The captains of these vessels had their hands full, as Confederate blockade-runners and commerce cruisers brazenly defied the Union navy and continued to run the blockade, using all manner of ingenious methods. These vessels roamed the oceans and pillaged and burned every Federal ship they found that was carrying commerce into Union ports. Their sole mission was to demolish American ocean commerce and hopefully to force wealthy shipowners to press Washington for an end to the conflict.[1]

But after the crews and valuable cargo were removed and the ships were fired, Confederate captains and crews secretly disliked the job of destroying ships. In fact, some raider crews looked on in sadness as beautiful ships were set adrift, burned to the waterline, and left eventually to sink. James Dunwody Bulloch, who was in charge of the Confederate shipbuilding program in England, said, "There could be no doubt that the destruction of unarmed and peaceful merchant ships, while pursuing their voyages on the high seas, is a practice not defensible upon the principles of moral law; and it does not in these modern times harmonize with the general sentiments of commercial nations."[2]

Rebel commerce raiding did become a real thorn in the side of the Union. For example, the *Robert E. Lee*, a converted Irish ferryboat, ran the Union blockade 22 times in just one year before she was captured and converted into a gunboat. As late as 1865, $65 million worth of cotton came out of the port of Wilmington, Delaware, money that was used to keep Confederate armies in the field and to feed the populace. The profitability of blockade-running can be seen in just one example— salt could be bought in Nassau for $6.50 per barrel and sold to the Confederacy for $1,700.[3]

It is easy, then, to understand why the government in Washington called for an end to this brazen blockade-running and raiding: it threatened the very existence of Union commerce.

The burden fell on the shoulders of the U.S. Navy, which was hard-pressed to assign ships to hunt down and destroy commerce raiders, since such missions would pull much-needed ships from blockading duty.

Mobile Bay was a hot spot for blockade-running vessels and for commerce raiders as well. With only a handful of ships available to patrol the channel of Mobile Bay, the West Gulf Blockading Squadron was hard-pressed to control illicit traffic there. Many audacious blockade-runners would slip out of the bay at night, using shoal waters in which heavy warships could not navigate. They would burn anthracite coal to reduce their smoke, and their low silhouettes and dull gray-painted hulls would help get them past the blockading ships. Raiders, by contrast, were usually deep-draft vessels and had to navigate in deeper-channel waters; they depended upon stealth and speed to get by the Union flotillas. Escaping raiders used the cover of darkness and inclement weather to slip by the blockading ships.

For the U.S. Navy, blockade duty was no picnic. Lieutenant Horatio L. Wait, serving aboard a blockading vessel outside Mobile Bay, wrote that the "blockading service of the Port of Mobile was difficult, because there were so many entrances to the harbor that could be used by the light-draft blockade-runners, while the blockaders were obliged to lie at a distance from land."

Wait also revealed that "in spite of violent gales which were prevalent in the Gulf, the fleet was maintained without interruption of a single hour for three years." He gave a stark description of the rigors of blockade duty:

> The horizon was unremittingly scanned by watchful eyes on board the blockaders, day in and day out, for indications of the suggestive black smoke. It happened several times that our ship saw steamers attempting to run past us. . . . This was always at night, and usually when the weather was thick, we would pursue for hours, usually seeing enough smoke to be sure of the position of the vessel. The smoke would gradually increase in volume as if the pursued steamer was forcing her fire to the utmost; then we would do all we could to lift the speed of our ship. Suddenly, no more smoke and no vessel could be seen.[4]

In this subterfuge, a pursued blockade-runner would pour on smoke until it became quite dense. When she was a considerable distance from her pursuer, so that her hull and spars were invisible in the darkness, the crew would close her dampers to shut off the smoke entirely. Then they would change their course by a right angle.

This ruse was but one problem that Farragut's ships faced on blockade duty. The Confederates used every trick in the book to escape being detected and pursued by the blockading ships. Keeping up with these subterfuges constantly taxed the ingenuity of Union ship captains.

Even Flag Officer Farragut wrote about the frustrations of blockade duty, especially during the furious, unpredictable Gulf storms: "There are times that try the commander of a squadron. I could not sleep last night, thinking about the blockaders. It is rough work, lying off a port month in and month out. . . . I have 6 vessels off Mobile, so that one can always come in for coal. They are all the time breaking down and coming in for repairs."[5]

Occasionally an encounter with a blockade-runner would break the monotony of blockade duty. For example, in December 1861 two Union vessels—the 1,000-ton *Potomac* and the 840-ton *Huntsville*—while on blockade duty off Mobile Bay, spotted the Confederate gunboat

Florida (not the cruiser of later fame) lurking off Pelican Island, to the south of Dauphin Island. A running fight ensued, and gunfire was exchanged. The *Florida* returned fire from both Union ships, and it was decided that "three of her pills" had hit the *Huntsville*, while she herself sustained no damage. According to the *Richmond Dispatch*, the engagement "was lengthy and many shots were fired on both sides, and ended by the [*Huntsville*] backing out as usual."6 This was a case of Confederate press acrimony and falsification. An official report from Captain L. M. Powell of the *Potomac* stated that none of the enemy's shots had hit either of the two Union ships, whereas the *Florida* had been hit and "retreated to the protection of Fort Morgan."7

Blockading duty in the Gulf was not always boring, then, because many such skirmishes occurred between Confederate and Union vessels.

PERHAPS the most famous encounter with a Confederate cruiser took place off Mobile Bay on September 4, 1862: the successful run of the C.S.S. *Florida*, under the command of John Newland Maffitt, past a blockade squadron. This event had far-reaching repercussions in the U.S. Navy and almost ruined an officer's naval career.

When we last saw the *Florida*, she had arrived at Cárdenas, Cuba, after being fitted out at Nassau following her launching, commissioning, and arrival from England in March 1862. She was a magnificent British-built screw sloop of 700 tons, with an iron hull, two funnels, and a proposed armament of six 6-inch rifles, two 7-inch rifles, and one 12-pounder howitzer.

Her skipper, John Maffitt, had literally been born at sea to his Irish-born mother. In 1832, he entered the U.S. Navy as a midshipman and became a career navy man, rapidly rising to lieutenant. When war broke out, he resigned his commission and joined the Confederate navy.8 As we saw earlier, he had taken a load of cotton to England, and while there he was given command of the *Oreto*, which he later commissioned as the *Florida*.

Maffitt took his ship into Cárdenas and anchored her there, after receiving permission from the governor. Then tragedy struck. A malady had felled many of his crew since departing Nassau; at first he thought it was the result of hard work in the hot, tropical sun. Later, however, it was diagnosed undeniably as the dreaded yellow fever. Maffitt himself was on the brink of death, barely staying alive for days, but he rallied long enough to proclaim that he was "not ready to die."[9] Sadly, he lost his beloved stepson Laurens, who was stationed on the ship with him.

When he was able to be up and around, Maffitt acted as a nurse and did all he could to tender assistance to the sick, in spite of his own suffering from the effects of the fever.

Then on August 30 the governor of Cárdenas informed Maffitt that it was too dangerous for the *Florida* to stay in his harbor, as there were no forts to protect him from the Union ships waiting outside the port. Ignoring his own illness, Maffitt decided to have it out with the enemy ships offshore. He had the anchor hoisted up and broke out the British flag and ensign. But the enemy ships had run off in pursuit of a Spanish vessel that they mistakenly thought was the *Florida*. Taking advantage of this fantastic stroke of luck, Maffitt steered his ship close to the shoreline, to avoid detection. He entered Havana harbor on September 1, where he anticipated completing his ship's armament and obtaining a fresh crew.

But Maffitt soon discovered that his ship and crew were unwelcome in Havana harbor because of the fever. Moreover all the available officers and men whom Maffitt might have recruited had fled the city in fear of a plague. Only one course remained open to Maffitt: He had to find a Confederate port that he could enter, where he could take care of the problems of his ill-fated ship. But he was still plagued with illness. A Captain Smith, who was present in Havana, offered to act as pilot and take the *Florida* to Mobile—where, he said, there were only two Union ships off the bay. Maffitt agreed, and the voyage was chartered. By hugging the shoreline once again, the *Florida* steamed out of Havana harbor practically under the noses of Union warships on station. They set a course for Mobile, and hopes were high that Captain Smith was right that only two Federal ships lay off Mobile Bay.

Smith was wrong. Three Union warships were on blockade duty: the screw sloop *Oneida*, with 10 guns, commanded by Maffitt's old friend Commander George Henry Preble; the screw gunboat *Winona*, with 12 guns, commanded by Commander James S. Thornton; and the armed schooner *Rachel Seaman*, with two guns. Four other warships had been present but had been sent to Pensacola for repairs. It was a formidable squadron. Maffitt, upon being apprised of the situation, decided to do what had always worked for him—bluff it out—even though he was still suffering from the fever and had to be carried up on deck to con the ship. So began a drama that has entered into the annals of naval history.

Onboard the *Oneida*, Captain Preble was wrestling with a serious problem: a leaky boiler. His chief engineer had reported that a donkey engine had to be used constantly to keep up with the leakage. Preble gave the engineer permission to pull the fire from under the boiler long enough to fix it, while keeping another going with a full head of steam—with the proviso that he have the first boiler repaired by night-fall.[10] Meanwhile, in the rest of the squadron, the *Winona* was patrolling the northwestern segment of the bar, watching for shallow-draft vessels; and while the *Oneida* was guarding the main channel, the *Cayuga* was watching the western channel.

At 5:00 P.M. on September 4, the cry "Sail ho!" came from *Oneida*'s mainmast lookout. A square-rigged sailing vessel had been spotted hull-down on the horizon. Preble and his crews relaxed, thinking it was the Union side-wheel frigate *Susquehanna* returning from Pensacola to take her station with the flotilla. But when the vessel began to pour out volumes of black smoke and to increase speed, Preble became suspicious. As the ship drew near, it was identified as a bark-rigged sloop-of-war. Suddenly the familiar red British ensign and pennant flew up her halyards. Preble decided it was a British man-of-war coming over to observe the block-ade procedures, a practice that was not unusual. But her course, set directly for the *Oneida*, unnerved him a bit. As she drew near, Preble hailed her for identification, but no answer came. He and his officers thought it strange that only one man was visible on the deck of the sloop; their suspicions grew stronger.

Preble decided to challenge the vessel and swung his ship around until she was abreast the British vessel's port beam. Then his worst suspicions were confirmed; it was the Confederate raider *Florida*, which was known to have been built in British shipyards along the lines of a British sloop-of-war. Receiving no answer to his second call for identification, Preble ordered a shot over her bow from his forward 11-inch pivot rifle, followed by another and a third, all of which landed near her forefoot, or bow waterline.

Then Preble ordered a full starboard broadside poured into the *Florida*. One shot tore through her hammock nettings and standing rigging; another smashed into a port coal bunker, striking a boiler, killing one man and wounding nine others. (During the court of inquiry held after the incident, Maffitt maintained that if that shot had exploded, he would have lost every man on the vessel, because he had ordered all crewmen below.) Maffitt's armament was not complete, and he lacked firing equipment for his guns, such as rammers, sponges, quoins, and elevating screws.[11] The *Oneida's* aft pivot gun passed high over the rail between the fore- and mainmasts. Some of the shots contained shrapnel.

Maffitt ordered the ensign and pennant hauled down and the Confederate flag raised in their place, but a signalman had lost a forefinger from shrapnel and the flag was never raised. Meanwhile shrapnel was raining down on the *Florida's* deck, loudly whapping into sails and spars.

Maffitt was frustrated because he could not return fire. However, his superior speed held and distance was rapidly put between him and *Oneida*.

Meanwhile the *Winona*, firing her guns, came up on the *Florida's* port, crossed her wake, and headed for a position along her starboard quarter. She never made it because the *Florida* was too swift; the *Winona* dropped behind. The *Rachel Seaman* managed to fire her guns but to little or no effect; she too watched helplessly as the *Florida's* stern moved up under the protection of Fort Morgan's guns. There Maffitt would lick his wounds and search for a crew.

Preble fired off a message to Farragut, explaining his position in the skirmish, and repercussions came swiftly. Farragut reported to Welles that Preble had apparently demonstrated neglect (he erroneously reported the *Florida* as being the British ship *Captain Bulloch*), and in a later despatch he recommended that Preble be dismissed from service.

The press insisted on Preble's dismissal, and Welles became the butt of invective. He wrote in his diary that "there must be a stop put to the timid, hesitating and I fear, sometimes traitorous course of some of our officers."[12] Smarting at the criticism, he decided to honor Farragut's recommendation. He sent a letter to Preble coldly informing him that he would "from this date [September 20, 1862] cease to be regarded as an officer of the navy of the United States."[13]

Preble fired back, claiming that he had been informed of his dismissal through the newspapers before Welles told him. The accusation of negligence was unjust, he said, since the truth of the matter was that he had fired at the *Florida* (which was strangely referred to as *Oreto*, its old name, in all correspondence from Washington) and heavily damaged her. He had not reacted until *Florida* came within 600 yards of his ship because he had been convinced the vessel was British, and he had hesitated to take action against a foreign flag.

Preble energetically responded to the accusations from Farragut and Welles and even wrote to President Lincoln about the injustice. He asked some of his officers and petty officers to write letters of defense as well. Farragut became impressed enough to write Welles that the secretary should soften his censure of Preble. President Lincoln, deeply moved, sent a letter to Congress, nominating Preble to be restored to the rank of commander.[14] Happily, the court agreed and restored Preble's commission.

On April 20, 1872, a naval court of inquiry was convened to hear the case, and all participants, including Maffitt, were called to testify. During testimony the true story about the incident came out, all of it favorable to Preble.

As for Maffitt and the *Florida*, a period of healing and repairing began within the protection of Mobile Bay, far beyond the reach of Union guns.

There was much to heal. The *Florida* had been hit in more than a thousand places, and the fever was still prevalent among the remaining crew members, including Maffitt. Admiral Buchanan sent down a hospital ship to aid the sick, and the assistant surgeon of the Confederate navy, Dr. F. Garretson, came aboard to attend to the patients.

As months went by, repairs were made and the sick were healed or replaced by fresh officers and crewmen. Maffitt himself recovered and soon became restless, eager to get back to sea. He made a trip to Fort

Morgan, on Mobile Point, where he peered over the parapets to note the number and positions of the blockading Union ships. By now they had been augmented by 10 new vessels. But more delays, caused by training new crewmen and by a couple of groundings, postponed his departure.

On January 15, during a violent storm, the *Florida* got under way and headed out of the bay—directly into the teeth of the blockade. Because of a fortuitous combination of bad weather, a low silhouette, and a dull gray paint job on the hull, Maffitt managed to slip by the first line of ships. But he was spotted when one of his funnels shot out sparks; the chase was on. There was no contest; the *Florida's* speed made the difference, and even the one Union warship present, the *Cuyler*, whose speed might have matched hers, was unable to catch her. At the first sighting of the Confederate vessel, the *Cuyler's* captain had hesitated to go after her, causing a delay. Try as he might, the skipper could not catch up with the fleeing *Florida*.

After a close call with another Union vessel, the *Mississippi*, whose captain thought *Florida* to be friendly, Maffitt continued on unhindered to the open ocean. There, in the months that followed, he chalked up an impressive 58 Union ships captured as prizes.

Another furor erupted in Washington, putting Secretary Welles once again in the hot seat. He was mercilessly castigated both in the press and in Congress; his department was described as a "nest of red tape and old-fogyism."[15] Welles fussed and fumed, threatening to demote a host of officers, including the flag officer of the flotilla off Mobile Bay at the time of the *Florida's* escape, but he never did.

Maffitt's depredations upon Northern shipping went unchecked until October 7, 1864, at which time the Union navy captured his ship and towed it to a Union port at Newport News, Virginia. On November 28, the *Florida* was sunk in a collision with a transport—an event that came under suspicion for many years afterward. Some claimed it was an act of sabotage by someone on the transport; however, nothing substantial ever came to light regarding the incident.

Thus ended a longtime scourge of the Union navy.

Meanwhile, on the far western end of the Gulf, events demanded the full attention of both Farragut and the leaders in Washington.

CHAPTER TWELVE

THE HAPPENINGS AT GALVESTON

The blockade in the Gulf of Mexico was, for a considerable time, centered on the central and eastern segment of the Gulf rim—New Orleans, Mobile, and Pensacola. The large fleet action in April 1862 resulted in the capture of New Orleans, while the blockading fleet of Mobile was strengthened. Before and during Farragut's spectacular passage past Forts St. Philip and Jackson and his subsequent occupation of New Orleans, Galveston, the one Texas port off which lay a sizable flotilla, seemed to be relatively forgotten.

For all practical purposes, Galveston *was* forgotten, until Farragut decided something had to be done about the Texas sieve through which there was a heavy leakage of small-craft blockade-runners that ran with impunity along the rugged 700-mile coast of Texas.

The passages they used extended from the Sabine Pass to the mouth of the Rio Grande. Farragut's desire was to seal off this sieve and extend the blockade to the west. The area around Brazos Santiago, at the mouth of the Rio Grande River, was too remote as a base for his flotillas, because they would be out of range of home base at Pensacola. Therefore Farragut turned his attention to the port of Galveston.

The island of Galveston, located about 50 miles southeast of Houston, extends for 32 miles northeast and southwest of the Texas coast. The largest city in Texas and a major seaport in 1862, it was connected to the mainland by a railroad. Its capture would be a major blow to the Confederacy, choking off a sizable conduit through which Texas—and hence Confederate civilians and armies eastward—received its foreign commerce.

Galveston was founded in 1785 by José de Evia, who was surveying the Gulf Coast for Galvez, the Spanish governor of Louisiana. Evia named the tiny colony "Galveztown." The city of Galveston was established in 1836 by Michel Branamour Menard, who was granted the land by the new Republic of Texas. He platted the original town site, and the city was incorporated in 1839. Up to the Civil War, Galveston grew and prospered, because of its vast bay and five-mile-wide entrance.

After the Civil War broke out, Texas seceded from the Union, even though strong Union sentiments were prevalent throughout. Those strong Union sentiments were shared by Governor Sam Houston, and as a result, he was removed from office. The state later supplied more than 50,000 volunteers for the Confederate army.

Union interest in Texas went beyond Galveston as a supply depot for Confederate causes and as a haven for blockade-runners. Napoleon III had designs on Mexico as a possible French colony, and in 1862, after convincing England and Spain that a joint Mexican venture would be in their best interests, he led a landing of the combined land forces at Vera Cruz. Napoleon III wanted to march on Mexico City and take possession of the capital city, but England and Spain demurred, deciding it was not after all to their advantage; they withdrew their troops, giving the French forces full rein. The United States saw this incursion as a violation of the Monroe Doctrine, and it was of deep concern to the Lincoln administration.[1]

But wring their hands as they might, Union commanders could not do much without sufficient land forces, so naval activities had to suffice. As a first move, Galveston, the major port of the state, had to be seized and occupied. While it was true that a smattering of warships were on duty off the Texas coast, a much larger force would be needed. Farragut therefore turned to Commodore William B. Renshaw on the gunboat *Westfield* to lead a squadron of warships into Galveston Bay and capture the port.[2]

It was a wise choice. Renshaw had been with Farragut's fleet since July 1862, when the Confederate gunboat *Arkansas* had bluffed its way past the Union fleet on the Mississippi. A career navy man who rose rapidly from midshipman to commodore, he served for a time in the Navy Ordnance Bureau until he was given command of the *Westfield*, in time for the Mississippi River campaign. In addition to his own command, Renshaw was put in command of four powerful gunboats: the 892-ton, side-wheel former ferry *Clifton*, with eight guns; the 750-ton side-wheeler *Harriet Lane*, with five guns; and the 1,370-ton screw gunboat *Owasco*, with 10 guns. Renshaw's own command, *Westfield*, was an 831-ton, side-wheel ex-ferryboat with six guns.[3] Serving with him would be such able commanders as Commander Richard Wainwright on the *Harriet Lane* and Lieutenant Commander Richard Law on the *Clifton*. These men had enjoyed distinguished naval careers and would feature prominently in the actions to come.

On November 4, 1862, Renshaw led his powerful squadron, plus a supply train, to Galveston and took station off the mouth of Galveston Channel. He wished to study the situation before entering the bay channel, because it was well defended by enemy batteries at three critical spots. Point Bolivar covered the entrance of the channel from the north; the north end of Galveston Island contained a battery that covered the channel from the south; and on the north end of Pelican Island stood another battery, plus a smaller one on the tip of Pelican Island spit, guarding Galveston Channel. The latter two emplacements would cover the entrance to the mile-wide channel, which runs between Pelican Island and Galveston itself.[4]

On October 5, Renshaw tried to run the mortar schooner *Henry James* over the bar, which could be traversed only at high tide. It was met with gunfire from the Point Bolivar battery. Renshaw replied with broadsides from his 29 heavy guns, sending the Confederates fleeing. He then led his flotilla over the bar, past the weak batteries on Pelican Island, and down the Galveston Channel to anchor off the town. To guard against enemy vessels approaching from the east, he positioned the *Harriet Lane* on the east (south to mapmakers) end of the channel.

While his ships sawed at their anchors in the channel, Renshaw received a group of Confederate army officers to discuss surrender plans. But instead of surrender, they arranged a truce to allow the Confederates to evacuate all noncombatants, women, children, and foreigners. At Eagle Grove, at the southern end of the two-mile railroad bridge leading from Galveston to Virginia Point, an artillery battery was established. Meanwhile, Renshaw sent a contingent of marines ashore to raise and lower a U.S. flag over the customs house, as a symbolic gesture of military occupation.[5]

The town had been captured, but troops were sorely needed to occupy it, especially with the enemy nearby. Renshaw sent out an urgent request to General Banks at New Orleans, to furnish troops for occupation duty.

The general, pleading a paucity of men, could spare only Companies G, D, and I—260 men from the 42nd Massachusetts Infantry Regiment. It was not what Renshaw and Farragut had desired, but it was enough to partially occupy Galveston.

From November to December naval reinforcements trickled in to Renshaw: the 197-ton *Sachem*, with five guns, arrived, and so did the small armed schooner *Corypheus*, with two guns. The latter, ironically, was a former Confederate blockade-runner, captured in 1862. Other vessels arriving were the steamer *Mary Boardman*, the 87-ton schooner *Velocity*, a supply ship, and six coal schooners.

In late December, the transport *Saxon* arrived with 240 of the men from the 42nd Massachusetts Infantry Regiment, under the command of Colonel Isaac S. Burrell. These troops were quickly landed on the largest of the waterfront wharves, called Kuhn's Wharf, where they quartered under the protection of the fleet's guns until the remainder of the regiment would arrive. As added protection from land assaults, the troops tore up the front planking at the foot of the wharf and built a barricade, leaving a wide gap from the shore over which attackers would be hard-pressed to traverse. These defenses were necessary because Confederate troops and artillery personnel at both ends of the railroad bridge had renewed their activity, causing concern for both Renshaw and Burrell. Renshaw stationed four of his gunboats in front of the town, in the following order from west to east: the *Harriet Lane*, followed inline by the *Sachem*, the *Owasco*, and the *Corypheus*.

Because of her deep draft, Renshaw decided to anchor his flagship, the *Westfield*, off the tip of Pelican Island, along with the *Clifton*, *Mary Boardman*, *Saxon*, and the coal schooners. This would offer protection from the east end of the channel. Such was the situation as January 1863 dawned—and as Confederate Major General John Bankhead Magruder was about to launch his meticulous attack plan.

Magruder, called "Prince John" because of his courtly manner and flamboyant style, had been hand-picked by President Davis to take charge of all Confederate forces in Texas. A veteran of the Seminole and Mexican campaigns, Magruder had joined the Confederacy in May 1861 and thereafter won plaudits as a colonel leading Confederate troops at Yorktown in October 1861 and at the battles of Mechanicsville and Gaines' Mill. Because of his propensity for drink, he committed serious blunders, causing him to be reassigned to command the District of Texas.[6]

One of Prince John's first acts was to create a navy with which to challenge the Federals at Galveston. But Texas had no viable gunboats and could offer him only river craft, including steamers and packet boats. Of these, Magruder picked two: the side-wheel river steamer *Bayou City* and the side-wheel mail packet *Neptune*. In addition to this "main body" of a flotilla, he picked the stern-wheel riverboat *Lucy Gwinn* and the river steamer *John F. Carr* to act as tenders. This mini-navy was placed under the command of Confederate Major Leon Smith, a former merchant marine sailor and steamboat captain.

The bulwarks of the two leading vessels were strengthened by cotton bales, which not only protected the vital parts but provided concealment for Texas cavalry sharpshooters. A 32-pound rifled gun was placed on the bows, as was an iron prow for ramming. After completion the fleet retired to Halfmoon Shoals, some 15 miles from Galveston, to await an opportunity for attack.

On land Magruder strengthened the artillery positions at Virginia Point and at Eagle Grove on the island. The resourceful Confederate general also pioneered the first rail-propelled artillery—an eight-inch columbiad mounted on a railroad flatcar, strengthened with bulwarks of rail iron. With these forces, Magruder planned to attack the Union troops at Galveston and the warships in the channel. Unable to match the Federals in firepower, he would depend on stealth and surprise maneuvers. Union land forces would be hit head-on with troops and artillery, and their warships would be rammed and boarded.

For the assault, New Year's morning of 1863 was picked. At 3:00 A.M., the small Confederate flotilla got under way while Magruder's troops opened an attack on the Federals, forcing them to retreat to Kuhn's Wharf. Confederate artillery roared at them, tearing at the timber bulwarks and sending lethal splinters flying everywhere. In the channel the Union fleet was alerted, and *Harriet Lane* opened with a firestorm of grapeshot at the advancing enemy troops and their artillery. Then the *Corypheus* and the *Sachem* joined in the ship-to-shore barrage, laying down a withering fire.

It became a pitched battle, and the resulting devastation was heavy, with the city rent by shot and shell. A Galveston doctor was killed when a piece of grapeshot passed through his head while he was attending to a patient. Many Confederate soldiers dropped as grape and shrapnel tore the air asunder. The Confederate attack slowed to a halt, and the attackers, unable to cope with the withering fire from the fleet's guns, began to fall back. Artillery was deserted where it stood, as was the rail-borne columbiad. An enemy attempt to board the wharf was thwarted when their ladders proved to be too short to reach from the water to the level of the wharf.

Meanwhile in the channel the Union ships moved in closer, in order to cover the troops on the wharf and enfilade the retreating Confederate forces. The area became a firestorm of blazing guns. One Confederate military man, in a remarkable understatement, wrote: "The enemy's fire was deadly."[7]

To the west of Pelican Island, the "Magruder navy" swung around and entered the channel, led by Major Smith, who ordered his boiler crews to pour rosin into the boilers and get "all the steam you can crack on. We must get there as quickly as we can and attack them."[8] His course was set directly for the Union ships, while those vessels were engrossed in pouring heavy fire on the Confederates in the town; they therefore failed to see the encroaching naval force. Finally lookouts on the *Westfield* and the *Harriet Lane* simultaneously spotted the oncoming enemy flotilla and quickly spread the alarm.

The Magruder floating juggernaut came on with a vengeance, exchanging shots with the *Harriet Lane* while some of her guns were still firing at the town. One shot struck her, knocking a hole in her "big enough for a man to crawl through." The gun captain on the *Bayou City* told his gunners to fire again, saying, "Here goes your New Year's present!" As he pulled the lanyard, the gun exploded, killing him and wounding three others.[9] The vessel's Captain Henry Lubbock had received instructions to strike the *Harriet Lane* forward of the port wheelhouse, as she was slipping her chains.

Lieutenant Commander Henry Wilson, captain of the *Owasco*, received a message that Confederate forces were attacking Kuhn's Wharf, then weighed anchor from his berth off Pelican Island. He headed into the channel directly for the oncoming Confederates, firing the ship's bow gun.[10]

At the *Westfield* anchorage, Commander Renshaw, alerted to the opening of hostilities in Galveston, ordered his vessel under way; unfortunately, the ship went hard aground in shoal waters and for all intents and purposes was out of the action. When attempts to free her failed, Renshaw was forced to watch from afar.

Back in the arena, the action was getting hotter minute by minute as the Confederates closed the Union vessels. The advancing *Harriet Lane* lunged at the *Bayou City*, tearing off the port planking of the wheelhouse and side. Both vessels sheared away from each other at the impact. Then, with her side-wheels slapping water vigorously, the *Bayou City* lunged in turn at her opponent.

Meanwhile, the *Neptune* came up and struck the *Harriet Lane* on her starboard side. The blow, however, so damaged the Confederate mail packet that she was forced to back into the mud flats, receiving heavy fire as she passed astern of the *Harriet Lane*; she sank in eight feet of water. The *Owasco*, which by now had steamed up, also started to blast away at the *Neptune*.[11]

By this time the channel between Galveston and Pelican Island was a mad, swirling tangle of ships, as thunderous reports from guns filled the air with smoke. In the narrow, shallow channel normally used peacefully for ocean-bearing commerce, it was an insane ballet of death.

The *Neptune*, while receiving heavy hits from the *Harriet Lane*, swung around and rammed the Union ship with such force that her prow was driven deep, hopelessly locking the vessels together. This was the moment the troops on board the cottonclad were waiting for. With ear-piercing yells, they swarmed over the bulwarks, their cutlasses swinging and pistols firing. Furious hand-to-hand fighting followed, until the overwhelmed Federals were driven belowdecks.

During the fight on deck, Commander Wainwright defended himself with two pistols until he was mortally wounded, as was his executive officer, Lieutenant Commander Edward Lea.[12] The *Harriet Lane* was now taken, and a white flag quickly went up. In a final sad note, Lieutenant Commander Lea was discovered dying by his father, Confederate Major Lea, who boarded after the ship surrendered. Major Lea took his son into his arms, and after a few words of greeting, the young Union naval officer expired.

After the *Harriet Lane* surrendered, Captain Wilson of the *Owasco*, not wanting to be outdone, swung his ship by the captured vessel and poured a few shots into her. In reply, another flag of truce went up the *Harriet Lane*'s halyards.

In the channel the Union ships ceased firing and raised white flags of truce. The capture of the *Harriet Lane* had shocked the rest of the fleet into a sort of immobility. Under a flag of truce, General Magruder sent a messenger, with a demand for surrender, to the *Clifton*'s Captain Law. The latter replied that he had no authority to surrender while the fleet's commander was up in the grounded flagship. But he told Magruder that three hours would be needed to place his personnel on a ship, to evacuate the harbor, leaving behind the rest of the flotilla as spoils to the Confederates.[13] Commander Law then went by boat to the *Westfield* to deliver the terms of surrender to Commodore Renshaw.

Renshaw was furious; he instructed Law to return to his ship and lead the flotilla out of the bay and into the Gulf. Law did what he was told and left with his ships, past the fire of the Point Bolivar batteries, past the bar, and into the Gulf. He was pursued by angered Confederates on the *John F. Carr,* but being too slow to catch the retreating Union flotilla, they returned to Galveston to deal with Renshaw and the hapless *Westfield.*

Determined that his ship would not fall into enemy hands, Renshaw decided to destroy her. He had sent the majority of his crew to the other vessels that were leaving the bay, but he kept a small boat crew onboard.

Renshaw had barrels of turpentine placed in the magazine, and a fuselike stream of turpentine laid on deck. Then, with a boat and crew standing by, he touched a slow match to the stream; it flashed too rapidly, and before he could leave the deck, the *Harriet Lane* exploded with a thunderous roar, killing Renshaw and his crew. Debris was sent spiraling into the air for hundreds of feet; a revolver even landed on the tip of Galveston Island.

The battle for Galveston was over, and it handed a humiliating defeat to the Union navy and a much-needed victory to the Confederates. The spoils of victory included, besides the *Harriet Lane,* two coal vessels, the auxiliary ship *Cavello,* and the supply vessel *Elias Pike.* The three Massachusetts infantry companies were left behind to be taken prisoner, along with their commander. One can only imagine their chagrin as they watched their protectors, the Union flotilla, retreating toward the mouth of the bay.

THE victory was quickly and loudly lauded by the Confederate press. The *Houston Telegraph* painted a glorious but exaggerated detailed account of the battle, loudly cheering on the Confederates. Jefferson Davis fired off a letter of commendation to Magruder, praising him for his "brilliant exploit in the capture of Galveston and the vessels in the harbor." Then on a note of optimism, he wrote, "I trust your achievement is but the precursor of a series of successes which may redound to the glory and honor of yourself and our country."[14]

Major General John Bankhead Magruder, of the Confederate army, congratulated the soldiers and crews of the two tinclads that had routed the Union navy, calling it "an enterprise so extraordinary and apparently desperate in its character and the bold and dashing manner in which the plan was executed, [are] certainly deserving of the highest praise."[15]

In Washington, Secretary Welles deplored the Union defeat and admitted that the navy was justifiably subjected to scathing criticism, not so much for the loss of Galveston as for the fact that five powerful vessels mounting 25 guns had been defeated by two riverboats mounting three light guns.[16] It was a red-faced Navy Department that had to face the president about the affair. All in Washington were agreed that it was fortunate the second contingent of the Massachusetts Regiment, on their way to Galveston during the battle, had been warned away in time and thereby escaped the fate of their captured comrades.

In New Orleans, Farragut was infuriated by the defeat and considered charging Captain Law for his "pusillanimous conduct" in leaving the Galveston area without being relieved. (At the time he was unaware that Law was acting under orders from Commodore Renshaw.) Later he recanted and even recommended Law for promotion. He vowed to send a powerful fleet to Galveston, take back the town, and destroy every Confederate vessel around. Captain Bell talked him out of it, suggesting instead that he would personally take an expeditionary force to rebuild the broken blockade.[17]

Farragut reluctantly agreed, because of his high regard for the acumen and abilities of his chief of staff.[18] Bell promptly took the *Brooklyn* and five gunboats, proceeded to the Texas coast, and took station off Galveston in January. He was careful to stand away from the heavy artillery that Magruder had brought up and placed along the coast side of the town, but he was ready to deal with any sorties by Magruder's cottonclad fleet.[19] All he could do himself was shell the city occasionally, to keep Confederate heads down, but he could not send in an expeditionary force. He could not spare them; big doings were afoot up at Vicksburg, and every available foot soldier was needed. Therefore Bell and his flotilla settled down for what they considered to be a typical, boring blockade routine.

But he had not foreseen the arrival of Raphael Semmes in the Gulf.

WHEN last we saw Commander Semmes, he had just embarrassed the blockading squadron off New Orleans with his daring escape on the cruiser *Sumter*. Later, after abandoning her, he went to England and took command of a new bark-rigged, screw sloop-of-war, Hull 290, which he named the *Alabama*. A Laird-built ship, she displaced 1,050 tons, was 220 feet long, and had a 32-foot beam. She was powered, in addition to sail, by two engines and a screw propeller. Her normal complement, which varied during cruises, was 280 men.[20] For six months Semmes cruised the Atlantic, taking 69 Union ships as prizes while evading the searching Union navy vessels that considered the *Alabama* a priority.

During December 1862 Semmes took the *Alabama* to Arcas Island, near Jamaica, for repairs and for refueling from the coal ship *Agrippina*. While the ship was undergoing repairs, the crew was allowed recreational time on the island. During this hiatus, Semmes received word that Union General Banks was preparing a large land and naval force to retake Galveston. He decided to intervene by sailing to the Galveston area and trying to intercept Banks's seaborne expedition, thereby serving his country and in the process obtaining a rich source of prizes.

Semmes weighed anchor on January 5, 1863, and set course for Galveston, arriving off the Texas coast 30 miles south of the town. Orders had been given to lookouts to keep a sharp eye for a large transport fleet of Union ships off the entrance to Galveston Bay. As the *Alabama* drew near, however, a lookout spotted, not the expected transport fleet, but five Union men-of-war. Semmes, fully expecting to intercept a force of troop-laden transports, was puzzled, but with Union warships around, this was a most difficult situation. Suddenly one of the warships opened fire and sent a shell exploding over Galveston. Semmes and his staff correctly inferred that the city was still in Confederate hands—since a Union ship commander would not be firing at his own people. The warships gave Semmes pause as he reasoned that he had not come into the Gulf to "do battle with five ships of war, the least of which was probably my equal."[21]

On January 11, while Semmes was pondering this turn of events, one of the Federal warships swung around and headed for him. It was the U.S.S. *Hatteras*, a 1,126-ton, iron-hulled, three-masted schooner with side-wheels and armed with four 24-pounders and one 20-pound rifle. When lookouts on Commodore Bell's flagship, the *Brooklyn*, spotted the "strange sail" on the horizon, Bell had dispatched the *Hatteras* to investigate. As the Union warship drew close, Semmes led her on a merry chase southward down the coast. According to Leander H. Partridge, acting master of the *Hatteras*, the strange ship had set a topgallant sail and swung around with a course southward. The chase was on.[22]

After 20 miles the *Alabama* hove-to, with steam up, waiting for the Federal ship to catch up. The skipper of the *Hatteras*, Lieutenant Commander Homer C. Blake, had his crews beat to quarters as he approached to within 200 yards of the *Alabama*. Through a speaking trumpet, he shouted, "Ahoy! What ship is that?" After a short but tense time, the answer came back from Lieutenant J. M. Kell, "Her Britannic Majesty's steamer *Petrel*." Blake replied, "If you please, I will send a boat on board of you." Kell answered that he would be happy to receive the boat.[23] Whereupon Blake ordered a boat lowered with Acting Master Partridge and five crew members aboard.

When the boat approached within 100 yards of the *Alabama*, Kell shouted out over the trumpet, "This is the Confederate steamer *Alabama*!"

The voice hail was followed by a roaring broadside from three of the *Alabama*'s starboard battery. But the *Hatteras* gunners were not caught off guard; they replied with their port broadside. As the exchange continued, the ships maneuvered into positions parallel with each other: The *Alabama* was still firing her starboard battery, while the *Hatteras* replied with her port battery.

One can only speculate what it must have been like for Partridge and the crew aboard the boat caught in the middle when the *Alabama* fired her broadside. Their ears must have been deafened by the report, and they must have been whipped by the concussion. Left in the lurch, the hapless crew managed to escape from the battle area by rowing up to the fleet anchorage. Partridge lived to make a full report on the incident.

The battle raged for about 20 minutes, in which the *Hatteras* received severe punishment. Shells smashed into her engine room, cutting off all power; great sheets of iron were peeled off her sides, admitting water to the extent that she developed a list and was in a sinking condition. Blake ordered the magazine flooded and a shot fired from the stern, indicating capitulation.

Semmes's boats picked up the *Hatteras* crew, just before she sank in 10 fathoms of water. When the *Brooklyn* arrived on the scene, they discovered masts above the water with the pennant still flying from the main trunk. Her hurricane deck was afloat, and some survivors were clinging to her masts.[24]

Bell informed Farragut that a "dangerous enemy" was in the Gulf and that "he had probably destroyed numerous vessels in the track between Key West and New Orleans and doubtless intends to sweep away the blockading vessels of inferior force along the whole extent of the Gulf Coast, trusting to his celerity of movement."[25]

By this time Semmes had sailed away and was headed back to Jamaica. There he dropped off his prisoners and commenced repairs and refueling, later to sail off into the Atlantic to pillage and plunder more Union ships. The *Alabama* was finally cornered and sunk off Cherbourg, France, in June 1864, by the U.S.S. *Kearsarge*.

THINGS were not going very well for the Federals along the Texas coast. The Confederates still held Galveston and had managed to build a small but powerful fort at Sabine Pass, near the mouth of the Red River, which became a haven for blockade-runners. The Union commanders could only "hold" their blockade, now and then lobbing a shell at Galveston and keeping a wary eye on the *Harriet Lane*, now anchored in Galveston Bay. Then on September 8, 1863, another disaster struck the Federals.

For some time General Henry Halleck, in Washington, had been proposing an amphibious assault on Sabine Pass. Besides the blockade-runner situation, Halleck believed that if Texas were to be invaded, Sabine Pass was the most logical place to launch the attack.

If the Union could take the fort there, it would give them a base for operations within Texas. The state might eventually be won over, but more compellingly, a Texas under the protection of Union troops would discourage any possible French invasion from Mexico. On a more cynical note, President Davis wrote that a Union invasion of Texas "would relieve them [Union] from the discomfiture of their expulsion from Galveston Harbor."[26]

The assault would not be an easy one, because the Confederate stronghold near Sabine City, called Fort Griffin, was armed with 42 men and six big guns. In addition, the enemy was rumored to have some cottonclads and even a ram in the vicinity.

Major General Banks gathered 4,000 troops from his 19th Corps, as well as troop transports and a naval escort of four gunboats: *Clifton*, *Sachem*, *Arizona*, and *Granite City*, under command of Lieutenant Frederick Crocker. This formidable force was to launch an attack on the Confederate-held pass, destroy any naval resistance, and occupy the region.[27] The gunboats were picked because their light drafts would allow them to successfully cross the shallow six-foot bar off the mouth of the pass.

Under the command of General William Franklin, the expeditionary force arrived off Sabine Pass on September 6, 1863, and anchored, while reconnaissance measures were taken to assess the strength not only of Fort Griffin but of a battery at the mouth of the pass (which proved not a hindrance).[28]

The gunboats went over the bar first, followed by the seven transports. As they neared Fort Griffin, the Confederates opened fire with their six guns, plus those from a cottonclad steamer off the fort. The *Sachem* was hit in a boiler and went aground, as did the *Clifton*. The *Arizona*, receiving hard hits from the fort, backed downstream and out of range. Unable to free the vessels and after a fruitless attempt to repair them, the commanders of the two gunboats struck their colors.[29]

By this time, General Franklin realized the hopelessness of the situation and ordered the transports back into the Gulf, jettisoning supplies, horses, and mules in order to lighten the drafts for the shallow bar. The shattered expeditionary force skulked back to New Orleans, leaving behind two gunboats plus 315 prisoners of war, which came from the small contingent of troops that had landed before the naval defeat. Union casualties amounted to 70 men killed, wounded, or missing.

General Magruder hailed the Confederate victory as "another glorious victory won by Texans." Seventeen years later, in September 1880, the *Houston Daily Post* published the names and ranks of the troops at

Fort Griffin—still lauding the victory after all those years.[30] The Confederate casualty count was described as "strictly and positively, nobody hurt."[31]

For the Union, the defeat at Sabine Pass would have been an ignominious way to close out the year, but it was offset the next year, in August 1864, by a brilliant victory achieved by Admiral Farragut at Mobile Bay.

CHAPTER THIRTEEN

MOBILE—PHASE ONE: THE ENIGMA OF MOBILE AND BUCHANAN

After a long and bitter siege, the Confederate stronghold of Vicksburg capitulated to General Grant on July 4, 1863, and the last Confederate bastion on the Mississippi, Port Hudson, surrendered on July 9. With these victories completed, Grant cast covetous eyes on Mobile, Alabama.[1] He was convinced that his huge victorious army, with only the help of the navy, could overwhelm the Confederate garrison there, thereby relieving the pressure on Union armies fighting to the east.[2]

President Lincoln wrote to Grant that his proposal for an expedition against Mobile would have "proved tempting to me, were it not that in view of recent events in Mexico, I am greatly impressed with the importance of reestablishing the authority in Western Texas as soon as possible."[3]

Grant, of course, was aware of his government's concern that because of French sympathy for the Confederacy, Napoleon III's designs on Mexico could present a threat to Texas. Therefore, he divided up his army and sent some contingents to other war areas.[4] It would be two more years before any move was made against Mobile.

Like Grant, Admiral Farragut, fresh from the New Orleans and

Vicksburg campaigns, also had his eye on the Mobile area. But his concern was with Mobile Bay, through which an alarming number of blockade-runners were slipping in and out, despite his blockading ships. Back on December 4, 1862, he had written that he "had all the coast except Mobile Bay, and I am ready to take that the moment I get troops."[5]

The effort to capture Mobile was intensified in December 1863, when Commodore Bell reported to Secretary Welles that Confederate strength in Mobile Bay was growing ever more formidable. "Six vessels," he said, "[were] either built or building." Admiral Franklin Buchanan's flagship, according to Bell, was "strong and fast."[6] Three large rams were being built on the Mobile and Tombigbee Rivers, to be launched in the winter. (But once again, as always when it came to Confederate ship-building, lack of machinery and skilled mechanics made all but one of these vessels into "phantoms," frequently included in estimates of enemy strength.[7] In the case of the *Tennessee*, rumors far outran actuality.) All this speculation kept nervous eyes on the Mobile area for many months to come, Farragut's not least among them.

MEANWHILE the old sea dog was exhausted and needed rest. After all, he and his command had battled Forts Jackson and St. Philip, plus the powerful citadels of Vicksburg and Port Hudson. The *Hartford* badly needed repairs and overhauling, and the crew needed a much-deserved leave of absence. In fact, during her 18-month service in the Gulf, the *Hartford* had been hit over 240 times. Her sisters, the *Brooklyn* and the *Richmond*, were also damaged, mostly below the waterline, and needed drydock attention. Farragut made his wish known to Welles, who promptly granted it.

Long before he made his request for a leave of absence of duty from river waters, he returned from his leave, wishing to go back to Gulf blockade duty, with which he was more comfortable.

On July 15, 1863, he wrote to Commodore Porter:

> I feel the time has now arrived, contemplated by the Honorable
> Secretary of the Navy, when I should turn over the Mississippi to

you down at New Orleans, and then turn my attention to the blockade of the Gulf.

Farragut then mentioned his granted leave of absence from Welles and went on to say:

Prior to the work he [Welles] expects of me in the fall, I suppose some work to be done by the vessels yet to be sent to me, Galveston and Mobile, perhaps, and that will finish my job.[8]

Farragut had hoped to take more of his ships back to New York with him, but they were needed for operations planned for the Red River. When he departed the Gulf on August 1, 1863, he took only the *Hartford*, the *Brooklyn*, and the *Richmond*. The gunboats *Winona*, *Kineo*, and *Itaska* were reluctantly ordered to follow the flagship to New York, then be dispatched to shipyards at Baltimore and Philadelphia for repairs and overhauling.

On August 12 the flotilla arrived at the Brooklyn Navy Yard and docked for their scheduled repairs. Farragut went on to New York City to a joyous, welcoming citizenry and a happy reunion with his wife Virginia and his son Loyall. Secretary Welles sent a message of welcome to Farragut, saying, "I congratulate you on your safe return from labors, duties and responsibilities unsurpassed and unequaled in magnitude, importance and value to the country by those of any naval officer."[9]

THE secretary invited Farragut to visit Washington if he were so inclined. But the admiral was kept busy, being wined and dined in a dizzying array of dinners and banquets.

Still, there was no evidence that Farragut was enjoying himself through all of it. Every now and then he would slip away to the shipyard to check on the progress of his beloved ships. If all seemed to be going to his satisfaction, he would return to the city—and face a citizenry puzzled as to his whereabouts.

A group of 81 citizens signed a letter that was presented to Farragut at one of the functions he attended. It said:

The whole country, but especially this commercial metropolis, owes you a debt of gratitude for the skill and dauntless bravery with which, during a long life of public duty, you have illustrated and maintained the maritime rights of the nation, and also for the signal ability, judgment and courtesy with which, in concert with other branches of the loyal national forces, you have sustained the authority of the government, and recovered and defended national territory.[10]

Farragut's string of victories, overshadowing the less spectacular successes of land armies of late, cast him as the national hero for which the public had been waiting.

While he was resting with his family and friends, he met Captain Percival Drayton, who was on shore duty in New York. The two officers became friends; Farragut offered him the post of fleet captain, with command of the *Hartford*. A grateful Drayton accepted the offer, and a solid and workable partnership was born.

It was not long before the sailor in Farragut once again took over, and he was itching to get back to sea. Although two of the sloops-of-war at Brooklyn were not yet ready for sailing, he was anxious to return to the Gulf after receiving intelligence from Commodore Bell that there were not enough ships available to serve off the coast of Texas and at the same time maintain the blockade. Farragut then sent a message to Commodore Porter asking for more ironclads for duty off Mobile Bay. He also expressed to Welles a desire that he be allowed to leave on the *Brooklyn*, which had been repaired, while *Hartford* was still undergoing refurbishing. Welles refused, maintaining that Farragut's name was inextricably linked with the *Hartford* and that the two should always be together. Obediently, Farragut agreed to wait until his flagship was ready for him.

When the *Hartford* was ready, Farragut and Drayton boarded her, cast off, and headed out to sea, amid rumors that Admiral Buchanan was ready to challenge the Union blockading fleet with the reported "most powerful ironclad in the world," the *Tennessee*, a ram "more powerful than the *Merrimack*."[11] Farragut set course for the Gulf and arrived at New Orleans on January 17, 1864, where he officially resumed command of the West Gulf Blockading Squadron on January 20. Once the command transfer was accomplished, he and his staff turned their full attention to Mobile Bay and the recently strengthened Union flotilla there.

MOBILE, as we have seen, was one of the most important deep-sea ports in the Confederacy, second only to New Orleans, because its commerce with the West Indies and Europe was kept up in spite of the blockade. Mobile had a most fascinating history, having existed under different flags—it was known as the City of Six Flags, because it had been under French, British, Spanish rule, and had flown the flags of Alabama, the Confederate States, and the United States since its founding in 1702 as Fort de la Mobile. It had served as the capital of Louisiana Territory until 1722, when the capital was moved to New Orleans. In 1813 the city came into the possession of the United States, and it entered its greatest period of prosperity because it had a conduit through which vast agricultural resources were shipped to the world. That conduit was Mobile Bay.

Mobile Bay, resembling a partially collapsed bladder, is 31 miles long and from eight miles at its narrowest to 30 miles at its broadest point above the channel. Its average depth is from 13 to 24 feet, up to the nine-foot-deep pile of sand known as Dog River Bar, five miles south of the city. Deep-water ships, unable to cross the shallow bar, were forced to anchor and unload onto shallow-draft lighters, which would carry their cargo to and from the docks.[12]

Dog River Bar, an unwelcome natural obstruction, played an important part in the coming struggle for control of Mobile Bay.

Mobile Bay's channel was protected on both sides: by Fort Morgan on Mobile Point to the east, and by Fort Gaines on Dauphin Island to the west. Both forts were of the classic brick style, with two or three tiers of gun emplacements, plus water batteries.

The task of defending this vital portion of Confederate real estate with naval power fell to Admiral Franklin Buchanan. Known as "Old

Buck" by his Annapolis colleagues, Buchanan was born in Maryland in 1800 and entered naval service in 1815 as a midshipman. He saw service in the Mediterranean and in the Mexican War and later became a cofounder and first superintendent of the Annapolis Naval Academy. Thereafter he was appointed commander of the Washington Navy Yard. At secession, he resigned his commission as a captain, thinking that Maryland would also secede. When this failed to happen, he tried to cancel his resignation, but was refused and promptly dismissed from Union service. Buchanan then offered his services to the Confederate navy, which heartily accepted him and placed him in charge of the Bureau of Orders and Details, with the rank of captain.

Like many landlocked naval officers, he became desirous of a ship command and was given command of the new ironclad C.S.S. *Virginia*, which was the rebuilt Union sloop-of-war *Merrimack*. On March 8–9, 1862, he led this vessel into Hampton Roads to do battle with the Union squadron on station there, in the first important naval action in the Civil War.

During that historic event, the *Virginia* rammed the U.S.S. *Cumberland* and severely damaged the U.S.S. *Congress*. Buchanan was wounded in the thigh and had to relinquish command of the *Virginia*, thereby missing the epic battle with U.S.S. *Monitor* the next day. He was appointed admiral on August 21, 1862, and took command of the naval defenses of Mobile. His flagship was the fabled and much-speculated-over ironclad, the C.S.S. *Tennessee*, as well as a flotilla of four wooden gunboats.[13]

The indefatigable Buchanan utilized to the fullest the time given him by Union procrastination over Mobile. He initiated construction of the ironclads *Huntsville*, *Nashville*, *Tuscaloosa*, and *Baltic* and, of course, the *Tennessee*. Of these vessels, only the *Tennessee* was available for action at Mobile Bay against the Union fleet when the time came. She was built at a crude shipyard at Selma, Alabama, 150 miles north of Mobile, along with the hulls of three proposed ironclads. The ironclads were never finished because of the now-traditional shortage of men and materiel. In fact, Secretary Mallory informed President Davis on July 1, 1864, that due to a shortage of mechanics, the ordnance works at Selma could make no more than one gun a week; with the proper number of mechanics, however, the facility could have manufactured guns with carriages at a rate of three a week and in a few months one every day. This handicap the South could never overcome.

As word of Farragut's preparations for an assault on Mobile Bay drifted in, work on the ironclad was feverishly accelerated; the huge vessel was ready for launching in February 1864. At launching the hull of *Tennessee* was towed downriver for outfitting, not to Selma, with its shortage of manpower and equipment, but to a shipyard in Mobile.

The *Tennessee* was the most formidable of Confederate ironclads, apart from the *Virginia*. She was 209 feet long, with a 48-foot beam, a displacement of 1,273 tons, and a draft of 14 feet. Her frame was composed of 13-inch, square, yellow pine timbers covered with five-inch pine planks and overlaid by 11-inch planks of oak. Her casemate, which extended below the waterline, consisted of six-inch sheet-iron plates, with four-inch plates at the bow, all fastened with 1½-inch bolts. Her weaknesses lay in her sluggish engines, which were taken from a river steamer, and could push her only at six knots per hour; her tiller chains, which were placed in exposed channels leading to the stern; and her gunports, which were opened and closed by pivots easily disarrayed by shot and shell.

Her armament was strong enough, with six Brooke rifles, one with a seven-inch bore, the others with a six-inch bore.[14] With this monster Buchanan hoped to somewhat negate the ship and firepower advantage of the Union.

But once the *Tennessee* was outfitted and ready for action, she faced another problem: getting past Dog River Bar. With a draft of 14 feet, her crossing loomed as an impossible task even at high tide, with a level of nine feet. But the resourceful Buchanan had the answer—a caisson.

A caisson is a temporary wooden structure built to hold back water during repairs or construction. Buchanan had caissons built around the base of the *Tennessee*, forming a temporary undercarriage. Then the water would be pumped out of the caissons—they would rise, taking the vessel up with them. After several failed attempts, the ponderous *Tennessee* was finally raised high enough to be towed over the bar. She was anchored a little below, while workmen removed the caissons and then supplied her with ammunition, fuel, and provisions. Then she was towed down to Fort Morgan, where she took station a few miles inside the bay, northeast of the fort, along with her consorts, the *Selma*, *Gaines*, and *Morgan*. This flotilla, despite its small size, was fairly powerful in its own right, and even more remarkable considering it was all that Buchanan could muster for the coming fight with Farragut's fleet. And all bets were on the *Tennessee* to make up the difference in size and the firepower advantage of the Federals.

As for the consorts, the *Selma* was a 320-ton, medium-sized side-wheel steamer, 169 feet long, with a 30-foot beam; she was armed with three 12-pound howitzers. The *Gaines*, an 863-ton side-wheel gunboat, was 202 feet long, with a 38-foot beam and a seven-foot draft; she was armed with one seven-inch rifle, one six-inch rifle, two 32-pounder rifles, and two 32-pounder smoothbores. The *Morgan* was a sister to the *Gaines* and shared the same dimensions and characteristics.[15] One wonders what went through Buchanan's mind when he considered his small fleet against the huge armada that Farragut was assembling. But he doubtless had confidence that he would prove once and for all the advantage of iron over wood.

During the long period of preparations for the attack, Farragut found time to write his son Loyall about the *Tennessee* and Buchanan. He described the Confederate ram as long but slow. Then he added:

> I am lying here, looking at Buchanan and awaiting his coming out. He has a force of four ironclads and three wooden vessels. I have eight or nine wooden vessels. We'll try to amuse him if he comes. . . . I have a fine set of vessels here just now, and am anxious for my friend Buchanan to come out.[16]

Of course, Farragut erred as to the number of ironclads in Buchanan's flotilla, but it was the best intelligence that could have been gathered, considering that any Union excursions into the bay would have been met by the fierce firepower of Fort Morgan. Farragut's error also hints as to why he and his staff were under the impression that Buchanan would come out of the bay to give battle. The truth was that the *Tennessee*, because of her sluggish speed, could never have coped with the waters of the Gulf, and her weight could have caused her to be swamped. Therefore Buchanan was content to wait inside the bay for Farragut's ships to enter; he would attack them as they passed Fort Morgan within range of his guns and ram, in a David-versus-Goliath situation.

The stark reality was that at this point Buchanan had only 14 heavy guns, as opposed to Farragut's 113.[17] The Union command appears to have accepted the inflated and reported potentials of the *Tennessee* at face value and greatly overestimated her fighting abilities. Farragut thought that Buchanan considered the ironclad to be superior to the *Merrimack* and that he would face Farragut as child's play. Farragut did proclaim to Welles, however, that if he had one ironclad, he could destroy the entire Confederate force in the bay.[18]

Buchanan took a cautious approach to the Union's misconceptions. "Everybody has taken into their heads," he wrote, "that one ship can whip a dozen, and if the trial is not made, we who are in her are damned for life, consequently the trial must be made. So goes the world."[19]

Farragut, knowing a real confrontation lay ahead, badgered the Navy Department for more ironclads and troops. He hoped the troops would be landed east of the fort to besiege it, while his fleet steamed by, hopefully pounding it into submission. Unfortunately, the department stonewalled him, kept him in suspense and wondering if he had enough power both to tackle the Confederate fleet and to hammer Forts Morgan and Gaines at the same time—the same tactic that he had used for his successful assault on Forts Jackson and St. Philip. In essence, the same ingredients were there: two forts and an enemy fleet. There was no reason to believe victory could not be achieved again with the same strategy.

Nevertheless, Farragut continually inspected his fleet and crews, and using a typical command tactic, he kept them busy to take their minds off the anticipated fight ahead. In actuality the crews were looking forward to battle with the hated Confederate fleet.

Farragut expressed his anticipations to Welles, writing on May 9:

I am in hourly expectation of being attacked by an almost equal number of vessels, ironclads against wooden vessels, and a most unequal contest it will be, as the *Tennessee* is represented as being impervious to all their experiments at Mobile so that our only hope is to run her down, which we will do all in our power to accomplish; but should we be unsuccessful, the panic in this part of the country will be beyond all control. They will imagine that New Orleans and Pensacola must fall.[20]

Meanwhile Farragut had to content himself with being on station off Mobile Bay and keeping a wary eye on Buchanan's fleet and on Forts Morgan and Gaines.

CHAPTER FOURTEEN

MOBILE — PHASE TWO: AGAIN WE FACE TWO FORTS!

Forts Morgan and Gaines loomed as powerful sentinels guarding spacious Mobile Bay, as Farragut and his commanders saw it. No one—from a ship captain to a powder monkey—doubted that passing these sentinels would be a difficult and bloody affair that many would not survive. The endless procrastinations by officials in Washington had given the Confederates ample time to strengthen their defenses at the two forts. Farragut and his commanders knew, as did General Grant, that had the Union moved on Mobile Bay after the fall of Vicksburg, those citadels would have fallen like ripe plums. In the two intervening years, however, Brigadier General Richard L. Page had used the time wisely to build his fortifications to their greatest strength. It was a case of 20/20 hindsight, and Farragut had to make the best of it.

On August 3, 1864, the *Mobile Advertiser and Register* revealed that "23 Federal ships of war lie off the Mobile harbor, including three ironclads which were in the main channel, two and one-half miles from the guns of Fort Morgan and, of course, within range of their shot. . . . The assemblage of this large fleet is not without meaning, and the fortifications defending the mouth of the bay become points of great interest."[1]

The same newspaper also reprinted a letter from an officer in the blockading squadron, as it had originally appeared in a northern paper. The letter revealed that a steamer had been spotted under the guns of Fort Morgan. The Union gunboat U.S.S. *Octorara* had shelled a Rebel craft, which promptly took off but was hit and stopped dead in the water. A lively exchange took place between the fort and the gunboat, with other Union ships joining in. In the melee, a man on the *Itaska* was drowned when he became snagged in his own lead line and was dragged through the water.

Later, under a flag of truce, the *Octorara* carried in an English officer who wished to communicate with the English consulate in Mobile; while the gunboat lay off Fort Morgan, its officers and crew observed the fort at first hand. They reported that it had been "greatly strengthened" and that "the walls are now concealed and protected by a heavy embankment of sand, against which shot and shell vainly pound."[2] Farragut realized he was up against a very powerful bastion and that he would need more ships and, hopefully, troops to invest the forts in a land and naval assault.

As early as 1819 President James Monroe had recognized the strategic importance of protecting Mobile Bay by strengthening the fort on Mobile Point and establishing a similar fort on Dauphin Island. A possible attack on New Orleans, he foresaw, "could only be made by a great power, or a combination of several powers with a strong naval and land force using shallow-draft transports." He recommended entrenching the two forts that guarded the mouth of the Mississippi River. He also recommended the same defense program for Dauphin Island and Mobile Point.[3]

Construction of Fort Morgan began in 1819; it was designed as a Third System Coastal Defense fort. This option had been created by the War Department as a result of the War of 1812, when it recognized that stronger fortifications were needed along the eastern and southern coastlines. The fort was named after General Daniel Morgan, an officer of the Revolutionary War who had successfully fought the British at Monmouth, New Jersey, in July 1778. Built of brick, the fort was designed in the traditional star-shaped or pentagonal manner. It directly faced the quarter-mile-wide and 30-foot-deep channel leading into Mobile Bay and constituted a real protectorate over the bay and the city to the north. Unfortunately the fort fell into disrepair in 1841, after which a caretaker contingent manned the facility. It was seized by Alabama militiamen on January 5, 1861.

In May 1864 the fort was placed under the command of General Richard L. Page, a former U.S. Navy man and cousin of General Robert E. Lee, who had been appointed brigadier general in March of that year. He greatly improved the defenses of Fort Morgan, so that by the time of the Union assault in August, it had an impressive strength of around 40 varied, heavy-caliber guns and 700 well-trained troops.[4] A water battery of 29 guns was placed at water's edge, including four 10-inch columbiads. Page also had sandbags placed along the western glacis, in order to absorb heavy shot. This level of armament meant that Farragut faced a heavier opposition here than he had with the forts on the Mississippi River.

Four miles to the west, across the mouth of Mobile Bay, stood Fort Gaines, a smaller fort than Fort Morgan though similar in its pentagonal design. This facility was named after General Edmund Pendleton Gaines, whose distinguished career had included the pursuit and capture of former Vice President Aaron Burr, who had been accused of conspiracy to commit treason. Gaines enjoyed an exemplary career: During the War of 1812, he had participated in the defense of Lake Erie.

Fort Gaines was situated on the eastern tip of picturesque Dauphin Island. The island had been colonized in 1699 by Pierre Le Moyne, Sieur d'Iberville, who discovered a large pile of human bones there and promptly named it Massacre Island. In 1707 French colonists renamed it Dauphin Island, in honor of the dauphin of France, the son of Louis XIV, who was heir to the throne. (The title is similar to Prince of Wales in England.)

The island was subsequently occupied by successive garrisons of English and Spanish troops until it came under the control of the United States in 1813. Construction of Fort Gaines began in 1821 and was completed in 1861, but it was not fully armed and garrisoned until the Confederates seized it in 1862 and occupied it with 600 troops under the command of Colonel Charles D. Anderson. Although he failed to graduate from West Point, this former artillery captain had been promoted to colonel. He later commanded the 21st Alabama and was transferred to Fort Morgan.

Fort Gaines was armed with 27 guns, including three 10-inch columbiads.[5] Unfortunately the guns' range did not extend across the four-mile-wide channel. They therefore took no part in the battle (except for dueling with Union monitors during the Union siege of the fort from August 6 to 8).[6]

A third fort was constructed by the Confederates on a spit of land called Tower Island between Dauphin Island and Cedar Point on the mainland to the north. Called Fort Powell, it had been established to cover the Mississippi Sound entrance to Mobile Bay and was placed under the command of Lieutenant Colonel James W. Williams. Fort Powell was armed with six guns, including a 10-inch and an eight-inch columbiad, plus two 32-pounders. At the time of Farragut's passage of Fort Morgan, it was still unfinished and not fully armed. Yet it was able to challenge any passage through the sound, and Union gunboats had to keep it neutralized until it was captured.

Dauphin Island was, and still is, an enchanting piece of real estate. In 1864 it was roughly 15 miles long and a quarter-mile at its widest point.[7] Its vegetation consists of tall, stately southern pines, hummingbird trumpets, fragrant mimosa and scrub grasses, and bushes along the beaches. The deep-blue skies are populated with an array of seabirds, including brown pelicans, herring gulls, laughing gulls, and terns. On land the melodious sounds of mockingbirds, mourning doves, and thrushes permeate the atmosphere. With all this Elysian beauty around them, the soldiers' garrison life must have been much tempered. In fact, after the fort surrendered in 1864, a Union soldier described the emeraldlike water around the island as "very calm and beautiful . . . it is very pleasant riding the ocean when it is so calm."[8] The diaries and letters of other troops stationed there also reflect on the beauty of their surroundings. The same natural conditions existed on Mobile Point, east of Fort Morgan, although more troopers commented on the beauty of Dauphin Island. It is sad indeed when such natural beauty has to be torn asunder by instruments of war.

.   .   .

INSIDE the forts life was both hard and soft. The duties of strengthening a fort for battle consisted of setting up guns, storing ammunition, undergoing endless drills and practices, sometimes eating less-than-palatable fare, practicing firing, battling sometimes insufferable heat, swatting ubiquitous mosquitoes, and standing long, uncomfortable guard watches. This discipline, however, whipped the men of the garrisons into viable fighting units. This efficiency prompted General Dabney H. Maury to describe his men as "the handsomest and best body of troops I have ever seen, either in the old service or in the Army of the Southern Confederacy."[9]

This arduous garrison life was mitigated a great deal by the surrounding natural facilities and beauty, including swimming in the warm waters of the Gulf and the bay, gathering oysters, fishing, and picking wild fruits and berries. Most of the time ample food was available for the troops. On April 14, 1864, a Confederate soldier stationed at Fort Morgan wrote his parents that rations had improved: "We draw ½ pound of pork per day (no beef). We get corn bread a plenty [sic] and also we get plenty of cow peas." He described his appetite as being greater than at home. He ate smoked meats brought from furlough, adding: "I have eat up [sic] one ham."[10]

But the rigors of garrison life caught up with at least one Confederate trooper, W. C. Walker. On June 26 he wrote his parents and brothers that passes for leaves of absence were no longer being issued and that life consisted of "mounting guns, dismounting guns, unloading boats of wood and lumber on the wharf, and carrying it in the fort on our shoulders." As a result his shoulders became unbearably sore, and he added plaintively, "I am sick and tired of garrison life and Fort Morgan."[11]

Any veteran who has served in a military installation will echo Walker's plight. In one of his letters, Walker theorized that General Page was "scared half to death for fear the Yankees will attack the place." He speculated that if the general were to get over his scare, he—Walker—would get his furlough. Of course, there is no evidence that General Page was frightened by Farragut's fleet; it sounds more like wishful thinking on Walker's part. But it is indicative of how the rigors of life in a fort color the thinking of many soldiers.

Some of the officers fared better than the enlisted men. The fort's surgeon, Dr. James T. Gee, wrote to his wife that the officers had hard feelings about being ordered to send their wives home. Earlier his own wife must have brought him a fig tree for planting, because he mentioned that it had "yielded a supply of the most delicious fruit you ever tasted, and I never gather and eat one without wishing for my darling."

During the battle, the good doctor worried about the fig tree, but he never mentioned whether it survived the Union assault on the fort, as he himself did. He also mentioned in one letter that he had a "strange visitor"—a cat that "came now regularly to be petted."[12] Thus for officers, garrison life had its lighter moments. One cannot resist wondering what happened to the cat during the fierce bombardment; unfortunately Dr. Gee did not tell us.

Other military personnel found life pleasant at Fort Morgan as well. When Lieutenant Robert Tarleton came to the fort in February 1864, he wrote his sweetheart, Sallie Lightfoot, that he had wondered if any "mortal man could ever be fond of such a place, and for the first ten weeks, my opinion was decidedly in the negative." But his opinion changed: "At the end of that time I was astonished to find myself in very healthy and cheerful frame of mind." He ended his letter with: "the grand conclusion of it all was that Fort Morgan was a very pleasant place, and I would like to remain here very happily, till the end of the war."[13]

The lieutenant was also blessed with a whimsical sense of humor. On May 8, 1864, he mentioned the arrival of the ironclad *Tennessee*, after her successful crossing of Dog River Bar. "The unsuspecting Yanks," he wrote, "are quietly at anchor outside dreaming of the entertainment waiting for them. And as the clown used to say, 'the first thing they know, they won't know nothing.' "[14] Lieutenant Tarleton was also a poet: "The moon was up," he wrote, "and a thousand stars sprinkling the waves with silver spangles and flooding the desert, sandy shore with a fairy light." He fancied the ripples of water as the "low prolonged, measured hush of a mother to a restless child."[15]

A strange place—embattled Fort Morgan—to find a sensitive poetic soul like Tarleton. (After the surrender he was captured and taken prisoner for a time, but he escaped and found his way home to Alabama, where he married his beloved Sallie and happily lived out the rest of his life.)

Incidents of human compassion were recorded at both forts. At Gaines, after the fort's surrender, a Union enlisted man was taken to the dispensary with a fatal illness in March 1865. One of the fort's officers, Lieutenant William J. McIntire, befriended the young trooper, Martin A. Smith, and cared for him during his illness. The Confederate officer spent his own money to buy "delicacies that the army ration did not afford." When the young Union soldier died, Lieutenant McIntire oversaw the burial and kept Smith's personal effects, which he sent to his parents. He also paid for the grave marker that would identify its position, in case the parents desired to bring the body home for burial.[16]

Another young trooper at Fort Gaines complained to his wife that his parents were sending him shirts with too-small wristbands, explaining that he had "growed some since leaving home." He also missed "goin' a-cooning" with his brother.[17]

IT is hoped that the preceding sketches will give the reader an idea of military life in a fort during the Civil War. Although they took place in two particular Confederate forts, they are nevertheless universal and indicative of life at all such installations, Confederate and Union. Human nature has not changed over the years, and military life at an installation today is not much different from what it was yesterday.

Life aboard a Civil War warship was similar in design if not in nature. Navy men were not fed as well as those at the forts, lacking access to fresh food and meat. The exception was men on the river gunboats, who had the distinct advantage of being able to tie up to shore and send out raiding parties to gather fresh vegetables and meat from farms nearby. Navy men, for the most part, had to be content with dried or preserved foods. One navy man described his meals, during blockading duty, as consisting of cornbread and a great deal of pork and beans—the pork being salt pork, by the way. Occasionally, when ovens were available onboard, a ship's cook would turn out baked goods for officers and crews.

For the most part, boredom was the enemy of ships' crews and had to be dealt with wisely by the commander.

Like men in forts, warship crews were kept busy with endless drills and maintenance—holystoning decks, shining brass fixtures, coiling lines, and doing rigging drills, endless gun drills, and repair work of all kinds, especially after an engagement. There was not much time for boredom, if a ship was run right. The antiboredom principle was the same during the Civil War as it is in today's armed forces.

Life went on in the two forts on both ends of the mouth of the bay known as Mobile Bay and on the warships of Farragut's fleet, gathering in the waters, preparing for action.

CHAPTER FIFTEEN

MOBILE–PHASE THREE: PREPARATIONS FOR AN ONSLAUGHT

On the hot, humid, cloudless late afternoon of May 24, 1864, the 974-ton Union gunboat *Metacomet* entered Sand Island Bank, a few miles north of Sand Island, at the entrance to Mobile Bay. On board was the ramrod-straight, clean-shaven Admiral Farragut, accompanied by his bearded fleet commander, Percival Drayton. The purpose of the trip was reconnaissance—the admiral was determined to see for himself the Confederates' laying of torpedoes and the current status of the forts. What interested Farragut more than anything else was the purported lines of torpedoes that the Confederates had placed in the channel between Fort Gaines and the main shipping channel.

As early as 1861, to offset their disadvantage in warship strength, the Confederates had been experimenting with torpedoes (mines, in modern parlance). Ever since July 5, 1861, when Matthew Fontain Maury had successfully exploded a prototype torpedo in the James River, off Richmond, before an amazed Stephen Mallory and a host of dignitaries, the Confederacy had stepped up its development and production of the underwater weapons for use in vital waterways.

Although Maury's torpedo was triggered by a lanyard mechanism, more sophisticated methods of detonating torpedoes would clearly be needed when they were placed in deeper waters, such as ship channels and bays. The Rains keg torpedo was simply a beer keg filled with powder and sealed at each end with a cone. Its detonation device was a plunger that would strike a percussion cap, which in turn would ignite the powder charge when the torpedo was struck by a boat or ship bottom. Another device was a simple demijohn filled with powder and similarly detonated by a plunger mechanism. Both these devices would be anchored by long lines to the bottom and then allowed to sway with the current just below the surface—hence the term "sway torpedo." Such a torpedo sank the Union gunboat *Cairo* in the Yazoo River of Mississippi in December 1862.[1] Another such device sealed the doom of the U.S.S. *Baron de Kalb* on the same river on July 13, 1863.

The most popular and most widely used Confederate torpedo was the Fretwell-Singer mine, a pear- or cone-shaped device filled with around 75 pounds of powder. It was triggered by a springlike plunger on the top that, when released, hit a percussion cap. This torpedo, like many other models, was anchored to the bottom by a heavy length of railroad iron.[2]

In Mobile Bay, the Confederates had placed torpedoes in two diagonal lines in the channel near Fort Morgan—and staggered them to make sure nothing could slip between them. They abutted a line of below-the-surface pilings that ran southeastward from a sand spit offshore of Fort Gaines across the nose of the channel, forming an obstruction. The two lines of 30 torpedoes each ended at the edge of the ship channel in front of Fort Morgan. Given the lines of pilings and torpedoes, all water traffic would be forced to navigate under the fort's guns. The edges of the torpedo lines were marked with red buoys, as warnings to friendly traffic.

Farragut made note of the buoys and their locations and later wrote to Admiral Gustavus Baily, who was at Key West, that Admiral Buchanan was directing the laying of mines. "I can see his boats very industriously laying down torpedoes," the admiral wrote. "So I judge he is quite as much afraid of our going in as we are of his coming out. But I have come to the conclusion to fight fire with fire and therefore shall attach a torpedo to the bow of each ship, and see how it will work on the rebels—if they can stand being blown up any better than we can."[3]

Farragut was obviously concerned about the use of torpedoes, knowing of the fate of the *Cairo* and the *Baron de Kalb*. If they could be used successfully in the Yazoo River, then they could also be utilized in a deep harbor and ship channel like Mobile Bay. (History does not record his use of spar torpedoes at Mobile Bay.)

His concern was evident in a report dated May 25, 1864, to Secretary Welles about the presence of Admiral Buchanan and the *Tennessee* in Mobile Bay:

> I ran in shore yesterday, and took a good look at the Iron Clad *Tennessee*. She flies the blue flag of Admiral Buchanan. She has four ports of a side, out of which she fights, I understand from the refugees, our 7in. Brooks Rifles and 2 11in. Columbiads. She has a torpedo fixture on the bow. Their Four Iron Clads and Three Wooden Gunboats make quite a formidable appearance. I see by the Rebel papers, Buchanan is advertised to raise the blockade so soon as he is ready.

Then in a reference to the torpedo threat, he added:

> Torpedoes are not so agreeable when used by both sides, therefore I have reluctantly brought myself to it. I have always deemed it unworthy of a chivalrous nation, but it does [not] do to give your enemy such a decided superiority over you.[4]

On February 16, Farragut had already sent a hard message of resolve to the Confederate high command, by calling up six mortar boats and four gunboats from New Orleans and bombarding Fort Powell. (Interestingly, the attack coincided with General Sherman's marches into Georgia with the object of capturing Atlanta.) The bombardment of Fort Powell, Farragut reasoned, would convince the enemy that an assault on Mobile was soon to come, and therefore they would siphon off troops from General Johnston's army to defend the city. The bombardment caused little damage to the fort, but it did prompt General Dabney

Maury and the Confederate high command to ask Richmond to send more troops. A few weeks later Farragut recalled the bombardment group, but in March he ordered them to return to station.[5]

Farragut continued to ply Washington with requests for ironclads to counter the presence of what he mistakenly thought were four Confederate ironclads. By this time Welles too was sufficiently alarmed and ordered the 1,000-ton monitor *Manhattan* to sail from the Brooklyn Navy Yard to the Gulf. Another order went out to Commander Tunis A. M. Craven, skipper of the 1,000-ton monitor *Tecumseh*, on station in the James River, to report to Farragut's command.[6] Admiral Porter, on the Mississippi, was put on notice to send some of his ironclads to join the Mobile fleet. All this action was the result of Farragut's firsthand, sometimes-not-so-accurate reconnaissance reports of the Confederate military situation. One cannot help but wonder how much "ram fever" had affected the mind-sets of officers in the U.S. Navy.

Meanwhile the 970-ton monitors *Winnebago* and *Chickasaw* from Admiral Porter's riverine fleet arrived. The arrival of *Tecumseh* was temporarily delayed when she stopped at Pensacola for provisioning, coaling, and slight repairs after her long trip down the Atlantic seaboard.

Farragut was keeping a wary eye on Buchanan's movements in the bay. In his report of May 25, he was unsure whether the *Tennessee* was about to attack him. In actuality, Buchanan had decided not to sortie out into the Gulf because of the sluggishness of his flagship and the vulnerability of his light, lesser-armed gunboats. The *Selma* sported four guns, and the *Gaines* and *Morgan* had six apiece. The entire ordnance of his squadron was 22 guns in all, as against the 174 guns of the Federal fleet. His hopes of receiving reinforcements from up north were dashed when the *Baltic* was pronounced unseaworthy. So Buchanan decided to wait under the lee of Fort Morgan and attack the wooden Yankee ships that managed to slip by the torpedo lines with the guns of Fort Morgan, and with his six rifles and powerful ram.

Lieutenant Tarleton, stationed in Fort Morgan, wrote his wife, on May 27, 1864, about Buchanan's reluctance to sortie out to do battle:

> The contrasts between the two fleets is almost ridiculous. Nevertheless, we landsmen prepared ourselves to see a grand fight, but

our fleet, on getting opposite the fort, came to an anchor in the most harmless and pacific way. It seems the admiral did not like the looks of the fleet outside. It is said that he sent a dispatch to Richmond stating the strength of the two squadrons and his willingness to make the attack and asking for orders. So there the affair rests and I don't expect a fight.[7]

Tarleton also intimated that many of Buchanan's younger officers did not "fancy the expedition very much." But it was clear to everyone that Buchanan, rather than go to the Yankees, was going to wait for them to come to him.

That was precisely what Farragut had planned to do. In July he had written to Welles about his plan for attack on Mobile Bay. He would take his "fourteen vessels, two and two, as at Port Hudson; low steam; flood tide in the morning with a light southwest wind: ironclads on the eastern side, to attack the *Tennessee*, and gunboats to attack the rebel gunboats, as soon as [they are] past the fort."[8]

On July 12 Farragut sat down in his cabin aboard the *Hartford* and penned the famous Order No. 10 to his fleet, outlining the procedures for the assault on Fort Morgan and the Confederate flotilla. It is typical of the admiral's carefully thought-out and detailed battle plans; no contingency for safety was overlooked.

Strip your vessels and prepare for the conflict. Send down all your superfluous spars and rigging. Trice up or remove the whiskers. Put up splinter nets on the starboard side, and barricade the wheel and steersman with sails and hammocks. Lay chains or sand bags on the deck over the machinery, to resist a plunging fire. Hang the sheet chains over the side, and make any other arrangement for security that your ingenuity may suggest. Land your starboard boats or lower and tow them on the port side, and lower the port boats to the water's edge. Place a leadsman and the pilot in the port quarter boat, or the one most convenient to the commander.

The vessels will run past the forts in couples, lashed side by side, as hereinafter designated. The flagship will lead and steer from Sand Island N. by E. by compass, until abreast of Fort Morgan;

then N.W. half N. until past the Middle Ground; then N. by W., and the others as designated in the drawing, will follow in due order until ordered to anchor.

Farragut then outlined the battle line that all the commanders must observe and the types of shells and fuses that the gunners must use, plus the types of weapons, such as howitzers, to place in the topgallants.

Then, in Order No. 11, he outlined the procedures to be observed if any of the vessels were disabled:

> Should any vessel be disabled to any degree that her consort is unable to keep her on station, she will drop out of line to the westward and not embarrass the vessels next astern by attempting to regain her station. Should she repair damages, so as to be able to reenter the line of battle, she will take her station in the rear as close to the last vessel as possible.[9]

As history has recorded, the intricate details of a military operation may not all be followed to the letter because of unexpected contingencies. This would be true in the coming run past the fort.

With all preparations for the assault made, the admiral was dismayed by the continued absence of the *Tecumseh*, which was still at Pensacola.

On August 3, Fleet Captain Drayton wrote to the commander of the Pensacola Navy Yard, Captain Thornton A. Jenkins, that the *Tecumseh* was needed for the coming action. If the monitor could not be released, Drayton explained, Farragut would have to go in without her. Farragut followed this communication with a letter of his own, stating that he could not lose any more days waiting for the monitor. He added, with a touch of philosophy: "I must go in after tomorrow morning at daylight or a little after. It is a bad time, but when you do not take fortune at her offer, you must take her as you find her."[10]

The letters had their effect; the *Tecumseh* arrived on station on August 4. On that same day Major General Gordon Granger led his Union troops to a landing on Dauphin Island and commenced a siege of Fort Gaines. Also on that same day Farragut called his commanders to the flagship for a conference and outlined the order of attack. His fleet now consisted of 18 ships. The four monitors—*Tecumseh, Manhattan, Winnebago,* and *Chickasaw,* on station inside Sand Island—would act as the van, heading past the fort. The main body would follow, Farragut explained, with ships in pairs, led by *Hartford* and *Metacomet.* His captains once again insisted that Farragut should not be placed in harm's way by leading the main body. The *Brooklyn,* they argued, would be a better choice because of her bow chasers and the antitorpedo device attached to her bowsprit. (This device was probably a descendant of the one invented by Colonel Charles Ellet in 1862 for use on inland rivers.)

Farragut acquiesced, and the order was changed as follows: *Brooklyn* and *Octorara*; *Hartford* and *Metacomet*; *Richmond* and *Port Royal*; *Lackawanna* and *Seminole*; *Monongahela* and *Kennebec*; *Ossipee* and *Itaska*; and *Oneida* and *Galena.*[11]

Offshore Mobile Point, to the east of Fort Morgan, four Union gunboats took station, in order to bombard the fort from the rear. These were *Sebago, Genessee, Pembina,* and *Bienville,* all light gunboats that packed a sizable punch. Five more Union gunboats took station off Fort Powell at Grant's Pass: *Stockdale, Estrella, Narcissus,* and *J. P. Jackson.* Their task was to keep the fort's gunners' heads down during General Granger's investment of Fort Gaines, and to challenge any strange ships that appeared near the fort.

As in a good chess game, all the pieces were in place.

Within the fort these Union ship movements had been duly noted, but the members of the Confederate garrison had a resolve of their own. As W. C. Walker observed on August 1: "There are twenty Yankee vessels lying off the fort. One monitor, 2 iron clad gunboats & 14 vessels of war. The monitor & ironclads are lying within range of our guns & no telling how soon they will commence the attack. If they do or when they do as it [is] now considered a certain fact, they will meet with a warm reception. There is no unnecessary excitement at all although the bombardment may commence at any moment. The men intend to emulate the example of their glorious friends & brothers in arms & stand to their posts of duty until the foe shall leave our land & we all die in the attempt."[12]

The *Mobile Advertiser and Register* editorialized that the battle was imminent: "We are glad to hear the garrison at the fort is in fine spirits and ready to do its whole duty. The men think if they can at target practice hit a barrel at every shot at a range of 1,000 yards, so big an object as a Yankee ship cannot pass their guns and 'nobody hurt [sic].' "[13]

Artillery Captain M. M. Whiting, of an Alabama artillery company, stated in a letter to the *Mobile Register*: "We knew the Federals were making preparations for an attack, and many shots were exchanged between the fort and vessels that came within range, or nearly so; and, for several nights, gun detachments remained at their posts on the ramparts, expecting the fleet to make a passage of the fort."[14]

The Fort Morgan personnel were tipped off as to a possible run past their installation when Fort Gaines was invested. Lieutenant Jere Austill noted that "all our conjectures as to what the enemy's intentions were, were settled by their landing a force of infantry several thousand strong on the spit of Dauphin Island, West of Fort Gaines; they were brought through the sound on transports."[15]

Judging from these accounts, the Confederates in Forts Morgan and Gaines were not demoralized; in fact, they were ready and waiting for the Yankee onslaught.

As darkness closed around the mighty fleet in the Gulf, chow time was over and the smoking lamp was lit. Officers and men aboard the ships sat down and wrote letters home or smoked. They speculated on the coming battle and about their chances of survival—a common ritual in all navies on the eve of battle. Farragut sat in his cabin and penned a note home, as did most of his officers in their quarters.

Much the same rituals must have taken place aboard the ships of the Confederate fleet, now ensconced in the lee of Fort Morgan. Aboard the *Tennessee* Admiral Buchanan and his commanders probably also held a strategy session. Outnumbered and outgunned, they no doubt knew the odds were against them but counted on the giant ironclad's armor, effective rifles, and deadly bow ram to lessen those odds somewhat. To take on an entire fleet out in the Gulf would have been suicidal. To be sure, in the Mississippi River campaign of August 1862, the C.S.S. *Arkansas* had rammed her way through an entire Union fleet and, despite a severe beating, made it safely to Vicksburg. But that spectacular success was a fluke. The audacity of her commander, plus the element of surprise, had assisted her. In Mobile Bay the *Tennessee* was no *Arkansas*. She was too slow to battle her way through a fleet, as the *Arkansas* had done, and her armament, at six guns, was nowhere near that of the *Arkansas*, which carried eight guns.[16]

Buchanan and his commanders must have discussed the strategy of having the ram head for the flagship *Hartford* and cripple her, then turn her attention to whatever Union vessels were at hand, assisted by her three consorts.

Out in the Gulf the smoking lamp was extinguished, the night watch was set, and silence spread over the hot, humid night. No doubt little real sleep was gained that night.

In a few hours the silence would be shattered by a holocaust of gunfire, death, and destruction.

CHAPTER SIXTEEN

MOBILE—PHASE FOUR: INTO THE BREACH

Friday, August 5, 1864, 4:00 A.M.

The copper disk of the sun poked up over the eastern horizon, splashing orange against the sides of the Federal warships anchored three miles below Fort Morgan and approximately a half-mile below Sand Island. A slight warm wind from the southwest barely ruffled the smooth, mist-dotted waters of the Gulf.

Aboard the ships there had been much activity even before the first fingers of light appeared. All were busy preparing the ships for action. Gun crews were tending to their black lethal charges; deck gangs were clearing away all superfluous gear from the decks and spreading sand around the gun stations. Below decks the boiler- and engine-room crews were checking fires and gauges; all stations had to be ready for the order to get under way. The ship's surgeon and his assistants in the forward pantry had been putting tables and instruments in order, ready to receive the casualties that were sure to come.

All available crewmen were exchanging mooring lines, which they crossed and crisscrossed between their own vessels and the consorts, which were now sidling up to the port sides of the seven ships of the main body. The 14 men-of-war, locked together in twos, like floating Siamese twins, were now formed into one unit each.

In the lee of Sand Island, various sounds onboard the low black monitors attested that they too were preparing to cast off upon signal from the flagship. They would cross the bow of the lead ship and then steam parallel with the main body, placing themselves in the van, between the forts and the main column.

At 5:39, after Admiral Farragut and Captain Drayton had confirmed that the six gunboats to the east of Fort Morgan were primed and ready, as were the five gunboats off Fort Powell up in the Mississippi Sound, the admiral gave the order for the fleet to get under way. Signal flags flew up, screws churned the water, and slowly, like some huge awakening marine animal, the fleet began to move. The bloodred eastern sky was becoming partly cloudy.[1]

6:00 A.M.

The entire Union fleet was now under way: The slower monitors had crossed the bows ahead of *Brooklyn* and *Octorara* and were presently steaming along with the *Tecumseh*, parallel to the *Brooklyn*, forming two columns.

All hands in the fleet were now grimly waiting for the *Tecumseh* to fire the opening shot. The fleet gathered speed, and as the *Brooklyn* moved along with her consort at her side, white foam splayed away from both sides of her cutwater, and her bowsprit was thrust up, like the lance of a charging knight; with colorful bunting and flags strung along the masts of the vessels, the fleet looked more like one heading for a naval review than steaming into battle.

In Fort Morgan, the troops had been alerted before dawn, because Farragut's attack was anticipated for this very day. At 5:00 A.M. Joseph Wilkinson, of the 1st Tennessee Heavy Artillery, was alerted by musket fire from Fort Gaines across the bay that "something was up." He walked down to the fort from his barracks and, "by the time I reached the parapet," he wrote, "the whole [Union] fleet was under way and steaming slowly upon the following order—Single turretted [sic] monitor in advance, double-turretted next, the *Hartford* and *Brooklyn* with double-enders lashed to their port sides, the three masters and other gunboats lashed two and two following."[2] Another trooper in the fort described the line of ships as being "decorated with flags from deck to masts, presenting quite a formidable scene and one that I have never forgotten."

6:47 A.M.

The warships and Fort Morgan were now within range of each other.

As the *Tecumseh*, the "single-turretted monitor," approached, a bloom of white smoke shot out of her 11-inch smoothbore; the shot arched high over the fort to explode and spray everything below with shrapnel. This was followed by a round from *Manhattan*, next in line. Another shot from *Tecumseh* slammed into the brick lighthouse on the south end of the fort. The opening shots were fired in the battle of Mobile Bay.

7:00 A.M.

The gunners on Fort Morgan's parapets, along with the water's-edge batteries, opened up on the approaching Yankee vessels. The *Brooklyn* returned a broadside, followed by the heavy guns of the *Hartford*, while the monitors added their guns to the fray. Soon the air was rent by smoke and flame and the thunderous reports from the belching cannons of both antagonists.

"The enemy did not open till within three quarters," wrote Joseph Wilkinson, "when broadside after broadside shook the very earth, though apparently that was the only trembling, for our men stood nobly to their guns."[3]

"The noise from the firing was terrific," wrote Captain Whiting. "Commands to the nearest men had to be yelled, and the smoke so obscured the hulls of the wooden ships, that we had to guess by their masts about where to direct our guns."[4]

By now the battle was in full swing, fort guns against ship guns.

Shells were bursting overhead or inside the fort and smashing the bulwarks of ships, reducing men to bloody shreds. Blinding, choking smoke swathed everything, setting eyes to burning and throats to coughing. The roar was deafening, as the big guns spewed their lethal projectiles. The very earth shook under the fort, and the water seemed to shake under the ships. Still the fleet moved forward, in spite of the relentless pounding.

On the *Tennessee*, Admiral Buchanan, who had long before been alerted about the approaching fleet, gave the order for his flotilla to get under way, with the flagship in the lead. His three ships formed a line abreast of the channel, standing ready to sortie out as soon as Farragut's lead ships had passed the fort.[5]

The flagship, with Farragut's blue pennant flying from her mast, received the fort's attention, and she took a fierce pounding. Ahead, the *Brooklyn* also came under an intense shelling, not only from the fort but from Buchanan's vessels. Now in place across the channel, the Confederate flotilla formed a classical crossing-the-T formation, in which they could enfilade an approaching column on both sides, while the ships in the column could respond only with their bow guns.[6]

At Fort Gaines, Colonel Anderson's garrison watched the heavy fighting across the channel—but not for long. General Granger, on cue from Farragut's run, soon opened a heavy artillery barrage on the fort.

The fort's gunners responded, but they were no match for Granger's guns, and Fort Gaines quickly suffered much damage and many casualties. Most of its guns were dismounted by the heavy fire from the Union artillerists.[7]

Across the bay the Union fleet was now abreast and slightly beyond the fort. The heavy pounding had taken a toll on the *Hartford* and had caused heavy damage, with fearful casualties; blood ran freely in her scuppers, and cannonballs ripped through her bulwarks, decimating men at their gun stations; shards of bone and fragments of flesh were splattered everywhere.

Frustrated because he could not observe the action through the heavy, acrid smoke, Farragut sought a clearer view by grasping the ratlines and climbing up the futtock shrouds until he was just below the maintop. On deck Fleet Commander Drayton worried lest the admiral be wounded by a stray shot hitting the rigging and tearing it away. He ordered the signal quartermaster aloft with a small line, intent on lashing his commander to the rigging. At first Farragut waved the man away, but upon further reflection he allowed himself to be lashed a few times with the line.[8] The admiral was able to communicate with the pilot, Martin Freeman, who was on the maintop, by grasping his feet when he wanted to communicate. He used a speaking trumpet to communicate with the deck and with the captain of the *Metacomet* alongside.

The fleet sailed on, coming within 200 yards of the fort, exchanging heavy fire, receiving punishment but handing it out as well. As Lieutenant Austill observed, "Everything was enveloped in smoke that little could be seen except their [Union ships'] brilliant banners which could be moved on, despite the terrific fire levelled upon them above the clouds of smoke."[9] Austill also observed the armed Union transport *Philippi*, which was holed below her waterline; she was hit and sank about a mile west of the main channel. Her crew was taken off, and she was burned by a crew from the *Morgan*. It began to look as if the Union fleet would get by the fort with a minimum of damage.

7:45 A.M.

Suddenly the *Tecumseh*, which was slightly ahead of the *Brooklyn*, swung to port. Captain Tunis A. M. Craven, on his own, had decided to engage the enemy fleet ahead, and in so doing he passed in front of the *Brooklyn*, causing Captain James Alden to ring a full stop to avoid a crash. The big sloop-of-war was not quite dead in the water, as the incoming tide moved her forward. But her sudden stop affected the ships behind her. The *Hartford* too rang to a stop, as did the other vessels behind, to avoid a massive collision. The fleet was now bunched up in front of Fort Morgan. The Confederate fort's gunners, concluding that the fleet had been severely damaged and was backing down, gleefully poured on the heat with a hail of shot and shell.

The situation suddenly no longer boded well for Farragut's fleet.

Captain Craven was now approaching the red buoy marking the eastern edge of the lines of torpedoes. Farragut had warned his fleet about them earlier, but Craven's single thought was to engage the *Tennessee*, which was now approaching from the east. As he swung his ship, his port side extended beyond the red buoy, where a Singer mine lay in wait.[10]

Suddenly the *Tecumseh* veered hard, and a huge geyser of water shot up along her port side. The monitor nose-dived, her screw still turning in the empty air. As the ship began to sink, whichever crew members had access to topside abandoned ship. Inside the vessel, Captain Craven and the pilot, John Collins, met at the ladder leading to the turret, but there was room for only one person. Craven stepped aside, saying, "After you, pilot." As Collins reached the last rung of the ladder, the ship fell away from beneath his feet. It sank, taking Captain Craven and 90 men with it to a watery grave.[11]

Some of the crew members swam ashore to be captured; others were picked up by Union fleet boats, one from the *Metacomet*. The rescue boat drew close to the fort and was exposed to fire, but Acting Master Henry Nields put an ensign in the stern sheets of the boat to signal his intent. At Fort Morgan, Brigadier General Page, the commander, spotted the signal and passed the word for his gunners not to fire on the boat because she was picking up "drowning men." The gun crews on the *Tennessee* held their fire upon orders from Admiral Buchanan, who had also observed the brave action of the Union boat crew. Nields managed to pick up four of the *Tecumseh*'s survivors.

It was likely one of the most heroic acts in the battle, and it showed that even in the thickest of fights, acts of mercy may occur on one side for the other.

The sinking of the *Tecumseh* moved Joseph Wilkinson to comment, "The foremost ironclad *Tecumseh* sinks to war no more and a tomb for one hundred and six corpses." (His estimate of fatal casualties was erroneous.) On the *Brooklyn*, Captain Alden proclaimed the sinking to be an "assassination at its worst form! A glorious though terrible end for our noble friends, the intrepid pioneers of that death-strewn path."[12]

When he learned of the *Tecumseh*'s sinking, Farragut signaled the *Brooklyn* that he intended to take the lead. As he passed her, he was informed that torpedoes lay ahead, whereupon Farragut shouted to

Drayton on the deck: "Damn the torpedoes! Four bells, Captain Drayton. Go ahead!"[13]

The *Hartford* and her consort *Metacomet* now passed to the port of *Brooklyn*, and in so doing they passed the east end of the buoys and entered into the torpedo line. Crew members later reported hearing the thumps of torpedoes striking her bottom. Their firing mechanisms failed to go off, however, and the flagship passed through safely. Most likely the primers had become corroded after a long immersion in salt water.[14] Nevertheless, it was a brave action on Farragut's part, and it reinforced his earlier argument that the torpedoes were "innocuous." The sinking of the *Tecumseh* seemed, for a moment, to fly in the face of that view, but examinations of the underwater weapons after the battle proved him right.

8:00 A.M.

The overall picture was now altered. Most of the Union fleet cleared the fort—except for the hapless *Oneida*, at the tail end of the column. A rifled shot struck her boiler, wounding and scalding 30 of her crew and putting her out of action. She was in a position to be sunk, but her consort *Galena* was undamaged and led her to safety.[15] The fleet had now changed course to a northwesterly direction.

Meanwhile Admiral Buchanan had been observing all this action, waiting for an opportunity to inflict a lethal strike on the approaching fleet. His ships kept up their enfilading actions and could be responded to only by the bow guns of the Union ships. But when the *Hartford* hove into view in the bay's middle ground, Buchanan's ships swung into action. The *Selma* placed herself in the path of *Hartford*, blasting away with her bow guns and managing to keep a thousand yards or so ahead. The Union flagship's excellent gunners managed to keep the *Morgan* and the *Gaines* at bay with devastating broadsides, while Farragut came to grips with the annoying, molesting *Selma*.

At 8:12 he ordered the *Metacomet* cast off to engage the *Selma*. The *Octorara* was then separated from the *Brooklyn*, and the two gunboats were ordered to attack their Confederate counterparts.[16] The two Union warships took off after their antagonists, who fled after spotting the faster and heavily armed vessels standing toward them.

Now was the time for Buchanan to act decisively. Instead of being content with firing his guns at lead ships, he headed the *Tennessee* directly for *Hartford*, intending to ram her amidships. The huge ram, smoke billowing from her single stack, lumbered on slowly but surely. Then, as she neared the *Hartford* to within a half-mile, she unexpectedly veered off and headed downstream toward the vessels in line with the flagship. As she passed by the stern of the *Hartford*, she poured out a broadside from her rifled guns, receiving a shower of shot and shell in return. The projectiles just bounced off her thick hide, like Ping-Pong balls against a granite wall. The shower failed to bother Buchanan; the much more adroit *Hartford* had already begun to move out of the way. The *Brooklyn* also managed to outmaneuver the ram and avoid a devastating blow, but she, like the *Hartford*, received punishment from the rifled guns.[17]

With a vengeance, Captain James E. Jouett of the *Metacomet* raced his fast vessel after the retreating *Selma*, firing his bow guns as he steamed. The Confederate gunboat answered with her stern guns. At 9:10 Jouett caught up with the *Selma* and pummeled her severely with gunfire. But the Confederate crew had had enough. With dead and dying men on her decks and with her chief officers and captain wounded, the white flag of surrender went up on the stern line. She was boarded by an assistant engineer and three firemen from the *Metacomet*. The wounded captain, P. U. Murphey, came onboard the *Metacomet* and was greeted by Captain Jouett. When he was offered the surrendered officer's sword, Jouett replied, "Pat, don't make a damned fool of yourself; I have a bottle on ice for you for the last half-hour."[18]

In the meantime, the *Hartford*'s gunners were having a field day with the *Gaines*. After taking a brutal punishment, the *Gaines* limped away to the lee of Fort Morgan, where she was abandoned, burned, and sunk in six fathoms.

Captain George Harrison of the *Morgan* attempted to assist the *Selma* by standing up and engaging the *Metacomet* for a time, but faster Union ships pursued her until she went aground at Navy Cove, to the east of Fort Morgan, still under the protection of the fort's guns.[19] Later, upon pulling loose, she stood down and anchored next to the fort to lick her wounds.

Down the line Buchanan was working the *Tennessee* with good effect—until he learned that his consorts had either been sunk or driven off. He then took his lumbering vessel to anchor near the fort, while he pondered his next move. By this time Farragut's fleet was past the fort and had anchored about six miles above Fort Morgan and around four miles to the northeast of Dauphin Island. The admiral ordered breakfast for his crew, plus the removal of debris on deck, in order to make the *Hartford* shipshape again.[20]

A similar routine was taking place on the *Tennessee*. The crew was at breakfast, gulping warm water, coffee, and hardtack on the afterdeck, because of the insufferable heat below. Several times the heat would reach over 100 degrees within the iron casemate. Life was not often easy in Civil War ironclad vessels.

Buchanan paced the deck in deep thought, trying to decide his next move now that his fleet was shattered. A run up the bay was out of the question, because he would never get over Dog River Bar again. He only had about six hours of coal left, so he decided to go out fighting. He ordered his captain, "Follow them up, Johnston. We can't let them off that way." The *Tennessee* moved out and stood for Farragut's fleet, hoping at the very least to sink a few enemy ships by ramming.[21]

Up on the main topsail yard of the *Hartford,* the approaching Confederate ram was spotted by Lieutenant Joseph Marthon, who spread the warning. Farragut was thunderstruck. He replied, "I did not think that old Buck was such a fool." Then he ordered the fleet to "destroy the enemy's principal ship" by ramming her.

As the monstrous ironclad approached, the *Monongahela*, with her consort *Kennebec* still lashed alongside, swung around and headed for the ram. Then with a loud crash the *Monongahela* hit the *Tennessee* squarely, knocking many men off their feet on all three vessels. Unfortunately for the Union sloop, the ram's casemate extended below the waterline, and though the impact spun her around, she received little damage. The *Monongahela*, on the other hand, suffered a crushed bow and shattered butt ends of her planking. At the moment of impact, the

Confederate gunners had managed to fire a shot that passed through the Union ship, causing many casualties. The *Monongahela*, managed to get off a few rounds, but as usual they bounced off the ram's iron overcoat.

Other Federal ships—*Ossipee, Lackawanna,* and *Chickasaw*—joined in the fray, striking the ram amidships, starboard quarter, and stern. Such blows would have sunk any ship in the Union navy, but the *Tennessee* persevered and even dished out some punishment of her own in the process.

Buchanan later wrote: "The engagement with the whole fleet soon became general at very close quarters and lasted about an hour, and notwithstanding the serious injury inflicted upon many of their vessels by our guns, we could not sink them." He continued, "Frequently during the contest, we were surrounded by the enemy and all our guns were in action almost at the same moment."[22]

The *Lackawanna*, under a full head of steam, charged in and struck the *Tennessee* at her starboard stern. Once again the Union ship suffered damage, and all *Lackawanna* could show for her effort was a smashed bow. As the two vessels swung parallel to each other, Confederate crewmen thrust their heads out of gunports and shouted obscenities at the Federal sailors. The response was a volley of pistol and rifle shots, plus some holystones and even spittoons from the Union sailors.[23] The *Lackawanna* did manage to fire shots that struck the *Tennessee*'s exposed rudder chains and a port gun shutter.

By this time, Farragut had the *Hartford* under way, and the big sloop-of-war was about to take her own chances with the *Tennessee*. He set course directly for the ironclad, fully intent on ramming her to the bottom of the bay.

The ram swung around to meet the oncoming ship, and as the vessel approached, a head-on collision seemed imminent. This possibility worried Buchanan, because if he were to ram the *Hartford* bow to bow, the *Tennessee* would be driven so far into the wooden sloop that she would be pulled down with her adversary. At the last moment, he ordered a starboard helm, and the two vessels struck each other starboard to starboard. As the ram scraped by the *Hartford*, with Farragut back up in the futtock shrouds looking on, his gunners opened a full broadside. Once again the shots bounced off harmlessly. The *Tennessee*'s gunners attempted to respond with their own broadside, but because of defective primers, she got off only one shot. (Many historians believe that such defective primers kept Buchanan from dishing out more severe damage to the Federal fleet.)[24]

Then the twin-turreted *Chickasaw* and *Winnebago* moved in astern of the sizable ram and unlimbered their hefty 11-inch guns. It would be the coup de grâce for the Confederate ironclad. Big shell after big shell slammed repeatedly into the *Tennessee's* aft shield and managed to loosen the shield and jam the iron port cover. As crewmen were trying to pry it loose, another shot hit it squarely, killing one man and sending iron splinters into the vessel; one of them struck Admiral Buchanan in the leg. The wounded admiral sent for Captain Johnston and ordered him to continue fighting but, if all else failed, to surrender. Johnston knew he could not hold out much longer, but orders were orders, and he encouraged his crews to fire as long as they were able.

But the devastating, relentless pounding from the monitors continued, reducing the *Tennessee* to a near wreck. Her steering chains and relieving tackles were shot away and her smokestack was knocked down, flooding the interior with acrid, choking smoke and lowering the boiler draft to a dangerous level. Captain Johnston realized the hopelessness of the situation and to prevent more of the crew from being killed or wounded, decided to surrender. He went to the gun deck and retrieved a boat hook, to which he attached a white flag of surrender. His action was not quick enough to stop the momentum of the charging *Ossipee* from ramming the *Tennessee* with one final blow. The skipper of the *Ossipee* turned out to be Commander William LeRoy, an old friend of Johnston's, who sent over a boarding party shortly after the surrender. Buchanan's sword was later sent to Farragut by way of a lieutenant from the *Ossipee*.

10:00 A.M.

The battle of Mobile Bay was over.

The cost to the Union was heavier, with 150 killed, including those on the *Tecumseh*, and 170 wounded or missing. Confederate losses came to only 12 killed and 19 wounded. It was a hard-earned victory for Farragut.[25]

The gunboat *Morgan* was the only Confederate survivor of the battle, and she was presently anchored as close to Fort Morgan as water depth would allow.

Captain Harrison was anxious to save the *Morgan* for the Confederacy, so he considered making a dash up to Mobile, hopefully to the safety of the floating batteries on and above the Dog River Bar. But he would have had to pass the anchored Federal fleet "unobserved with a noisy, high-pressure steamer making black smoke." Nevertheless, he decided to risk the run at night. He unloaded all unnecessary weight on board, including three-quarters of his provisions and most of his coal. Important papers were sent upstream in two boats under the command of Lieutenant Commander John W. Bennett, instructed to follow the shoreline northward.

That night, after 11:00 P.M., he cast off. The fleet became alerted and quickly dispatched two gunboats after him, but he managed to slip by. "Fortune found us," he wrote later. "And although hotly pursued and shelled by the enemy's cruisers, for a large portion of the way, we successfully reached the outer obstructions near Mobile at daybreak, having been struck but once."[26] A portion of the pursuit was observed by Commander Bennett and his men, rowing their way up the coast.

Mobile Bay was now in Union hands, but the forts themselves remained in Confederate hands. They would have to be dealt with next.

CHAPTER SEVENTEEN

MOBILE—PHASE FIVE: TO THE VICTOR . . .

Admiral Farragut's stunning victory at Mobile Bay brought a swift, warm response from Secretary Welles:

> In the success which has attended your operations, you have illustrated the efficiency and irresistible power of a naval force led by a bold and vigorous mind, and insufficiency of any batteries to prevent the passage of any fleet thus led and commanded. You have, first on the Mississippi and recently in the Bay of Mobile, demonstrated what had been previously doubted, the ability of naval vessels, properly manned and commanded, to set at defiance the best constructed and most heavily armed fortifications. In these successive victories you have encountered great risks, but the results have vindicated the wisdom of your policy and the daring valor of our officers and seamen.[1]

Accolades or not, Forts Morgan, Gaines, and Powell were still intact and operative, although Fort Gaines was under siege by artillery and troops. The Confederate fleet had been reduced to only four entities—

the *Morgan*, the unfinished *Nashville*, and two floating batteries, *Huntsville* and *Tuscaloosa*. For all intents and purposes, the Confederate navy was nonexistent in the Gulf area, because the *Morgan*, the only survivor of Buchanan's fleet, remained immobile for the duration.

Farragut moved swiftly to subjugate the forts. On August 5, the gunboats *J. P. Jackson*, *Estrella*, *Stockdale*, and *Narcissus* opened a heavy bombardment on Fort Powell. The monitor *Chickasaw* also stood down to the fort from the bay side and added her big guns to the barrage. Colonel James W. Williams, who was commander of the fort with two companies of the 20th Alabama, finally wired General Page at Fort Morgan that his situation was untenable. Page told him to evacuate the fort and save the men. At 10:00 P.M. on August 5, he set a slow match to the magazine and then at low tide led his men wading to Cedar Point. Behind them, the fort disintegrated in a stupendous blast. The Mississippi Sound was now open to Federal water traffic.[2]

The *Richmond Enquirer* dourly reported the fall of Fort Powell but added with a note of false optimism: "The people are satisfied with the conduct of lieutenants Johnston, Murphey and Bennett of the navy."[3] (Why Colonel Charles Anderson was not mentioned is a mystery; perhaps there was confusion as to Fort Gaines's status.) On August 9, the *Mobile Advertiser and Register* wrote a scathing indictment of Fort Powell's young commander Williams. After listing some of the reasons for its surrender, such as danger to the magazine, the driving away of the men from their guns, and the destruction of ordnance, the editor wrote: "An isolated fort like that may be held long after its big guns are silenced. Sumter was held in that way. Unfortunately, the commander thought too much of his garrison and not enough of the permanent value of the actual key to the Bay of Mobile."[4] But General Page himself later concurred with Colonel Williams's assessment of the situation.

Meanwhile at Fort Gaines on Dauphin Island, the situation was becoming critical for Colonel Anderson. Federal forces of 2,000 men had planted artillery positions on the Gulf shore dunes, on the center of the island, and on Little Dauphin Island. Pickets had moved up to within 100 yards of the fort. The monitor *Chickasaw* had stood down from the fleet anchorage to add more firepower to the besieging artillery forces.[5] In spite of General Page's morale-building visit to the fort on August 4 and his later message urging Anderson to "hold the fort to the last extremity," it soon became too much for Anderson. In the spirit of discretion being the better part of valor, he decided to surrender the fort before he lost any more men and armament.[6] The white flag of surrender was hoisted on the parade ground staff.

When Page found out about the surrender of Fort Gaines—the flag had been spotted by sharp-eyed men in Fort Morgan—he was enraged. He fired off a despatch to General Dabney Maury, bitterly castigating Anderson for his surrender. He had tried to contact Anderson by telegram and signal guns but received no reply. He added: "Colonel Anderson's conduct [was] inexplicable and disgraceful."[7]

When Union troops marched through the sally port of Fort Gaines, they took 818 prisoners of war, including Anderson, 26 guns, and an enormous supply of ammunition and provisions. Unquestionably the fort could have held out a lot longer than it did, but Anderson was concerned about the welfare of his men when the bombardments increased, as they most certainly would have.

From a military prison—probably the customs house building in New Orleans—Anderson wrote a letter to the *Mobile Advertiser and Register* defending his actions. It was published on September 22:

> I was compelled to surrender Fort Gaines through feelings of mercy for my officers, who earnestly appealed to me. The position was utterly untenable, the fleet having passed and an overwhelming force besieging by land, the only three guns with which I could have responded to the fleet disabled, my picket line driven back to the last notch, the ditches and parapets swept from every direction by the enemy's shot and shell, no safe shelter in the miserable apology for a fortification, two sick men having been killed in what was considered the best casemate, threatened with a tremendous conflagration from the buildings within and the magazines in great danger of being blown up, and all hope of escape, or of accomplishing the slightest good by holding out, gone. . . . Under these circumstances my command was seized with the appalling conviction that our case was hopeless, and seemed paralyzed with the prospect of certain and useless destruction.[8]

Anderson's letter flies in the face of those who condemned him for a useless surrender. The weaknesses he mentioned were never brought out in any of the literature surrounding the saga of Fort Gaines. It did not matter much to the Union, but the Confederacy felt that they had to have what today is called a "fall guy" for the loss of the fort.

With Forts Gaines and Powell now in Union hands, only Fort Morgan was left out on the vine, either to wither or to carry on as best it could. But it was besieged by several thousand troops, under the command of General Granger, who were landed on Navy Cove and covered by the guns of three gunboats. The fort's pickets were driven back, and the Union men burned all the wooden buildings outside the stronghold.

This powerful force would besiege Fort Morgan from the rear, but in order to assault it by water, Admiral Farragut brought up monitor *Manhattan*, screw gunboat *Itaska*, and sloop-of-war *Monongahela*, plus the surrendered *Tennessee*, towed up for the mission. Their water assault would coordinate with that of Granger's artillery.[9] "The siege has commenced," wrote Joseph Wilkinson, "and God only knows how long it will last, though in the end there can be no favorable result."[10]

On August 9, Farragut demanded the unconditional surrender of the fort, in a message to General Page. But the general refused, claiming, "I am prepared to sacrifice life and will only surrender when I have no means of defense." Page also crabbed about Farragut's use of the *Tennessee* in the bombardment group.[11]

Granger moved his troops and guns to three positions spanning the narrow peninsula on both water sides, placing one artillery group less than a mile from the fort. Austill took time to admire the Union resolve by writing that "the enemy never stops work for the hardest showers. Their energy is indefatigable and should grace a better cause."[12]

The bombardments continued—both from the warships in the bay and from the land artillery positions. Most of the fort's guns were dismounted and the powder magazine was nearly flooded; only by a diligent effort did Page's troops save most of the powder. The citadel was burned to the ground, and the commissary and quartermaster stores were flooded. The situation was desperate, and the fort could not prevail much longer.

The Yankees were making it hot for the fort's occupants; but in spite of the shelling, morning prayer services were inaugurated. "No place is safe," wrote Wilkinson. "We are in the hands of the Almighty and may He be merciful to us."[13]

Finally, at 6:00 A.M. on August 23, Fort Morgan was surrendered to General Granger. The Confederate troops were taken prisoner, and the wounded and sick were sent to Mobile hospitals. More than 1,700 troops were captured in the Mobile Bay assault.[14]

General Page later wrote that his surrender had been the result of attrition: "My guns and powder had been destroyed, my means of defense gone, the citadel gone and nearly all of the quartermaster stores and a portion of the commissariat burned by the enemy's shells. It was evident the fort could hold out but a few hours longer under a renewed bombardment."[15]

MOBILE Bay was now completely in Federal hands, and Mobile was cut off from the Gulf and overseas commerce. The Confederate navy had faded into history, and the war effort now focused on the land battles to the north, in Georgia and Virginia.

Once again, as at New Orleans, the smashing victory by Farragut's fleet—in passing the forts, destroying the Confederate naval strength, capturing the *Tennessee*, and finally taking the forts—brought enormous acclaim to Farragut from a grateful nation and its president. Lincoln tendered national thanks to him and ordered that a 100-gun salute be fired at the arsenal and the navy yard in Washington on September 5 and 6, 1864.

The president lauded Farragut for "the brilliant achievements of the fleet and land forces of the United States in the harbor of Mobile and in the reduction of Fort Powell, Fort Gaines, and Fort Morgan."[16]

Secretary Welles wrote to Farragut that "the possession of Mobile Bay, which you have acquired, will close the illicit traffic which has been carried on by running the blockade in that part of the Gulf, and gives point and value to the success you have achieved."[17]

But the admiral was tired and wanted to take a leave of absence to rest and visit his family. At first Welles wanted him to command a squadron in the Atlantic, but he changed his mind and ordered Farragut, with his *Hartford*, back to New York and his family. The adoring public gave him a hero's welcome of huge proportions; Farragut soon found himself a national hero. On December 22, 1864, Congress bestowed on him the rank of full admiral, and he became the first Admiral of the United States Navy in history.

Farragut served the navy until the end of the war, and after receiving his commission as full admiral, he raised his flag on the new 4,000-ton *Franklin*, with 39 guns and a crew of 750. An exception was made to the old rule that wives could not travel onboard warships with their husbands. Virginia joined her husband, and they traveled extensively around the world until his death on August 14, 1870.

David Glasgow Farragut became a true legend in naval history. Some of his military strategies were used in World War II by General MacArthur, when he bypassed Japanese military strongholds in his drive across the Pacific for an assault on the Japanese homeland.

After the Federal occupation of Mobile Bay, Union gunboats, now under the command of Rear Admiral H. K. Thatcher, still sortied around the bay. They bombarded enemy positions and covered the landings of troops right up to the surrender of Mobile itself on April 12, 1865. Unfortunately, torpedoes still took their toll, as eight vessels were lost to them. Union efforts to sweep the waterways clear of them were hampered by Confederates who, at nighttime, dropped more of the weapons into the waters.

ONE important aspect of the Mobile Bay campaign remained controversial for years afterward—the sinking of the *Tecumseh*. Was she sunk by shot or torpedo? The generally accepted explanation was that when she veered to port and beyond the buoy marking the eastern edge of the torpedo line, she went down as a result of striking a torpedo. All eyewitnesses on the Union side, and most historians since, have insisted she was sunk by the torpedo. But some of the personnel in Fort Morgan disagreed, insisting that their gunfire had sunk the vessel. After the battle, many Fort Morgan personnel came forward and gave testimony that the big guns of Fort Morgan had been responsible.

Captain Whiting, in a report to Major General Matthew Maury, claimed to have seen the bottom of the monitor as she sank and said there was no visible sign of torpedo damage. He was of the opinion that "she was sunk before reaching the line of torpedoes." He was backed by pilots on the lookout and a contingent of privates who participated in the planting of the weapons.[18] Napoleon Smith, who was also in the fort, corroborates Whiting's statement by reporting that the *Tecumseh* was "sunk by our guns when she came immediately abreast of our fort."[19]

Confederate Brigadier General G. J. Raines, however, strongly disagreed with Captain Whiting and the others. He reported to President Davis that there was no evidence her magazine had been penetrated. "How otherwise," he wrote, "could a shot have occasioned her sinking in half a minute? The time of submersion would determine whether shot or torpedo sank the vessel."[20]

Secretary Mallory opined that the *Tecumseh* was sunk by a torpedo, because "this vessel was deep and could not probably have borne 30 inches of additional immersion without going down, the suddenness of her disappearance can be accounted for upon the supposition that she was struck by shot or shell, and it is not denied that she was over the place where torpedoes had been placed."[21] The torpedo theory was also supported by the army paymaster, Captain Douglas Vass, at Fort Gaines, who witnessed her sinking. He wrote that "a tremendous column of water [was] thrown up around her—evidently the work of a torpedo."[22]

But President Davis put forth a totally different theory in his book *Rise and Fall of the Confederate Government*. The monitor, he maintained, was actually sunk by her own torpedo. This theory was also propounded by General Dabney Maury in an article in the *Southern Historical Papers* of January 1877. Maury wrote that the *Tecumseh* carried a spar torpedo on her bow, intended for use against the *Tennessee*. But a shot from the fort cut away the stays by which the torpedo was attached, and it doubled under her, exploding under her bottom.[23] This theory was never offered by anyone else, and I have found no reference to the *Tecumseh*'s carrying a spar torpedo either in the general literature or in the archival material that I have examined. It is not mentioned in any of the official reports from Admiral Farragut, his staff, or the ship captains. In my opinion, the theory is to be taken with a grain of salt.

In 1967 the torpedo theory was conclusively proven when a team of divers and salvage personnel explored the wreck. A large gash on her port side was discovered, and all agreed that such a major wound could only have come from contact with a torpedo. They found no evidence that the vessel was fatally struck by either shot or shell.

CHAPTER EIGHTEEN

A GLANCE BACKWARD

With the capture of Mobile Bay, all naval actions in the Gulf of Mexico came to a halt, with the exception of minor skirmishes between Union warships and blockade-runners off the coast of Texas. This activity continued until Galveston surrendered to Federal forces on June 2, 1865. All further naval actions were centered on the Atlantic coast.

When General William T. Sherman's army rolled and burned its way through Georgia, Mobile became unimportant to the South. It was isolated and became a "Rebel Island."[1]

One could argue that the defeats in the Gulf constituted the nadir of the Confederacy itself. The closing of such important and vital ports as New Orleans, Mobile, and Galveston isolated it from the rest of the world and kept vital sustaining materiel from reaching its armies and its populace.

Before the war, New Orleans was clearly the South's main port of entry for European commerce, and an impressive number of blockade-runners ran in and out on errands of mercy for their government. Without blockade-runners, the Confederacy would have collapsed before April 9, 1865.

In spite of the Union blockade, which grew more effective as the months went by, the intrepid blockade-runners chalked up a remarkable number of successful runs—nine out of ten made the run without being caught. But that effectiveness weakened as more and more Union warships joined the blockading fleets. By 1865 the Union fleet had grown to 700 vessels, and by the end of the war, the Union navy had captured 1,149 blockade-running vessels, of which 210 were steamers; it burned or sank 200 more. The value of the cargo in these actions amounted to $31 million. A large number of the vessels were captured in the Gulf.

The most important naval actions in the Civil War were most likely those fought on the Mississippi River and in the Gulf of Mexico. A possible exception would be the epic battle between the *Monitor* and the *Merrimack*. But this encounter involved only two warships as opposed to whole fleets.

Some Southern apologists maintain that the naval engagements of the war were lopsided, what with the clear superiority of the Union fleet over that of the Confederates. This may be true to a certain extent, but the Confederates offset that superiority with cunning and ingenuity in their weaponry. Historian Raimundo Luraghi writes, "The South's ingenuity was remarkable, with outstanding sagacity not only in creating new tools, but using them in exceptional and creative ways—to transform them into tested elements that would change forever the conduct of war at sea."[2]

One need consider only the innovation of the torpedo, or mine, and the first successful submarine to agree with this assessment of Confederate "sagacity." These awesome weapons were created out of necessity, "the mother of invention." Because the Confederacy lacked naval vessels and the facilities with which to build and service them, Mallory's resourceful technicians used technology to take up the slack. They succeeded to a remarkable extent, in that 33 Union vessels were sunk or damaged by torpedoes. (This crude weapon was to have its legacy in the terrible engines of destruction of World Wars I and II.) The same could be said of the submarine—the primitive *Hunley*—whose descendants today are the monstrous nuclear submarines.

The brief appearances of the *Monitor* and *Merrimack* notwithstanding, the ironclad warship came into prominence on the Mississippi

River and in the Gulf campaign. These lumbering, iron-coated vessels blazed their way into naval history and became the progenitors of to-day's sleek and powerful steel warships. They had their limitations, to be sure, in their sluggishness and their sometimes-intolerable living conditions. The *Tennessee* at Mobile Bay exemplifies these limitations, entirely due to the lagging technology of Southern shipbuilders. But they were used with firm and resolute determination on both sides.

The Confederacy was sorely lacking in industrial prowess. She was hampered by a lack of skilled manpower—especially skilled artisans—material shortages, and inadequate building and repair facilities for warships. These inadequacies crippled the Confederate navy from the start. Even the attempts to buy warships from Britain and France failed, because of the ambivalence of those countries. The Navy Department did all it could, but during the war the South produced only 29 ironclads as opposed to 60 for the Union.

To be fair, the problem was not all Secretary Mallory's fault. He was an efficient and intelligent leader, and had he had the resources of the Union, the naval war might have had a different outcome. His problem was that whenever he should have acted decisively and with absolute authority—to which he was entitled as the head of the Confederate navy—a coordinated infrastructure stayed his hand.

New Orleans was an example of this unfair hand-tying. The Confederate naval forces were splintered into three different commands—civilian, army, and navy—and therefore had no central command structure. Consequently a small naval force, which could have inflicted heavier damage to Farragut's fleet, suffered an ignominious defeat. Although Admiral Buchanan was not saddled with such a command situation at Mobile Bay, his *Tennessee* did suffer from poor workmanship and lack of quality materiel. The vessel had the potential to inflict major damage on the Federal fleet, but instead its surrender led to the eventual destruction of its fleet.

The Union successes were impressive, but its naval commanders had their own problems. One was poor judgment, as in the Galveston fiasco, when Captain Winslow divided his forces and failed to put out pickets to warn of approaching enemy ships. The destruction of his ship and the capture of the *Harriet Lane* and other vessels of his squadron were inexcusable. They led to a serious defeat that closed the port of Galveston to the Federals until the capture of New Orleans negated the defeat. The Union successes in the Gulf were made possible only after the capture of New Orleans and the fall of Vicksburg. These two victories opened the Mississippi to the Gulf, split the Confederacy in two, and cut it off from the rich resources of Arkansas, Louisiana, and Texas.

Another result of these victories was that Confederate armies were forced out of Tennessee and Kentucky and back east, to join their embattled armies there. Vicksburg's surrender not only opened up the Mississippi but it came almost simultaneously with the victory at Gettysburg—indeed, many historians are of the opinion that the South essentially lost the war in July 1863. Grant wrote in his memoirs: "The capture of Vicksburg, with its garrison, ordnance, ordnance stores and the successful battles fought in reaching them, gave a new spirit to the loyal people of the north. . . . The Mississippi was entirely in the possession of the national troops."3

The capture of New Orleans, for its part, disproved the old maxim that wooden ships could not prevail against stone forts. Not only did Farragut's fleet prevail against the stone forts of St. Philip and Jackson, but he managed to defeat a Confederate fleet sent down to stop him. The forts simply withered on the vine, so to speak (anticipating the military strategy of General MacArthur in World War II, in his amazingly successful island-hopping campaigns in the Pacific).

The Confederate navy might have presented a more formidable threat to Union naval forces had their river fleet been more aggressive and had their new ironclads not been hampered by the incredible parade of difficulties that dogged their building and launching.

The Confederate defense fleet consisted of a few river craft converted into gunboats. The two existing ironclads were ineffective and unable to take an active part in the battle for New Orleans. One was burned at the dock when Farragut ran the forts; the other was tied to a bank and used as a floating battery, but the use of her stern ordnance against Farragut's big guns was ineffective.

Another Confederate deficiency was in ground troops. New Orleans simply had no army to oppose General Butler's formidable forces—no thanks to General Lovell's hasty retreat with his troops.

The climax of the struggle for the Gulf came at Mobile Bay. Once again, Farragut flew in the face of conventional ship-against-fort wisdom when he brilliantly fought his way past one of the most powerful forts in the Gulf area, Fort Morgan. His loss of the magnificent monitor *Tecumseh* was due primarily to her captain's eagerness to tackle the Confederate fleet single-handedly, or so it appears from the evidence. Captain Craven brought his ship inside the eastern edge of the torpedo line and directly over a Singer mine, thereby losing his ship, his crew, and his own life.

The ignominious surrender of the *Tennessee* was yet another stark example of the sad state of Confederate technology and workmanship. The *Tennessee* had the potential to inflict a great deal of damage on Farragut's wooden ships. Some historians speculate that she might even have stopped the Union onslaught cold.

But the fact remains that shoddy workmanship, weak engines, and insufficiently protected steering cables hampered the *Tennessee*. Her defective gun primers could have heavily damaged more Union ships, possibly even sinking the *Hartford*, but they did not work when they were desperately needed.

In the end, as I have pointed out, the battle of Mobile Bay closed that last major Confederate port in the Gulf. One of the major consequences of that defeat was the eventual self-destruction of the entire Savannah flotilla, before the city was captured by General Sherman. The Confederate navy had finally reached its nadir.

The paltry remains of the Confederate navy survived the war physically but impotently. When Lee surrendered his army, the Confederate navy was also surrendered. As historian Luraghi points out, "The Southern Navy survived the war. It was the collapse of armies that dragged the navy into disaster."[4]

After the Gulf of Mexico became a Union lake, fleet operations continued in the Atlantic and culminated in a gigantic Union fleet action off Fort Fisher, North Carolina. The largest amphibious operation to date took place from January 13 to 15, 1865. Eight thousand Union men stormed ashore, after a bombardment by the 627 guns of 60 warships, and captured the last Confederate fort. The smashing victory was due to the incredibly powerful Union naval forces in the Atlantic. (It was another precursor—of the enormous amphibious landings at Normandy and in the Pacific, more than 80 years later.)

The inevitable fact of Union naval supremacy came to fruition in 1864–65. It had been proven again and again—in the muddy waters of the Mississippi River; in the deep blue waters of the Gulf of Mexico; and in the cold green waters of the Atlantic Ocean—that troops supported by sufficient naval strength could assault and capture any enemy stronghold, be it fort or city. The amphibious operations on the Mississippi, the Gulf, and at Fort Fisher gave Union armies a decided advantage. As the editors of CWNC point out:

> Employing the mobile heavy artillery of ships, their carrying capacity, range and speed of operations, armies gained the advantages of the sea. They could strike by surprise, swiftly and massively. They could promptly shift the heavy artillery of ships or concentrations of troops to attack where the foe was vulnerable or their own lines weak. Ships could strike on the flank or break through and roll up the most powerful position. They could pour in supplies or reinforcements to a key base or shift it at will.[5]

The South could not match the Union in amphibious warfare, in either ships or troops, not even in transports, let alone in powerful steam frigates or ironclads.

This combined strength of amphibious operations drew the Anaconda Plan coils tight around the Confederacy, squeezing it and in some cases pounding it into submission. The war at sea was coming to a close, and with it would go the fate of the South.

Finally, it comes down to commanders, the men who plan and lead the campaigns. Farragut stands out as the shining example of what a good leader should be, in the tradition of a Lord Nelson or a John Paul Jones. The outstanding characteristic of Farragut's genius was that he paid no attention to the skeptics and naysayers. Like his army counterpart, General Grant, he threw away the book and fought the battles his way. Both men had masters they could have followed—Grant had his

Jomini and Farragut his Nelson—but they both ignored the traditional methods and tried tactics of their own, Grant at Vicksburg and Farragut at Mobile.

Farragut was exceptional in his refusal to follow the old axiom that wooden ships could never prevail against stone forts. He put that rule away for all time at New Orleans and Mobile, and whether he was aware of it or not, he launched the era of ironclad ships and ushered in the demise of the wooden war vessel.

Admiral Buchanan was a tragic figure, saddled with inferior vessels and materiel. There was no doubt in the minds of some historians that Buchanan was an able commander and might have made a difference at Mobile had he better ships and materiel. Considering the state of his health and the debilitating wound he received, we may never know the man's true capabilities.

But we do know about the capabilities of Farragut. Historian T. Henry Williams sums them up in his discussion of the genius of Napoleon:

> The first quality of a General-in-Chief is to have a cool head which receives exact impressions of things, which never gets heated, which never allows itself to be dazzled, or intoxicated, by good or bad news.[6]

These qualities apply to David Glasgow Farragut more than to most military men.

ABBREVIATIONS

B&L   *Battles and Leaders of the Civil War, Being for the Most Part Contributions by Union & Confederate Officers.* 4 vols. Edison, NJ: Castle Books, 1956 ed.

CWD   *The Civil War Dictionary*, ed. Mark M. Boatner. New York: Vintage Books, 1988.

CWNC   *Civil War Naval Chronology, 1861–1865.* 6 vols. Washington, DC: U.S. Government Printing Office Naval History Division, 1971 ed.

DAFS   *Dictionary of American Fighting Ships.* 8 vols. Washington, DC: U.S. Government Printing Office Naval History Division, 1959–1981.

ORA   *The War of the Rebellion: A Compilation of the Official Records of the Union and Confederate Armies.* 128 vols. Washington, DC: U.S. Government Printing Office, 1880–1901.

ORN   *Official Records of the Union and Confederate Navies in the War of the Rebellion.* 31 vols. Washington, DC: U.S. Government Printing Office, 1894–1922.

WCWN   *Warships of the Civil War Navies*, by Paul Silverstone. Annapolis: Naval Institute Press, 1989.

NOTES

CHAPTER ONE

1. Some referred to Scott as being "older than our Constitution." Physically feeble, the general even had a system of ropes and pulleys to get himself in and out of bed. For more information, consult the excellent biography by David W. Jordan, *Winfield Scott: A Soldier's Life* (Bloomington: Indiana University Press, 1988). There is a fine capsule biography in *Who Was Who in the Civil War* (New York: Facts on File, 1988).

2. The river-war phase of the Civil War is amply covered in Jack D. Coombe, *Thunder Along the Mississippi* (New York: Sarpedon Publishers, 1996). A fine treatment is also found in M. F. Force, *From Fort Henry to Corinth* (New York: Charles Scribner's Sons, reprint, 1992). See also H. Allen Gosnell, *Guns On the Western Waters* (Baton Rouge: Louisiana State University Press, 1992).

3. On Magoffin and the Kentucky affair, see John G. Nicolay, *The Outbreak of the Rebellion* (New York: Charles Scribner's Sons, reprint, 1992).

4. The best source of technical information on Civil War navies is WCWN. The old standard on naval information is DAFS.

5. Ulysses S. Grant, *Personal Memoirs of U.S. Grant. Selected Letters 1839–1867* (New York: Literary Classics of the United States, 1990). Grant maintained that contrary to his critics, the battle was neither unnecessary nor barren of results. If the battle had not been fought, Colonel Oglesby and his detachment of 3,000 men would have been captured or destroyed.

6. A fine recent account of Fort Donelson is James J. Hamilton's *The Battle for Fort Donelson* (South Brunswick, New Jersey: Thomas Yoseloff, 1968).

7. Ellet's ram fleet is excellently covered in many sources, including Coombe, *Thunder Along the Mississippi*, pp. 125–27. A detailed explanation of the construction of the rams is found in *Warfare Along the Mississippi: The Letters of Lieutenant-Colonel George E. Currie* (Mount Pleasant, MI: Clark Historical

Collection, Central Michigan University, 1961). This rare work contains a treatment of the letterpress books by Currie, who served under Ellet in the ram fleet.

8. Coombe, *Thunder Along the Mississippi*, p. 219. A fascinating study of the Vicksburg campaign as seen by participants is Richard Wheeler's *The Siege of Vicksburg: The Seven-Month Battle That Sealed the Confederacy's Fate* (New York: HarperCollins, 1978).

CHAPTER TWO

1. *The Life and Writings of Abraham Lincoln,* ed. Philip van Doren Stern (New York: Modern Library, 1940), pp. 661–62.

2. Jefferson Davis, *The Rise and Fall of the Confederate Government* (New York: Thomas Yoseloff, 1958), vol. 1, p. 327.

3. E. B. Potter and Chester W. Nimitz, *Sea Power: A Naval History* (New Jersey: Prentice Hall, 1960), pp. 250–51; Howard P. Nash, Jr., *A Naval History of the Civil War* (New York: A.S. Barnes & Co., 1972), pp. 15–16; ORN, series 1, vol. 4, p. 306.

4. John Niven, *Gideon Welles: Lincoln's Secretary of the Navy* (Baton Rouge: Louisiana State University Press, 1973), pp. 389–90. There is no dearth of material on the man. Other works include Richard S. West, Jr., *Gideon Welles: Lincoln's Navy Department* (Indianapolis: Bobbs-Merrill, 1943), and his own *Diary of Gideon Welles* (Boston: Houghton Mifflin, 1911).

5. For more information on Mallory, see Joseph T. Durkin, *Stephen R. Mallory: Confederate Navy Chief* (Chapel Hill: University of North Carolina Press, 1954). Capsule biographies may be found in *Who Was Who in the Civil War* and the *Dictionary of American Biography*, 22 vols (New York: Scribner's, 1928–1932), vol 1.

6. CWNC, vol. 3, p. 74.

7. CWNC, vol. 2, p. 91.

8. Raimundo Luraghi, *A History of the Confederate Navy* (Annapolis: Naval Institute Press, 1996), p. 348. This work, twenty years in the making, is an amazing and definitive account of the Confederate navy. Luraghi displays an unmistakable admiration for Mallory. See also William M. Fowler, *Under Two Flags: The American Navy in the Civil War* (New York: Norton, 1990), p. 44.

9. Niven, *Gideon Welles*, pp. 359–60; Fowler, *American Navy,* pp. 53–59.

10. WCWN, p. x. The blockade routes were from Charleston to Bermuda, 978 miles, and from Brownsville to Havana, 960 miles.

11. A skilled blockade-runner could make a profit of more than $5,000 on one trip, such as by carrying cotton to the mills in England.

12. CWNC, vol. 1, pp. 1–9.

13. Nicolay, *Outbreak of the Rebellion*, p. 78.

14. Butler, one of the most controversial figures in the Civil War, caused no end of trouble for Lincoln's administration. A good biography is Richard S. West, Jr.'s, *Lincoln's Scapegoat General: A Life of Benjamin F. Butler, 1818–1893* (Boston: Houghton Mifflin, 1965). His orders to command the troop expedition can be found in ORN, series 1, vol. 6, p. 112.

15. An excellent account of the Port Royal expedition is found in Potter and Nimitz, *Sea Power*, pp. 252–54; Fowler, *American Navy*, pp. 71–78; Fletcher Pratt, *A Short History of the Civil War* (New York: Pocket Books, 1956), pp. 45–47; and ORN, series 1, vol. 6, p. 112.

16. On Semmes, see his *Memoirs: My Service Afloat During the War Between the States* (Baltimore: Kelly Piet, 1868).

17. Buchanan has been well documented. Consult Charles Lee Lewis, *Admiral Franklin Buchanan: Fearless Man of Action* (Baltimore: Norman Remington Co., 1929); and *Captains of the Old Steam Navy*, ed. James Bradford (Annapolis: U.S. Naval Institute Press, 1986). The latter contains an excellent short biography by Charles M. Todorich. See also *Who Was Who in the Civil War*.

18. For more on Porter, see his *Incidents and Anecdotes on the Civil War* (New York: Sherman, 1886). Brief biographies are found in CWD and *Who Was Who in the Civil War*.

19. No definitive biography of Hollins is known at this time. A fine capsule version is in CWD, p. 405.

CHAPTER THREE

1. I am indebted to the Pensacola Historical Society for the Stockton B. Colt paper "The Civil War in Florida Waters," which provided me with some of the information on Florida in 1860.

2. CWNC, vol. 1, p. 2.

3. ORA, series 1, vol. 1, p. 332.

4. ORA, series 1, vol. 1, p. 334; *Dateline Pensacola*, published by the Pensacola Historical and Research Library. The latter is an excellent, detailed account of Pensacola's early history. Coastal forts were intended mainly for defensive purposes and did not require much manpower to maintain. In most cases only a caretaker and a small military unit occupied these forts in 1860.

5. Thomas Muir, Jr., and David P. Ogden, *The Fort Pickens Story* and *Dateline Pensacola*, both from the Pensacola Historical Society. The author is indebted to the society for access to these important materials.

6. Lieutenant Colonel Gilman, "With Slemmer in Pensacola Harbor," B&L, vol. 1, pp. 26–28; Slemmer to Cooper, ORA, series 1, vol. 1, pp. 30–32. Slemmer's impatience with the recalcitrant command structure shows through clearly in this series of reports.

7. Gilman, ibid., pp. 30–32. Gilman, who by virtue of the manpower shortage held a number of positions under Lieutenant Slemmer, reported the conference dialogue in full. The dialogue sometimes sounds a bit stagey and may not be accurate.

8. ORN, series 1, vol. 1, pp. 340–41. Slemmer's pride shows clearly through this report.

9. Mallory to Slidell, ORA, series 1, vol. 1, p. 354. Mallory seemed ready to unleash all-out war if the Union reinforcements came. The Union Navy Department took his threats seriously and issued precautionary measures to the commanders aboard the *Brooklyn*. Quite a brouhaha ensued over a reluctance to order landing of troops.

10. Ibid., p. 364; Virginia Parks, Alan Rick, and Norman Simons, "Pensacola in the Civil War," *Pensacola Historical Society Quarterly* (Spring 1978); reissued as a pamphlet in 1995.

11. ORA, series 1, vol. 1, p. 426.

12. An excellent account of salt-making in Florida is in Ella Lamm, "The extent and importance of Federal Raids on Salt-Making in Florida, 1862–1865," *Florida Historical Quarterly, 1862–1865,* vol. 10 (July 1932), pp. 167–85. See also ORN, series 1, vol. 17; ORA, series 1, vol. 14; and CWNC, vols. 1–4.

13. Lamm, ibid., p. 172.

14. Muir and Ogden, *Fort Pickens Story,* pp. 7–9; *Pensacola in the Civil War,* pp. 17–20; CWNC, vol. 1, p. 26; Richard S. West, Jr., *Mr. Lincoln's Navy* (New York: Longmans Green & Co., 1957), p. 71.

15. West, *Mr. Lincoln's Navy,* p. 72.

16. Eagle to McKean, ORN, series 1, vol. 1, p. 18.

17. Quoted in CWNC, vol. 2, p. 24.

18. ORN, series 1, vol. 16, pp. 605–07; WCWN, vol. 1, p. 18.

CHAPTER FOUR

1. B&L, vol. 1, p. 107; Nash, *Naval History of the Civil War,* p. 29; Luraghi, *History of the Confederate Navy,* p. 21.

2. WCWN, p. 24. This is far and away the best work on the Union and Confederate navies in print, aside from DAFS, and it is used extensively in this book.

3. For a description of the Memphis shipbuilding facility, consult Coombe, *Thunder Along the Mississippi*, pp. 128–29.

4. CWNC, vol. 2, pp. 91–92. The iron shortage became so critical for the Confederacy that it launched a concerted effort to collect scrap iron and old train rails for ship plating.

5. B&L, vol. 1, p. 628.

6. For a detailed account of these Confederate weapons, see Milton E. Page's excellent book *Infernal Machines: The Story of Confederate Submarine and Mine Warfare* (Baton Rouge: Louisiana State University Press, 1965). For many references to torpedoes, see ORN, series 1, vol. 4; and Davis, *Rise and Fall of the Confederate Government*, vol. 2, p. 208. Curiously, both sides experimented with land mines made from cannonballs buried in the ground, but later they dismissed them as too uncivilized.

7. ORN, series 1, vol. 23, pp. 593–94.

8. Davis, *Rise and Fall of the Confederate Government*, vol. 2, p. 40.

9. The saga of the *Arkansas* is covered in Coombe, *Thunder Along the Mississippi*, pp. 163–65. See also William N. Still, Jr., *Iron Afloat* (Memphis: Vanderbilt University, 1971), pp. 62–79.

10. David Horner, *The Blockade Runners* (New York: Dodd, Mead & Co., 1968), pp. 13–14.

11. The fascinating but complicated subject of blockade-running is treated in Luraghi's *History of the Confederate Navy*; Horner, *Blockade Runners*; and Philip van Doren Stern's *The Confederate Navy: A Pictorial History* (New York: Da Capo Press, 1992). These excellent reference works are dedicated to the blockade.

12. Horner, *Blockade Runners*, p. 10.

13. Ibid., p. 6; and WCWN, pp. 221–26. The 1,000-ton side-wheeler *Colonel Lamb*, with its 16 knots, outran blockading ships and managed to survive the war.

14. Potter and Nimitz, *Sea Power*, p. 256.

15. Quoted in Stern, *Confederate Navy*, p. 36.

16. Davis, *Rise and Fall of the Confederate Government*, p. 36, pp. 250–51. Both vessels originally had only hull numbers. Rumor had it that it had taken 290 Englishmen to build the *Florida*. Davis cleared this up, maintaining that the hull number of the Laird vessel was 290.

17. Mallory to Semmes, April 18, 1861, ORN, series 1, vol. 1, p. 613.

18. Semmes to Mallory, ORN, series 1, vol. 1, p. 615. Semmes was literally quoting the admonition given him by Mallory in a letter.

19. Semmes to Mallory, ibid., p. 615. See also Chester G. Hearn, *Gray Raiders of the Sea* (Baton Rouge: Louisiana State University Press, 1992), p. 11, and Luraghi, *History of the Confederate Navy*, p. 83.

20. Semmes to Mallory, ibid., p. 615. Interestingly, Semmes ordered copies of an English dictionary, one of which he sent to Mallory, and worked out an ingenious system of codes based on the page numbers and columns in the book.

21. ORA, series 1, vol. 1, p. 491. The only excuse given by the *Brooklyn's* Captain Poor was that he was concerned about being off station and about a report that a strange sail was standing in that direction. The good captain appears to have underestimated the enemy cruiser.

22. Luraghi, *History of the Confederate Navy*, p. 84.

23. Davis, *Rise and Fall of the Confederate Government*, p. 247.

24. CWNC, vol. 1, pp. 228–29; Nash, *Naval History*, p. 274.

25. Hearn, *Gray Raiders of the Sea*, (Baton Rouge, Louisiana State University Press, 1992) p.54.

26. It is interesting to note that the commerce raider concept was effectively used by the Nazis during the early days of World War II. Usually raiders were merchant ships that were heavily armed, but the armament was concealed until a victim was sighted, then the false bulkheads were removed and the guns were unmasked. What appeared to be a noncombatant merchant vessel quickly turned into a deadly warship. These vessels took a frightening toll upon Allied ship convoys, until at last technology and the superior shipbuilding capabilities of the Allies turned the corner, and Nazi raiders were swept from the oceans.

CHAPTER FIVE

1. Onsted to Onsted, Onsted Letter Collection, 1861–1863, Missouri State Historical Society.

2. For the *Carondelet* story, see ORN, series 1, vol. 22; Walke, "Western Flotilla," B&L, vol. 1, pp. 439–40; Nash, *Naval History*, p. 99; and John Fiske, *The Mississippi Valley in the Civil War* (Boston: Houghton Mifflin, 1900), p. 104. Fiske's is by far the most cogent of the accounts. Also consult Coombe, *Thunder Along the Mississippi*, pp. 90–91.

3. Herbert Asbury, *The French Quarter* (New York: Pocket Books, 1996), pp. 75–76; Porter, "The Opening of the Lower Mississippi," B&L, vol. 2, pp. 30–31.

4. Nash, *A Naval History of the Civil War*, p. 122.

5. Fiske, *Mississippi Valley in the Civil War*, pp. 111–13. Fiske points out that in 1891 the city was practically indefensible and that two warships could have

conquered it and pushed all the way upriver to Cairo. But because of the Union propensity for slowness at the time, the Confederacy was able to quickly fortify its works all the way down to the Gulf.

6. Niven, *Gideon Welles,* pp. 299–380; Nash, *Naval History,* pp. 122–23; Bern Anderson, *By Sea and by River: The Naval History of the Civil War* (New York: Alfred A. Knopf, 1962), pp. 116–17.

7. Niven, *Gideon Welles,* p. 382; West, *Mr. Lincoln's Navy,* pp. 134–35.

8. James P. Duffy, *Lincoln's Admiral: The Civil War Campaigns of David Farragut* (New York: John Wiley & Sons, 1997), p. 19.

9. Ibid., p. 22; CWD, pp. 275–76.

10. ORN, series 2, vol. 17, p. 187.

11. Duffy, *Lincoln's Admiral,* p. 60.

12. ORN, series 2, vol. 1, p. 622.

13. Fowler, *American Navy,* p. 117; Duffy, *Lincoln's Admiral,* p. 69. One of the insidious features of this obstruction was the loose chains and cables that were allowed to trail in the water, thus fouling the screws of ships. Fortunately Union commanders managed to cope with this threat.

14. WCWN; B&L, vol. 2, p. 77.

15. ORN, series 2, vol. 1, p. 573. This volume contains the long exchange of information between the Tifts and Mallory.

16. An excellent account of the concept and construction of the *Louisiana* is found in Luraghi, *History of the Confederate Navy,* pp. 120–31.

17. ORN, series 2, vol. 1, p. 598.

18. Davis, *Rise and Fall of the Confederate Government,* vol. 2, p. 227.

19. Duffy, *Lincoln's Admiral,* p. 71. See also Robert W. Patrick, *Jefferson Davis and His Cabinet* (Baton Rouge: Louisiana State University Press, 1961), p. 254.

20. ORN, series 1, vol. 1, p. 610. The governor himself seemed to have no idea of what was involved.

21. *New Orleans Picayune,* January 29, 1862. For responses to the article, see Charles L. Dufour, *The Night the War Was Lost* (New York: Doubleday, 1960), pp. 175–76.

22. Welles to Du Pont, *Report to the Secretary of the Navy in Relation to Armed Vessels* (Washington, DC: U.S. Government Printing Office, 1864).

23. Duffy, *Lincoln's Admiral,* p. 61.

CHAPTER SIX

1. *Who Was Who in America,* Historical Volume 1607–1896 (Chicago: A.N. Marquis Co., 1963), p. 348.

2. Winslow to McKean, ORN, series 1, vol. 16, p. 714. The reconstruction of

the battle in this chapter is based mostly on ORN, vol. 16, which contains, in my opinion, the best and most accurate account.

3. Edward Stokes Miller, *Civil War Sea Battles: Seafights and Shipwrecks in the War Between the States* (Mechanicsburg, PA: Combined Books, reprint 1995), pp. 29–30; Nash, *Naval History,* pp. 70–71; and Fowler, *American Navy,* pp. 96–97; WCWN.

4. Extract from *New Orleans Daily True Delta,* October 15, 1861; ORN, series 1, vol. 16, p. 724.

5. Ibid; abstract log of *Water Witch,* p. 724.

6. ORN, series 1, vol. 16, p. 723.

7. Pope to McKean, ibid., p. 699.

8. French to McKean, ibid., p. 712.

9. French report, ibid., p. 713.

10. Ibid., p. 714.

11. Ibid., p. 714.

12. Ibid., Handy report, p. 109.

13. Pope to McKean, McKean to Pope, in ibid., pp. 711–12; Miller, *Civil War Sea Battles,* p. 35. It is difficult to fathom the confusion among the Union ship commanders at the Head of the Passes.

14. Handy report, ORN, series 1, vol. 16, p. 721.

15. Ibid., p. 721.

16. *New Orleans Daily True Delta,* October 15, 1861.

17. Pope to McKean, ORN, series 1, vol. 16, p. 711.

CHAPTER SEVEN

1. Dean S. Thomas, *Cannons: An Introduction to Civil War Artillery* (Gettysburg, PA: Thomas Publications, 1985), pp. 49–50. This is one of the most informative publications on Civil War weaponry.

2. Bartlett, "The *Brooklyn* at the Passage of the Forts," B&L, vol. 2, p. 56.

3. Duffy, *Lincoln's Admiral,* pp. 61–68; Chester G. Hearn, *Capture of New Orleans* (Baton Rouge: Louisiana State University Press, 1995); ORN, series 1, vol. 18, pp. 64–68.

4. Duffy, *Lincoln's Admiral,* p. 62; Fiske, *Mississippi Valley in the Civil War,* pp. 120–21.

5. Log of the *Portsmouth,* entry for April 8, 1862, courtesy Historic New Orleans Collection at the Research Center, Williams Foundation, New Orleans. Many officer-of-the-day entries in the ship's log bear the stamp of a man with a romantic soul.

6. Farragut's concern for his men is aptly illustrated in an August 16, 1863,

letter to a governmental tribunal concerning Ensign Charles D. Jones, who was found guilty of sleeping on watch. Farragut intervened on behalf of the hapless ensign and asked for mercy, because the ensign "had already suffered some punishment in the mortification that his fault occasioned him." The letter appeared in the Farragut letter book, Western Gulf Blockading Squadron, dated August 1, 1863 to December 14, 1863, courtesy Historic New Orleans Collection, Research Center, Williams Foundation.

7. *Portsmouth* journal. One cannot help but wonder where a "first-class hotel" would be found in a ramshackle town built mostly on stilts.

8. Bartlett, B&L, vol. 2, p. 58.

9. Alden to Farragut, ORN, series 1, vol. 18, p. 199.

10. Farragut to Bailey, ORN, series 1, vol. 18, p. 132. Captain T. Bailey was commander of the First Division. Farragut's trusty second-in-command, Commander Henry H. Bell, was commander of the Second Division.

11. Farragut, general order, ORN, series 1, vol. 18, pp. 133–34.

12. This proposition can be read in its entirety in ibid., pp. 133–34.

13. *Portsmouth* journal, entry for April 16, 1862. Note the colorful descriptions, which the unknown officer of the day could not resist.

14. Quoted in Davis, *Rise and Fall of the Confederate Government*, p. 213.

15. Ibid., p. 213.

CHAPTER EIGHT

1. From *Plaquemines Parish, Fort Jackson*, published by the Plaquemines Parish Commission, 1962, p. 3. The author is indebted to Wayne Everard, archivist, Louisiana Division, New Orleans Public Library, for a rare copy of this important publication.

2. "Fort St. Philip Budget Request, 1860," courtesy of the Louisiana Division, New Orleans Public Library.

3. *Plaquemines Parish, Fort Jackson*, p. 4.

4. Davis, *Rise and Fall of the Confederate Government*, vol. 2, p. 211; Hearn, *Capture of New Orleans*, p. 67; Duffy, *Lincoln's Admiral*, p. 67; and Dufour, *Night the War Was Lost*, p. 119. Among the sources there seems to be some discrepancy as to the number of guns in each fort. I am inclined toward the figures in Davis and Hearn.

5. Davis, *Rise and Fall of the Confederate Government*, vol. 2, p. 213.

6. Alfred Thayer Mahan, *Admiral Farragut* (New York: Haskell House, reprint 1968); Duffy, *Lincoln's Admiral*, p. 69.

7. Lovell to Benjamin, ORA, vol. 6, pp. 560, 575; Duffy, *Lincoln's Admiral*, pp. 78–79; and Fiske, *Mississippi Valley in the Civil War*, pp. 118–19.

8.   Quoted in David D. Porter, "The Fight for New Orleans, April, 1862," *In Their Own Words: Civil War Commanders* (New York: Berkley Publishing Group, 1995), pp. 80–81; CWNC, vol. 2, p. 42. Bell made a note of concern to the effect that two guns on St. Philip "reached downriver as far as any from Fort Jackson."

9.   ORN, series 1, vol. 18, pp. 684–86; Dufour, *Night the War Was Lost*, pp. 222–23.

10. Davis, *Rise and Fall of the Confederate Government*, p. 214.

11. Dufour, quoting from Porter's manuscript journal, in *Night the War Was Lost*, p. 225.

12. Ibid., p. 226.

13. *Portsmouth* journal, entry for April 18, 1862. (Pages in the journal are not numbered.)

14. Farragut, report to Welles, ORN, series 1, vol. 18, p. 135.

15. John Hart diary, entry for April 16, 1862, courtesy Historic New Orleans Collection, Research Center, Williams Foundation.

16. Porter, "Fight For New Orleans," *In Their Own Words,* p. 82.

17. *Portsmouth* journal, entry for April 17, 1862.

18. *New Orleans Picayune,* April 24, 1862, New Orleans Public Library Archives.

19. Moore to Davis, Davis to Moore, ORN, series 1, vol. 6, pp. 650, 878; Dufour, in *Night the War Was Lost,* comments that there was no logical reason for President Davis to have been so out of touch with the situation at New Orleans. But Davis, like his advisers, still believed the greater threat lay upriver.

20. CWNC, vol. 2, p. 51; Duffy, *Lincoln's Admiral,* p. 79; ORN, series 1, vol. 2, p. 135. Farragut's last quote reveals his affection for Bell. They were more than just flag officer and chief of staff; they were close friends for the rest of their lives.

21. Welles to Farragut, Barnard's memorandum, ORN, series 1, vol. 18, pp. 14–23; Dufour, *Night the War Was Lost,* pp. 219–22.

22. Fiske, *Mississippi Valley in the Civil War,* pp. 122–23. Fiske, who published this venerable book in 1900, was still close enough to the war to draw upon the accounts of many participants and therefore is remarkably accurate, as later research has revealed.

23. Davis to Baily, ORN, series 1, vol. 18, p. 137.

24. Farragut, general order regarding plan of attack, ORN, series 1, vol. 18, p. 162.

25. *New Orleans Crescent,* April 21, 1862; Dufour, *Night the War Was Lost,* p. 242.

26. B&L, vol. 2, p. 41.

27. Mahan, *Admiral Farragut,* p. 134.

CHAPTER NINE

1. ORN, series 1, vol. 18, p. 156; CWNC, vol. 2, p. 58; Duffy, *Lincoln's Admiral,* p. 83; Stern, *Confederate Navy,* p. 98.

2. Duffy, *Lincoln's Admiral,* p. 83.

3. *Portsmouth* journal, April 24, 1862, 2:00 P.M.

4. Based on ORN, series 1, vol. 18, p. 166; Hearn, *Capture of New Orleans,* p. 269; and CWNC, vol. 2, p. 55.

5. Porter, "Opening of the Mississippi," *In Their Own Words,* p. 85.

6. *Portsmouth* journal, April 24, 1862.

7. John Hart diary, entry for April 24, 1862. According to Hart, the *Portsmouth* was struck by two 68-pound solid shots, fatally wounding one man and doing enough damage to force the vessel to drop downstream to the protection of the mortar schooners.

8. George Perkins, "Commodore Farragut Captures New Orleans," *The Blue and the Gray,* ed. Henry Steele Commager, (New York: Meridian, 1973), vol. 2, p. 20.

9. Commager Ibid., p. 209.

10. *Cayuga* log, ORN, series 1, vol. 18, p. 336.

11. Commager Ibid., p. 336.

12. Boggs to Farragut, ORN, series 1, vol. 18, pp. 210–11; B&L, vol. 2, pp. 42–43; Hearn, *Capture of New Orleans,* p. 222.

13. Craven to Craven, ORN, series 1, vol. 18, pp. 195–96. That night the *Brooklyn* was being conned by Lieutenant George Dewey because Captain Craven was suffering from poor eyesight.

14. Warley to Mallory, ORN, series 1, vol. 18, p. 336.

15. Craven to Craven, ORN, series 1, vol. 18, p. 198.

16. Farragut, report to Welles, ORN, series 1, vol. 18, p. 153; Stern, *Confederate Navy,* p. 98.

17. Farragut, report to Welles, ibid, pp. 153–54; Hearn, *Capture of New Orleans,* p. 227.

18. Bartlett, "The *Brooklyn* in the Passage of the Forts, " B&L, vol. 2, p. 66; ORN, series 1, vol. 18, pp. 205–06; Duffy, *Lincoln's Admiral,* p. 87; Porter, *In Their Own Words,* p. 89; and Fiske, *Mississippi Valley in the Civil War,* p. 123.

19. WCWN, p. 206; Ivan Musicant, *Divided Waters: The Naval History of the Civil War* (New York: HarperCollins, 1995), p. 228.

20. Quoted in Davis, *Rise and Fall of the Confederate Government,* p. 215.

21. Niven, *Gideon Welles,* p. 386.

CHAPTER TEN

1. CWNC, vol. 2, p. 54.

2. Davis, *Rise and Fall of the Confederate Government*, p. 222; Hearn, *Capture of New Orleans*, p. 238.

3. Davis, *Rise and Fall of the Confederate Government*, p. 862.

4. ORA, series 3, vol. 1, p. 862.

5. Quoted in William Meredeth, "Farragut's Capture of New Orleans," B&L, vol. 2, p. 72.

6. Alden to Farragut, ORN, series 1, vol. 18, p. 198.

7. Farragut, report to Welles, ORN, series 1, vol. 18, p. 158; Fowler, *American Navy*, p. 123; Nash, *Naval History*, p. 124; Duffy, *Lincoln's Admiral*, p. 94; Topographic Map of Louisiana, United States Geological Survey.

8. Farragut, report to Welles, ORN, series 1, vol. 18, p. 158.

9. Asbury, *French Quarter*, p. 166.

10. Farragut, report to Welles, ORN, series 1, vol. 18, p. 158.

11. Ibid.

12. ORN, series 1, vol. 18, pp. 351–52; Still, *Iron Afloat*, pp. 58–59.

13. George Cable, "New Orleans Before the Capture," B&L, vol. 2, pp. 20–21; Perkins, in Commager, *Blue and Gray*, vol. 2, pp. 298–309.

14. Perkins, in Commager, *Blue and Gray*, p. 211.

15. *New Orleans Daily Picayune*, April 27, 1862.

16. Ibid., April 29, 1862.

17. Farragut, report to Welles, ORN, series 1, vol. 18, p. 155; Albert Kautz, "Incidents in the Occupation of New Orleans," B&L, vol. 2, pp. 91–92. Kautz reported that the crowd pushed children in front of his marines, daring them to shoot.

18. Farragut, report to Welles, ORN, series 1, vol. 18, p. 155; Duffy, *Lincoln's Admiral*, p. 108.

19. *New Orleans Picayune*, April 30, 1862. This article would be heart-wrenching, were it not for the writer's ridiculous, pedantic style.

20. Ibid., April 29, 1862. This long diatribe becomes wearisome because Admiral Farragut would obviously never have bombarded a helpless city, killing innocent civilians. Still, one wonders what he would have done, had the shore party been harmed in any way.

21. Julia LeGrand journal, in Commager, *Blue and Gray*, vol. 2, p. 212.

22. Musicant, *Divided Waters*, p. 235.

23. ORN, series 1, vol. 18, p. 274; Still, *Iron Afloat*, p. 60. Commodore Mitchell maintained that he was never informed of the surrender, while he was trying to get the *Louisiana*'s machinery in working order.

24. John Hart diary, entry for April 29, 1862.

25. *Portsmouth* journal, entry for April 29, 1862.

26. George Strong, "The Rebellion Record," in Commager, *Blue and Gray,* vol. 2, pp. 214–15.

27. Walton Glenny Family Papers, courtesy Historic New Orleans Collection, Research Center, Williams Foundation.

28. Davis, *Rise and Fall of the Confederate Government,* p. 232.

29. Ibid., p. 225.

30. Niven, *Gideon Welles,* p. 387.

31. Fiske, *Mississippi Valley in the Civil War,* p. 132.

CHAPTER ELEVEN

1. Hearn, *Gray Raiders of the Sea,* p. xii.

2. Quoted in Stern, *Confederate Navy,* p. 114.

3. Stephen T. Foster, *Blockade Running* (New York, Atlas Editions, 1993).

4. Quoted in Otto Eisenschiml and Ralph Newman, *The American Iliad* (Indianapolis: Bobbs-Merrill, 1947), pp. 363–64.

5. CWNC, vol. 2, p. 98.

6. Extract from *Richmond Dispatch,* January 2, 1862, ORN, series 1, vol. 17, p. 13.

7. Ibid., p.13.

8. Biographical information on Maffitt can be found in CWD, p. 500; *Who Was Who in the Civil War,* p. 427; Emma Maffitt, *The Life and Services of John Maffitt* (New York: Neal Publishing, 1906); and his journal in ORN, series 1, vol. 1, pp. 766–67.

9. Maffitt journal extracts, ORN, series 1, vol. 1; Musicant, *Divided Waters,* p. 335; and Hearn, *Gray Raiders of the Sea,* p. 61.

10. *Florida* journal, Preble to Welles, ORN, series 1, vol. 1, p. 115.

11. Preble to Farragut, ORN, series 1, vol. 1, p. 437.

12. Niven, *Gideon Welles,* p. 430.

13. Welles to Preble, ORN, series 1, vol. 1, p. 437. Welles admitted that Preble had been led to believe *Florida* was a British ship; Preble's awareness of the sensitivity between the two countries, resulting from the *Trent* affair, would naturally have given him pause before taking aggressive action toward her.

14. Lincoln to U.S. Congress, ORN, series 1, vol. 1, p. 459.

15. Niven, *Gideon Welles,* p. 430.

CHAPTER TWELVE

1. Ralph Volney Harlow, *The United States: From Wilderness to World Power* (New York: Henry Holt & Co., 1949), p. 358.

2. Curiously little biographical information on Renshaw is available. There is one short piece in Donald S. Frazier's *Cottonclads! The Battle of Galveston and the Defense of the Texas Coast* (Fort Worth, TX: Ryan Place, 1996), p. 26.

3. WCWN.

4. Some of the early Civil War maps place Pelican Island far to the northwest of Galveston. In reality it is directly across the channel from the city, resembling a large basketball rebounding from a hit by the bat of Galveston Island. The most accurate Civil War map is that by Farragut in ORN, series 1, vol. 19, p. 450.

5. Frazier, *Cottonclads!* pp. 29–30.

6. CWD, p. 501; *Who Was Who in the Civil War,* p. 329; *Webster's American Military Biographies* (Springfield, MA: Merriam Publishers, 1978), p. 269.

7. Quoted in Magruder report, ORN, series 1, vol. 19, pp. 471–72.

8. "Naval Engagement at Galveston," ibid., p. 469.

9. Ibid., p. 469; Shelby Foote, *The Civil War: A Narrative* (New York: Random House, 1963), vol. 2, p. 58.

10. Wilson to Farragut, ORN, series 1, vol. 19, p. 439.

11. Farragut, report to Welles, ibid., p. 448; Wilson to Farragut, ibid., p. 439; Frazier, *Cottonclads!* p. 75.

12. Farragut, report to Welles, ibid., p. 447.

13. "Naval Engagement at Galveston," Ibid., p. 469; Miller, *Civil War Sea Battles,* p. 167.

14. Davis to Magruder, ORN, series 1, vol. 19, p. 470.

15. Quoted in CWNC, vol. 3, p. 4.

16. Niven, *Gideon Welles,* pp. 429–30.

17. Farragut to Welles, ORN, series 1, vol. 19, p. 440.

18. Duffy, *Lincoln's Admiral,* p. 164.

19. Foote, *Civil War,* p. 19; Duffy, *Lincoln's Admiral,* p. 164.

20. WCWN, p. 209. The unmistakable English cut of the jib of Semmes's ship fooled Union officers many times, usually resulting in disaster for them.

21. Raphael Semmes, *The Confederate Raider Alabama* (Greenwich, CT: Fawcett, 1972), p. 164.

22. Partridge statement, ORN, series 1, vol. 17, p. 510.

23. Semmes, *Confederate Raider Alabama,* p. 166. Kell was told to reply because of his "powerful, clarion voice."

24. Bell to Farragut, ORN, series 1, vol. 17, p. 507.

25. Ibid., p. 507.

26. Davis, *Rise and Fall of the Confederate Government*, p. 236.

27. CWNC vol. 3, p. 136; Banks to Lincoln, ORN, series 1, vol. 20, pp. 534–35.

28. Banks to Halleck, ORN, series 1, vol. 20, p. 533.

29. Ibid., Crocker to Welles, p. 544.

30. Davis, *Rise and Fall of the Confederate Government*, pp. 238–39.

31. Stern, *Confederate Navy*, p. 125.

CHAPTER THIRTEEN

1. The Vicksburg and Port Hudson campaigns are covered in Coombe, *Thunder Along the Mississippi*. Several excellent books on Vicksburg are available. On Port Hudson consult Edward Cunningham, *The Port Hudson Campaign, 1862–1863* (Baton Rouge: Louisiana State University Press, 1994).

2. Ulysses S. Grant, *Personal Memoirs, 1839–1865* (New York: Library of America, 1990), p. 338. Grant blamed Halleck for the denial of the proposed Mobile campaign, saying that it was easier for Halleck "to refuse a favor than grant one." Anderson, *By Sea and by River*, p. 236.

3. Abraham Lincoln, *Speeches and Writings, 1856–1859* (New York: Library of America, 1989), vol. 2, p. 490.

4. Grant, *Memoirs*, p. 388. Grant believed that the government's obsession with occupying Texas could be satisfied by sending a garrison to Brownsville on the Rio Grande River.

5. CWNC, vol. 4, p. 112; Musicant, *Divided Waters*, p. 307.

6. CWNC, vol. 3, p. 160. Bell was sadly misinformed on the *Tennessee*. She might have been "strong," but she was far from "fast."

7. Ibid., p. 160. This publication is one of the finest and most informative sources of Civil War naval activities in print.

8. Ibid., p. 116; Duffy, *Lincoln's Admiral*, p. 218.

9. CWNC, vol. 3, p. 126; Duffy, *Lincoln's Admiral*, p. 220; Musicant, *Divided Waters*, p. 307. Another momentous and happy event during Farragut's stay in New York was that his son Loyall was accepted into the Naval Academy.

10. Quoted in CWNC, vol. 3, p. 126. Charles Lewis, *David Glasgow Farragut* (Annapolis: Naval Institute Press, 1941–1942) is a penetrating biography of the famed naval hero.

11. Welles to Farragut, Hurlburt to Welles, ORN, series 1, vol. 21, pp. 21–25.

12. *Alabama: A Guide to the Deep South*, American Guide Series (New York: Hastings House, 1941); *Alabama and Mississippi: Confederate Military His-*

tory, ed. Clement A. Evans (Secaucus, NJ: Blue and Gray Press, 1899). Evans's venerable work is very reliable.

13. For information on Buchanan, consult Charles L. Lewis, *Admiral Franklin Buchanan: Fearless Man of Action* (Baltimore: Norman Remington & Co., 1929). For a short biography, see *Who Was Who in the Civil War*, pp. 83–84.

14. Technical information on the *Tennessee* came from: WCWN, p. 208; Chester G. Hearn, *Mobile Bay and the Mobile Campaign* (Jefferson, NC: McFarland & Co., 1993); Still, *Iron Afloat*, p. 195. Some sources say that she had two 32-pounders, but others negate that.

15. WCWN, pp. 219, 236; Francis X. Walter, *The Naval Battle of Mobile Bay and Franklin Buchanan on the Tennessee* (Birmingham, AL: Prester Meridian Press, 1993). Walter's very readable little book is full of information.

16. CWNC, vol. 3, p. 61.

17. Charles Lee Lewis, *Famous American Naval Officers* (Boston: L.C. Page & Co., 1924), p. 246; Walter, *Naval Battle of Mobile Bay*, p. 20.

18. Quoted in Musicant, *Divided Waters*, p. 308.

19. Ibid, p. 310; Duffy, *Lincoln's Admiral*, p. 229.

20. CWNC, vol. 3, pp. 58–59.

CHAPTER FOURTEEN

1. *Mobile Advertiser and Register*, August 3, 1864.

2. Ibid., January 16, 1864.

3. James Monroe, *Message from the President of the United States to Congress upon the Subject of Fortifications on Dauphin Island and Mobile Point, March 26, 1822* (Washington, D.C.: Gales and Seaton, 1822), courtesy Fort Gaines Archives, Dauphin Island Park and Beach Board.

4. Estimates of the number of guns at Fort Morgan vary from 45 to 79, including the water battery. Historian J.T. Scharf puts the number at 45 guns, but R.B. Hitchcock's report in ORN, series 1, vol. 19, puts the number at 67, including 11 guns at the lighthouse to the southwest of the fort. Based on much research, I agree with Blanton Blankenship, historic site manager at Fort Morgan, that the number was between 35 and 40. Incidentally, some sketches made before and after the battle show three lighthouses, but research reveals only one lighthouse outside the fort.

5. These figures came from a report by General Dabney Maury to James A. Seddon, Confederate secretary of war, in ORN, series 1, vol. 21, pp. 565–66.

6. A large gouge from a Union shot is still visible in the southwestern bastion of the fort. The shot came from gunboat *Chickasaw* on August 6, 1864.

7. *Mobile Advertiser and Register,* March 18, 1864, courtesy Fort Gaines Archives, Dauphin Island Park and Beach Board. Since the Civil War some of the island's western end has been washed away by hurricanes and storms.

8. Private Rufe Dooley, letter dated August 10, 1864, courtesy Fort Gaines Archives.

9. *Mobile Evening Telegraph,* February 16, 1864.

10. W.C. Walker Papers, letter dated April 13, 1864, courtesy Fort Morgan Archives.

11. Ibid., June 26, 1864.

12. Dr. James T. Gee, post dentist, letter to his wife dated July 28, 1864, courtesy Fort Morgan Archives.

13. "The Civil War Letters of Robert Tarleton," ed. William B. Still, Jr., *Alabama Historical Quarterly,* vol. 32 (Spring and Summer 1970).

14. Ibid., letter dated May 8, 1864.

15. Ibid., letter dated May 20, 1864.

16. Lieutenant William J. McIntire, 11th Illinois Infantry Volunteers, letter to Mrs. Johnson dated March 4, 1865, courtesy Fort Gaines Archives, Dauphin Island Park and Beach Board.

17. L. Taylor, letter dated September 14, 1864, courtesy Fort Gaines Archives. Taylor was one of the occupying troops at Fort Gaines.

CHAPTER FIFTEEN

1. Milton F. Perry, *Infernal Machines* (Baton Rouge: Louisiana State University Press, 1965), pp. 32–33; Coombe, *Thunder Along the Mississippi,* p. 173.

2. Hitchcock to Farragut, ORN, series 1, vol. 19; Perry, ibid. p. 40.

3. CWNC, vol. 3, p. 63.

4. Ibid., p. 65.

5. Duffy, *Lincoln's Admiral,* pp. 224–25; Fowler, *American Navy,* p. 237; ORN, series 1, vol. 21, pp. 91–92. On March 1, the bombardment fleet fired 564 shells at the fort, of which only 23 struck the island. The damage they caused was so minor that it was repaired in 10 minutes, according to an eyewitness.

6. CWNC, vol. 4, p. 82.

7. "Civil War Letters of Robert Tarleton," *Alabama Historical Quarterly,* vol. 32 (Spring and Summer, 1970), p. 62.

8. CWNC, vol. 3, p. 89.

9. ORN, series 1, vol. 21, pp. 397–98.

10. CWNC, vol. 4, p. 93.

11. ORN, series 1, vol. 21, p. 405; Nash, *Naval History,* pp. 239–40.

12. W. C. Walker Papers, letter dated August 1, 1864, courtesy Fort Morgan Archives.

13. *Mobile Advertiser and Register,* August 4, 1864.

14. Captain Whiting to *Mobile Advertiser and Register,* undated, courtesy Fort Morgan Archives.

15. Hurieosco Austill, "Fort Morgan—August, 1864," *Alabama Historical Quarterly* (Summer 1945), p. 255, courtesy Fort Morgan Archives.

16. Coombe, *Thunder Along the Mississippi,* pp. 151–61. This work narrates the story of the *Arkansas,* based on research at her birthplace, Yazoo City, Mississippi. It contains much hitherto unpublished material.

CHAPTER SIXTEEN

1. Farragut, report to Welles, ORN, series 1, vol. 21, p. 405.

2. Joseph Wilkinson diary, entry dated August 5, 1864, courtesy Fort Morgan Archives.

3. Ibid.

4. M.M. Whiting, letter to *Mobile Register,* courtesy Fort Morgan Archives.

5. Buchanan to Mallory, ORN, series 1, vol. 21, p. 576; James D. Johnston, "The Ram *Tennessee* at Mobile Bay," B&L, vol. 4, p. 402.

6. Johnston ibid., p. 576; Austill, "Fort Morgan," p. 257.

7. Duffy, *Lincoln's Admiral,* pp. 239–40.

8. J. Crittenden Watson, "The Lashing of Admiral Farragut in the Rigging," B&L, pp. 406–407; CWNC, vol. 4, p. 95; Loyall Farragut, *The Life and Letters of David Glasgow Farragut, First Admiral of the United States Navy* (New York: Appleton, 1879). There is some controversy over this incident. Most historians, including the admiral's son, agree that Farragut bowed to the wisdom of being lashed to the shrouds, thus freeing both of his hands. Lieutenant Commander Joseph Marthon, who was in charge of a howitzer on the maintop, attested to the fact that the admiral lashed himself to the rigging.

9. Austill, "Fort Morgan," p. 257.

10. ORN, series 1, vol. 21, p. 508; John Coddington Kinney, "Farragut at Mobile Bay," B&L, vol. 4, pp. 388–89.

11. ORN, series 1, vol. 21, pp. 442, 445, 490–92; Kinney, "Farragut at Mobile Bay," ibid., p. 388. One source offers that Collins begged to go up the ladder first, claiming he had five little children, but most scholars doubt that story. Today the *Tecumseh,* with her captain and most of her crew, still lies in 29 feet of water, about 300 yards from Fort Morgan, marked by a buoy. In 1967

a team of salvage personnel examined her remains and laid plans to salvage her, but unfortunately the cost proved prohibitive.

12. James Alden, report to Farragut, ORN, series 1, vol. 21, p. 445.

13. A great deal of speculation as to what Farragut shouted has been tossed around. There is no mention of it in ORN or any other government source; therefore it must have been some sort of familiar command. Some sources say that the admiral replied to the question as to how many bells should be rung: "Four bells, eight bells, sixteen bells—damn it! I don't care how many bells you ring." Perhaps, because of the din of battle, Farragut's exact words may never be known. I agree with James P. Duffy that he said: "Damn the torpedoes!" then added, "Four bells, Drayton." To the captain of the *Metacomet* alongside, he shouted, "Full speed ahead!" Over the years the two separate commands became compressed.

14. Kinney, "Farragut at Mobile Bay," B&L, vol. 4, p. 391; Hearn, *Mobile Bay and the Mobile Bay Campaign*, p. 92; Farragut, report to Welles, ORN, series 1, vol. 21, p. 417.

15. Whiting, letter to *Mobile Register*; ORN, series 1, vol. 21, pp. 478–80.

16. Alden, report to Farragut, ORN, series 1, vol. 21, p. 405.

17. Buchanan report, ORN, series 1, vol. 21, p. 445.

18. *Metacomet* log; Farragut to Welles, ORN, series 1, vol. 21, p. 417.

19. Hearn, *Mobile Bay and the Mobile Bay Campaign*, p. 98; Still, *Iron Afloat*, p. 209.

20. CWNC, vol. 4, p. 45; Austill, "Fort Morgan," p. 258.

21. Kinney, "Farragut at Mobile Bay," B&L, vol. 4, p. 395.

22. Buchanan to Mallory, ORN, series 1, vol. 21, p. 580; Musicant, *Divided Waters*, p. 320; Duffy, *Lincoln's Admiral*, p. 250.

23. Buchanan report, ORN, series 1, vol. 21, p. 577.

24. Musicant, *Divided Waters*, p. 321.

25. Kinney, "Farragut at Mobile Bay," B&L, vol. 4, p. 397.

26. Harrison, report to Buchanan, ORN, series 1, vol. 21, pp. 584–85.

CHAPTER SEVENTEEN

1. CWNC, vol. 3, p. 97.

2. Austill, "Fort Morgan," p. 259.

3. *Richmond Enquirer*, August 8, 1864; ORN, series 1, vol. 21, p. 441.

4. *Mobile Advertiser and Register*, August 9, 1864.

5. Ibid., August 11, 1864.

6. Maury to Cooper, ORN, series 1, vol. 21, p. 564.

7. Page to Maury, ORN, series 1, vol. 21, p. 561; *Mobile Advertiser and Register,* August 9, 1864.

8. Anderson to *Mobile Advertiser and Register,* September 22, 1864, courtesy Fort Morgan Archives.

9. CWNC, vol. 3, p. 100; Austill, "Fort Morgan," p. 259.

10. Wilkinson diary, August 5, 1864.

11. Page to Farragut and Granger, ORN, series 1, vol. 21, p. 563, Austill; "Fort Morgan," pp. 258–60; R. L. Page, "Defense of Fort Morgan," B&L, vol. 4, p. 409.

12. Austill, "Fort Morgan," p. 260; Wilkinson diary, August 9, 1864.

13. Wilkinson diary, August 15, 1864; Napoleon Smith Papers, courtesy Fort Morgan Archives, Fort Morgan, Alabama, p. 1.

14. Napoleon Smith, "Siege of Fort Morgan, Alabama."

15. Page report, CWNC, vol. 3, p. 108; Page, B&L, vol. 4, p. 411.

16. Lincoln proclamation, ORN, series 1, vol. 21, p. 543.

17. Welles to Farragut, ORN, series 1, vol. 21, p. 542.

18. Whiting to Maury, ORN, series 1, vol. 21, p. 598.

19. Napoleon Smith Papers, p. 1. Smith's matter-of-fact style attests to the general agreement among the fort's personnel as to the fate of the *Tecumseh.*

20. Gaines to Davis, ORN, series 1, vol. 21, p. 597.

21. Mallory to Davis, ORN, series 1, vol. 21, p. 597.

22. Vass letter to *Mobile Advertiser and Register,* dated August 11, 1864, courtesy Fort Morgan Archives.

23. Davis, *Rise and Fall of the Confederate Government,* vol. 2, p. 209.

CHAPTER EIGHTEEN

1. Mark McLaughlin and Curt Johnson, *Civil War Battles* (New York: Crown Publishers, 1977), p. 134.

2. Luraghi, *History of the Confederate Navy,* p. 346.

3. Grant, *Memoirs,* p. 348. Grant's thoughts, after the fall of Vicksburg, were to take his huge army and march on Mobile.

4. Luraghi, *History of the Confederate Navy,* p. 346.

5. CWNC, vol. 4, p. iii.

6. *Why the North Won the Civil War,* ed. David Donald (New York: Macmillan, 1960), p. 35. This short work on the economic, diplomatic, social, and military aspects of the antagonists is very informative.

BIBLIOGRAPHY

GOVERNMENT SOURCES

Civil War Naval Chronology, 1861–1865. 6 vols. Washington, DC: U.S. Government Printing Office, Naval History Division, 1971.

Dictionary of American Fighting Ships. 8 vols. Washington, DC: U.S. Government Printing Office, Naval History Division, 1959–1981.

Message and Documents: Message of the President of the U.S., Accompanying Documents at the 2nd Session of the 38th Congress. Washington, DC: U.S. Government Printing Office, U.S. Navy Department, 1864.

Official Records of the Union and Confederate Navies in the War of the Rebellion. 31 vols. Washington, DC: U.S. Government Printing Office, 1894–1922.

Report of the Secretary of the Navy in Relation to Armed Vessels. Washington, DC: U.S. Government Printing Office, 1864.

The War of the Rebellion: A Compilation of the Official Records of the Union and Confederate Armies. 128 vols. Washington, DC: U.S. Government Printing Office, 1880–1901.

JOURNALS

Alabama Historical Quarterly
Florida Historical Quarterly
Journal, U.S.S. *Portsmouth*
Pensacola Historical Society Quarterly

NEWSPAPERS

Mobile Advertiser and Register
Mobile Evening Telegraph
New Orleans Daily Crescent

New Orleans Daily Picayune
Richmond Enquirer

MAGAZINES
America's Civil War
Civil War History
Civil War Times Illustrated
Military History

BOOKS
Alabama: A Guide to the Deep South. American Guide Series. Writer's Program. New York: Hastings House, 1941.

Alabama and Mississippi: Confederate Military History, ed. Clement A. Evans. 13 vols. Secaucus, NJ: Blue and Gray Press, 1899.

American Heritage Battle Maps of the Civil War. Tulsa, OK: Council Oaks Books, 1992.

Anderson, Bern. *By Sea and by River: The Naval History of the Civil War.* New York: Alfred A. Knopf, 1962.

Angle, Paul M. *A Pictorial History of the Civil War.* New York: Doubleday & Co., 1967.

Asbury, Herbert. *The French Quarter.* New York: Pocket Books, 1996.

Atlas of the Civil War, ed. James McPherson. New York: Macmillan, 1994.

Battles and Leaders of the Civil War. 4 vols. New York: Thomas Yoseloff, 1956.

Beach, Edward L. *United States Navy, 200 Years.* New York: Henry Holt & Co., 1986.

Boatner, Mark M. *The Civil War Dictionary.* New York: Vintage Books, 1988.

Carnegie, Dale. *The Unknown Lincoln.* New York: Pocket Books, 1949.

Catton, Bruce. *Reflections on the Civil War.* Garden City, NY: Doubleday, 1981.

———. *This Hallowed Ground.* New York: Pocket Books, 1956.

Chaitin, Peter M. *The Coastal War: Chesapeake Bay to the Rio Grande.* Civil War Series. New York: Time-Life Books, 1984.

Commager, Henry Steele. *The Blue and the Gray.* 2 vols. New York: Meridian, 1973.

Coombe, Jack D. *Thunder Along the Mississippi.* New York: Sarpedon Publishers, 1996.

Craven, Amory. *The Coming of the Civil War.* Chicago: University of Chicago Press, 1966.

Davis, Jefferson. *The Rise and Fall of the Confederate Government.* 2 vols. New York: Thomas Yoseloff, 1958.

Duffy, James P. *Lincoln's Admiral: The Civil War Campaigns of David Farragut.* New York: John Wiley & Sons, 1997.

Dufour, Charles L. *The Night the War Was Lost.* New York: Doubleday & Co., 1960.

Durkin, Joseph T. *Stephen R. Mallory: Confederate Navy Chief.* Chapel Hill: University of North Carolina Press, 1954.

Eisenschiml, Otto. *Why the Civil War?* ed. Richard B. Morris. New York: Bobbs-Merrill, 1958.

———— and Ralph Newman. *The American Iliad.* Indianapolis: Bobbs-Merrill, 1947.

Farragut, Loyall. *The Life and Letters of David Glasgow Farragut, First Admiral of the United States Navy.* New York: Appleton, 1879.

Fiske, John. *The Mississippi Valley in the Civil War.* Boston: Houghton Mifflin, 1900.

Fowler, William M. *Under Two Flags: The American Navy in the Civil War.* New York: Norton 1990.

Frazier, Donald S. *Cottonclads! The Battle of Galveston and the Defense of the Texas Coast.* Fort Worth, TX: Ryan Place, 1996.

Gosnell, H. Allen. *Guns on the Western Waters.* Baton Rouge: Louisiana State University Press, 1949.

————. *Papers of U.S. Grant.* Carbondale: Southern Illinois University Press, 1979.

Grant, Ulysses S. *Personal Memoirs.* New York: Library of America, 1990.

Hattaway, Herman, and Archer Jones. *How the North Won: A Military History of the Civil War.* Urbana: University of Illinois Press, 1983.

Hearn, Chester G. *Capture of New Orleans.* Baton Rouge: Louisiana State University Press, 1995.

————. *Gray Raiders of the Sea.* Baton Rouge: Louisiana State University Press, 1992.

————. *Mobile Bay and the Mobile Campaign: The Last Great Naval Battles of the Civil War.* Jefferson, NC: McFarland & Co., 1993.

Hoehling, A.A. *Damn the Torpedoes! Naval Incidents in the Civil War.* Winston-Salem, NC: John F. Blair, 1989.

Holland, J.C. *Life of Abraham Lincoln.* New York: Paperback Library, 1961.

Horner, David. *The Blockade Runners.* New York: Dodd, Mead & Co., 1968.

Howarth, Stephen. *To Shining Sea: A History of the United States Navy.* New York: Random House, 1991.

Image of War, 1861–1865: The End of an Era, ed. William C. Davis. New York: Doubleday & Co., 1984.

In Their Own Words: Civil War Commanders, ed. J.N. Stiles. New York: Berkley Publishing Group, 1995.

Jones, Virgil Carrington. *The Civil War at Sea.* 3 vols. New York: Holt Rinehart Winston, 1961.

Katchor, Philip. *The Civil War Source Book.* New York: Facts on File, 1992.

Lewis, Charles Lee. *David Glasgow Farragut.* 2 vols. Annapolis: Naval Institute Press, 1941–43.

————. *Famous American Naval Officers.* Boston: L.C. Page & Co., 1924.

Lincoln, Abraham. *Speeches and Writings, 1859–1865.* 2 vols. New York: Library of America, 1974.

Lincoln in the Civil War, ed. Courtland Canby. New York: Dell Publishing Co., 1958.

Long, E.B., and Barbara Long. *The Civil War Day by Day: An Almanac 1861–1865.* New York: Doubleday & Co., 1971.

Lord, Francis, and Arthur Wise. *Uniforms of the Civil War.* New York: Thomas Yoseloff, 1970.

Luraghi, Raimundo. *A History of the Confederate Navy.* Annapolis: Naval Institute Press, 1996.

Mahan, Alfred Thayer. *Admiral Farragut.* New York: Haskell House, 1968.

————. *The Gulf and Inland Waters.* New York: Charles Scribner's Sons, 1983.

————. *The Influence of Seapower Upon History.* New Jersey: Prentice Hall, 1980.

Martin, Christopher. *Damn the Torpedoes: The Story of America's First Admiral, David Glasgow Farragut.* New York: Abelard Schuman, 1970.

McCormick, Robert R. *The War Without Grant.* New York: Bond Wheelwright, 1950.

Milhollen, Hirst Dillon, and James Ralph Johnson. *Best Photos of the Civil War.* New York: Fawcett Publications, 1961.

Miller, Edward Stokes. *Civil War Sea Battles: Seafights and Shipwrecks in the War Between the States.* Mechanicsburg, PA: Combined Books, 1995.

Mitchell, Joseph B. *Decisive Battles of the Civil War.* Connecticut: Fawcett, 1955.

Muir, Thomas, Jr., and David P. Ogden. *The Fort Pickens Story.* Pensacola: Pensacola Historical Society, 1989.

Musicant, Ivan. *Divided Waters: The Naval History of the Civil War.* New York: HarperCollins, 1995.

Nash, Howard P., Jr. *A Naval History of the Civil War.* New York: A.S. Barnes & Co., 1972.

Nevins, Allen. *The War for the Union: The Improvised War, 1861–1862.* New York: Charles Scribner's Sons, 1959.

Niven, John. *Gideon Welles: Lincoln's Secretary of the Navy.* New York: Oxford University Press, 1973.

Noel, John, Jr. *Naval Terms Dictionary*, 5th ed. Annapolis: Naval Institute Press, 1988.

Parks, Virginia, Alan Rick, and Norman Simmons. *Pensacola in the Civil War*. Pensacola: Pensacola Historical Society, 1995.

Patrick, Robert W. *Jefferson Davis and His Cabinet*. New Orleans: Louisiana State University Press, 1961.

Perry, Milton F. *Infernal Machines: The Story of Confederate Submarines and Mine Warfare*. Baton Rouge: Louisiana State University Press, 1961.

Potter, E.B., and Chester W. Nimitz. *Sea Power: A Naval History*. New Jersey: Prentice Hall, 1960.

Pratt, Fletcher. *A Short History of the Civil War*. New York: Pocket Books, 1956.

Reynolds, Clark G. *Command of the Sea*. New York: William Morrow & Co., 1974.

Robertson, James, Jr. *The Civil War*. Washington, DC: U.S. Government Printing Office, 1963.

Sandburg, Carl. *Abraham Lincoln: The War Years, 1861–1864*. New York: Dell, 1954.

Scharf, J. Thomas. *History of the Confederate States Navy*. New York: Rogers and Sherwood, 1887.

Silverstone, Paul H. *Warships of the Civil War Navies*. Annapolis: Naval Institute Press, 1989.

Stern, Philip van Doren. *The Confederate Navy: A Pictorial History*. New York: Da Capo Press, 1992.

Still, William N., Jr., *Ironclad Captains: The Commanding Officers of the U.S.S. Monitor*. Washington, DC: U.S. Government Printing Office, 1988.

———. *Iron Afloat: The Story of the Confederate Armorclads*. Memphis: Vanderbilt University Press, 1971.

Thomas, Dean S. *Cannons: An Introduction to Civil War Artillery*. Gettysburg: Thomas Publications, 1985.

Thwait, Philip Haythorn. *Uniforms of the Civil War*. New York: Macmillan, 1975.

Walter, Francis X. *The Naval Battle of Mobile Bay and Franklin Buchanan on the Tennessee*. Birmingham, AL: Prester Meridian Press, 1993.

Ward, Geoffrey C. *The Civil War: An Illustrated History*. New York: Alfred A. Knopf, 1990.

War on the Mississippi, ed. Jerry Corn. Alexandria, VA: Time-Life Books, 1985.

Webster's American Military Biographies. Springfield, MA: G & C Merriam Publishers, 1978.

Wertz, Jay, and Edwin Bearss. *Smithsonian's Great Battles and Battlefields of the Civil War*. New York: Smithsonian Institution and Master Vision, 1997.

West, Richard S., Jr. *Mr. Lincoln's Navy*. New York: Longmans Green & Co., 1957.

Who Was Who in America. St. Louis: A.N. Marquis & Co., 1963.

Who Was Who in the Civil War. New York: Facts on File, 1988.

Why the North Won the Civil War, ed. Daniel Donald. New York: Macmillan, 1960.

Woodworth, Stephen. *Jefferson Davis and His Generals.* Lawrence: University of Kansas Press, 1990.

LETTERS, DIARIES, PRIVATE PUBLICATIONS, AND JOURNALS

Alabama Historical Commission Report, ed. Blanton Blankenship.

Beauregard, P. G. T. Chief engineer for U.S. Army. Fort St. Philip Budget Request. Louisiana Division, New Orleans Public Library.

Cary, J. M. Letter to wife, July 30, 1864. Fort Morgan Archives.

Civil War Manuscript Series 524, Tulane University Library.

Crownover, I. H. Letter, August 8, 1864. Fort Morgan Archives.

———. Letters. Fort Morgan Archives.

Dooley, Pvt. Rufe, U.S.A. Letter to mother, August 10, 1864. Fort Gaines Archives.

Ellis, Wesley Crosby. *Gabriel Richard Ellis, His Life, His Descendants.* Mobile: Graphix House.

Farragut, Admiral David G. Letterbook and Papers, 1862–1864. Historic New Orleans Collection, Research Center, Williams Foundation.

Fort Gaines History and Guide. Fort Gaines Archives.

Gee, Dr. James T. Letters. Fort Morgan Archives.

General Order No. 28, "The Woman's Order," May 15, 1862. Historic New Orleans Collection, Research Center, Williams Foundation.

General Order No. 30. Headquarters 3rd Brigade DG, Fort Morgan. B. General Page. Fort Morgan Archives.

Hart, John. Diary, April 16–May 2, 1862. Historic New Orleans Collection, Research Center, Williams Foundation.

Hunter, William H., Collection. Forts Jackson and St. Philip. Historic New Orleans Collection, Research Center, Williams Foundation.

McIntire, Lt. William J. Letter. Fort Gaines Archives.

Monroe, James. *Message from the President of the United States Upon the Subject of Fortifications, on Dauphin Island and Mobile Point, March 26, 1822* (Washington, DC: Gales and Seaton, 1822). Fort Gaines Archives.

New Orleans Fire Alarm and Public Telegraph Record of Messages Received and Sent, 1860–1863. Louisiana Division, New Orleans Public Library.

Pensacola History Pamphlets and Papers. Pensacola Historical Society.

Plaquemines Parish Commission, *Plaquemines Parish, Fort Jackson.* Louisiana Division, New Orleans Public Library.

U.S.S. *Portsmouth.* Log, 1861–1863. Historic New Orleans Collection, Research Center, Williams Foundation.

Register of the Commissioned and Warrant Officers of the Confederate States to January 1, 1864. *An Act to Create a Provisional Navy of the Confederate States.* Pensacola Historical Society.

Smith, Napoleon Papers. #1105, Southern Historical Collection. University of North Carolina Library, Chapel Hill.

Taylor, T. Letter, September 14, 1864. Fort Gaines Archives.

Thomas, C. B. Letter, January 7, 1864. Historic New Orleans Collection, Research Center, Williams Foundation.

Tibbetts, Melvan. Letters, 1862–1864. Historic New Orleans Collection, Research Center, Williams Foundation.

U.S. Customs House Dedication as an Historic Building, October 10, 1972. U.S. Customs House, New Orleans.

Vickers, James R. Letters. Fort Gaines Archives.

Walker, W. C. Papers. Fort Morgan Archives.

Walton-Glenny Family Papers, 1855–1967. Historic New Orleans Collection, Research Center, Williams Foundation.

Whiting, Capt. M. Letters. Fort Morgan Archives.

Wilkinson, Joseph. Diary. Fort Morgan Archives.

Zielen, Colonel J. Letters. Tulane University Library.

MAPS

Fort Gaines Archives

Fort Morgan Archives

New Orleans Chamber of Commerce

U.S. Department of the Interior Geological Survey

INDEX